READINGS FROM THE HISTORY OF THE
EPISCOPAL CHURCH

10|1

to Jackie —
a fellow student of the
history of the church

READINGS
from the
HISTORY
of the
EPISCOPAL CHURCH

Edited by
Robert W. Prichard

Robert W Prichard

MOREHOUSE-BARLOW
Wilton, Conn.

Morehouse-Barlow Co., Inc.
78 Danbury Road
Wilton, Connecticut 06897

Library of Congress Cataloging-in-Publication Data

Readings from the history of the Episcopal Church.

Includes index.
1. Episcopal Church—History. 2. Anglican
Communion—United States—History. I. Prichard,
Robert W., 1949–   .
BX5880.R43   1986   283'.73   86–12741
ISBN 0–8192–1383–7

Printed in the United States of America

2   4   6   8   10 9   7   5   3   1

Contents

Preface

The following anthology contains selections from ten different periods in the history of the Episcopal church. I have written brief introductory essays to the selections and have also included a short comment on events in the life of the church since 1980. The chapter introductions focus on a continuing theme: what did Episcopalians understand themselves to be? The authors that are included offered, I believe, meaningful answers to this question. In some cases they summarized significant issues of their day. In other cases they were minority voices which indicated the way for future generations. All of them left their mark on their church.

R.W.P.

READINGS FROM THE HISTORY OF THE EPISCOPAL CHURCH

CHAPTER ONE

PLANTING THE CHURCH IN AN AGE OF FRAGMENTATION (1585–1688)

After unsuccessful attempts in 1585–87 to colonize Roanoke Island, North Carolina, the English established a permanent settlement at Jamestown, Virginia in 1607. In the years between the founding of this colony and the Glorious Revolution (1688), the English had no single coordinated plan for the colonial Anglican church. Indeed, they were still fighting with one another about the shape of the church in the mother country. Three parties contended for control: a royalist episcopal party, a puritan presbyterian party, and a puritan congregational party. In addition other groups—Roman Catholics, and Protestant Separatists such as the Quakers and Baptists—questioned the need for any national church. Adherents of each of these groups established footholds in the new colonies: the royalist episcopal party in Virginia, the puritan congregationalists in Massachusetts and Connecticut, the puritan presbyterians in New York and New Jersey, the Quakers in Pennsylvania, the Roman Catholics in Maryland, and the Baptists in Rhode Island.

These religious parties did not compete with the violence of their counterparts in the English Civil War of 1642–52, but seventeenth-century colonial Christians were less tolerant than American Christians of later centuries. In 1643, for example, the Virginia legislature banished all who did not support a royalist episcopal Church of England. The Massachusetts authorities could be even more harsh; they had four Quakers executed between 1659 and 1661.

The lack of a single English religious policy and the resultant patchwork of religious communities gave the colonists an extraordinary measure of religious self-determination. Members of the Massachusetts Bay Colony brought their own charter with them from England. Anglican vestries in Virginia claimed the right to choose their own rectors, a right they still do not have in England.

This divided situation, however, weakened the possibility that the church could exercise leadership in the formation of overall colonial policy. It could, for example, do little to influence the growth of slavery. During the seventeenth century colonial legislatures were adopting racial legislation that gave slavery a more permanent footing. Virginia, to which the earliest slaves had come in 1619, was the first to act. In 1662 the General Assembly passed an ordinance reversing English common law by making the legal status of a child born to a female slave and a male planter depend not on the father but on the mother. Later statutes outlawed marriage between blacks and whites, and imposed special penalties on white women who bore illegitimate children of mixed race. Other colonies soon followed suit. The relationship between the colonists and the Indians was also worsening. As settlers moved off the eastern coast, they claimed Indian lands, often sparking wars. The patchwork of colonial denominations was unable to speak with one mind on such issues.

The document that follows was written by Morgan Godwyn in 1680. Godwyn had served as a parish priest in Virginia from 1665 to 1670. He shared the party spirit of his day, regarding only the (royalist episcopal) Anglican church as legitimate and doubting the sincerity of Quakers and the Commonwealth men (supporters of Oliver Cromwell). It was not to air his attitudes about other denominations, however, that he wrote. He wanted to reclaim the church's role as a positive moral influence. He believed the church was the one institution that could serve as an advocate for blacks and native Americans.

In his five short years in Virginia, Godwyn was unable to convince his fellow Anglicans. Indeed, following a dispute with a vestryman, he left the colony. He could not give up the vision, however. After his departure, he carried on his crusade in print.

The text of Godwyn's *Advocate* is taken from the 1680 London edition, pages 106 to 150.

MORGAN GODWYN
(1680)

THE NEGRO'S AND INDIANS ADVOCATE, Suing for their Admission to the Church.

A Persuasive to the Instructing and Baptizing of the Negro's and Indians in our Plantations.

Shewing that the Compliance therewith can prejudice no man's just interest; So the wilful Neglecting and Opposing of it, is no less than a manifest Apostacy from the Christian Faith.

[The full text of chapter 3 follows.]

That the Inconveniences here pretended for this Neglect being examined, will be found nothing such, but rather the contrary.

I. n.1. The absolute necessity of a Christian's promoting Christianity, even in despite of the greatest Difficulties and Inconveniencies being shewed, I come now in the last place to examin those very Inconveniencies, and to try whether they are indeed such, as they are pretended; or whether the continuance of those practices for whose Justification this Plea was invented, will not upon a due trial be found more inconvenient and prejudicial to our Interest: At least whether Christianity, notwithstanding these pretences (whether true or false) may not, upon the score of its innocent deportment, and unquestionable blamelessness in all Ages, without the least hazard to any Man's just Right and Interest, be afforded a free course, and find entertainment amongst all Conditions and Degrees without prejudice, or offence to any.

2. And here I shall not conceal, what I have often within my own Brest considered and wondered at; how, and with what Front these Persons who proclaim to the World, the inconveniencies and dangers threatned by Christianity to their Estates and Lives, (for no less are the things in controversie) can utter things which I am certain themselves neither do, nor can, believe: It being impossible but that Men endued with common sense must know (and that with the highest certainty that they can have), that nothing of prejudice can really accrue to any Man by the Christian Religion. But much less can they be imagined ever to have enter-

tained any thoughts touching a future Account to be given for such blasphemous suggestions, which to the dishonour of their blessed Redeemer, and his Eternal Truth, they continually belch forth without the least shame or blush. For otherwise Christianity might doubtless have found more candid and civil usage from them, than to have thus put upon her such an hideous and frightful Dress, as these have taken the boldness to represent her in, unto the most ignorant and besotted Herd of Mankind, in these remote Quarters of the World.

3.   For it cannot but appear evident, even to the dimmest and most bleared sight, that no such extraordinary danger can possibly attend the Work, I am here suing for, on our Slaves Behalf; there being no persecuting Magistrates carrying in their Brests an hostile Enmity against either the Professors, or Promoters of it; nor yet breathing out slaughter and destruction to them. There are no Confiscations of Estates or Goods; no loss of Liberty threatned; nor is it a Crime now to be a Christian; the Civil Powers being such themselves, and Kings and Queens being long since become Patrons and Nurses of the Church.

4.   Yet notwithstanding this, they are not ashamed to infer ('tis true, not always in express words, as I have said) even as great Mischiefs from their Negro-Slaves becoming Christians (but not otherwise) as the Faithful in the Primitive Times sustained from the most persecuting Heathens. It being their common Affirmation, That

the Baptizing of their Negro's, is the ready way to have all their Throats cut, etc. which my self, and, I believe thousands of others have heard declared and insisted upon by them, with much vehemency and indignation; tho without any great shew of Reason to make it out. For being at any time demanded, from whence those fears could arise, they should never fail most pertinaciously to persist in the Affirmative, That it was so. Which, with the addition of a few angry words, and uncivil rude speeches, in reply to those demands, thereby to testify their displeasure thereat, as well as the danger of enquiring further into their secrets, was what was usuall to be gotten from them. [So Tertullian saith of the Gentiles, *Nolentes audire, quod auditum damnare non possint.* Apol.c.I.]

5.   But that which I have casually learned from certain False-Brothers of the Society, hath in their more retired Cabals, been alledged by them (and which indeed was no other than what I before suspected) was principally these three things.

6.   First, They object the Knowledg wherewith their Slaves would be thereby furnished; which they are sure will make them less governable, and like the Galileans of old, or our seditious Reformers in 1642, to mutiny and rebel, to free themselves from Tyranny and Oppression: Possess them with the Quakers, (of whom here are great numbers) and other Phanatic's Spirit of Obstinacy, against all Laws and Government, and dis-

pose them rather to suffer Death than to be subject, and at last out of pure Conscience, to murther their Masters.

7.   Secondly, They object the charge and loss of Time, *viz.* from their Sunday-work, etc. with divers other the like sore Inconveniencies, which in the end will (forsooth) strike deep at their Profit, and quite ruine their Estates. And therefore they often repeat this saying, If the Negro's get to be Baptized, they must then e'ne take the Island to themselves.

8.   Thirdly, They complain that the Terms of Christianity are in some things too large, but in some other too narrow for them; both ways inconsistent with the condition of Bondage: And therefore that their Negro's are not to be admitted to, nor entrusted therewith. In which three we have a brief Account of both the Principles and Men, that are such fierce Enemies to this way of propagating Christianity: Their Religion and Interest are of one and the same piece, nor are they ashamed to own it to the World. Doubtless, these do conclude the Merchant in the Gospel, who judged it worth his while to sell all that he had besides, to purchase that Pearl, to have had but a very shallow Pate, for setting such a high value upon nothing, or at most, but Toys and Fooleries, whose worth they believe lies only in the fancy and opinion of the Wearer, not in any intrinsic excellency of their own.

9.   But to undeceive the more well disposed, and to defeat their Malice by unfolding this Mystery of Anti-Religionism: I shall in answer to their first Objection, here demand of them, of what kind that Knowledg is they stand so much in fear of? Is it the knowledg of Vertue and Goodness? Certainly it cannot be other which Christianity instructs Men in. And how can there arise any danger from such knowledg should they receive in never so great a proportion? Can the Decalogue, Creed, and Lord's Prayer, with some few Catechistical and general Points of the more necessary parts of Christianity from thence deduced, prove so poysonous to the minds of Men, as to make them deserve a Character due only to the vilest Blood-suckers, and cruel Assassins? Or can these be a means to render them suspected, or dangerous to the World, when 'tis known that nothing but the non-observance of them, is the sole occasion of all, as well the greatest as the least evils? And therefore the Slaves Right understanding and instruction in these Doctrines, can no more be a motive to him to slacken his Duty, or prejudice his Master, than an Artizan's known skill in his Trade can unqualifie him for being imployed therein, or his tried Honesty, from being either trusted or dealt with. This knowledg therefore must in common Reason, be concluded to be the Master's chiefest Interest, being indeed a worthy inducement to the highest trust and confidence in his Servant, thus endued therewith, and no less ought to be his first care; That is, to make him Just, True, and Honest to himself. At least, none can reasonably be the more suspected for addicting

themselves to such a Study, which only directs to Integrity and Vertue. Where though they may be thought to begin but in Jest, yet 'tis probable, they may end in Earnest: Their Reason may be overcome by the force of its Arguments, or else their sight may be captivated: For, *Vidit hanc, visamq, cupit,* doth here very often follow; the thorow understanding of Vertue (as Plato observed) being apt to create most ardent affections to it. Nor can any genuine, or true principle of Christianity, give the least occasion for either Fears or Jealousies, because in their own proper nature the most innocent and opposite to all Frauds, guileful Practices, and worldly Policies, of any Religion ever yet professed or taught. Those Crafts and Circumventions, which the generality of Men do not once scruple, being most loathsom to the Mind of a true Christian. And therefore it is most evident, that no Master can be endangered by his Slaves instruction therein, which these Blasphemers, who affirm the contrary, cannot but know; unless we will suppose them like Owls and Bats, to be stark blind in the clearest Meridian light; and that amidst all the Books and Sermons, with which this latter Age hath been so abundantly stored, any Man can possibly still remain so ignorant, (tho subtile enough as to other less commendable and excellent things) as to be utterly unacquainted, with the first and greatest points of his Religion.

[10.]   But here withal, I must confess, that I am not of their mind, who hold none fit to be admitted for Christians and Members of the Church, but Gifted, Wise People only. Such as are able to Extemporize an hour or two, and speak to a Text, as they call it. This possibly, as being of that kind of Knowledg or Science which may be apt to puff them up, might in its consequence prove fatal: It being not to be wondred at, if their swelling Tympany of fancied Abilities do make them presume, since we read that when Hagar, (a Bond-Woman too) had conceived, she soon began to behave her self impudently towards her Mistress. The knowledg therefore which I here plead for, is such as tends to their Edification only, being of things absolutely necessary, as of God, our Blessed Saviour, and of the Holy Spirit; of Faith, Hope, and Charity, and of Repentance, of living uprightly, and of a conscientious discharge of their Duty both to God and Man. And if these can be hurtful, then I shall not be ashamed even with the Adversaries to confess, that the knowledg of Christ's Religion, is a thing Repugnant, and Inconsistent with the most honest and just Interest, and wholly tending to disturb the good Order and Peace of the World. And yet here I would not be misconstrued, as if intending to abridg any Masters kindness to his Slave, who hath a desire to furnish him with greater knowledg: Only my request is, That he would not damn him for the want of this; which as I am sure it is sufficient to save him, so neither is it considerable enough, for his Masters fears. And so much touching this first Point, *viz.* The danger arising from the Negro's knowledge.

[11.]   The second is an Implication of the foulest charge against

Christianity, which the worst Enemies of it did ever suggest, but could never prove, *viz.* That it instigates Men to Mutiny and Rebellion: Which cannot possibly be true of it, but by Principles directing thereunto, therein contained and taught. Which if so, then 'twere impossible for a Christian not to be a Rebel; and the better Christian the more Rebellious. But unto such Practices nothing is more diametrically opposite, than the genuine Doctrines of Christianity.

[12.]   For first, It presseth absolute and entire Obedience to Rulers and Superiors, as may be collected from almost innumerable places of Scripture; but more especially from the 13th to the Romans, and from St. Peter's and St. Judes Epistles. And our Lord's answer to the Herodians, is sufficient to silence all Cavillation touching this Duty. It gives the Title of Gods to Kings and Magistrates, forbidding so much as to surmise evil of them. And this is so plainly and evidently true, that amongst Atheists and Commonwealths-Men, (two Names for one and the same thing) it is the only Crime known to be by them charged with, *viz.* That it invests Governours and Monarchs with so independent and absolute a Power. And thereupon have for divers Years past, wisely endeavoured the suppression of it, to prevent (what they are pleased to term) Tyranny and Slavery, and in order to the advancing the liberty of the Subject.

[13.]   Secondly, It establisheth the Authority of Masters, over their Servants and Slaves, in as high a measure, as even themselves could have prescribed; in a due proportion placing them in a no less absolute degree of Power, than the former. Exacting the strictest Fidelity; and that without any respect to their Quality and Condition, but of their natural and true Right of Authority over them. Requiring service with singleness of heart, as unto the Lord, and not unto Men, Ephes. 6.5, 7. And so far it is from encouraging Resistance, that it allows them not the liberty of Gainsaying, or making undutiful replys to their Masters. And referring them to future recompence in Heaven, for their faithful services done to them upon Earth, Eph. 6.8. Of which Ties and Promises, Gentile Slaves being destitute, no such Fidelity can be from them hoped for, or expected. And so far is this Religion from a tendencie to Anarchy, or any Levelling Tenets (as being founded not in a Parity, but a Superiority, not in a Domocracy, but in an Aristocracie) that a conformity to that Axiom, *Aequalitate nihil iniquius*; Nothing is more dangerous than Equality; has been her most professed and constant Practice from her first appearance untill this very day.

[14.]   Thirdly, It enjoyns to all in general an abhorrencie of evil, tho such only in appearance. But much more prohibiting those things which are plainly such, and even of the grossest and wrankest kind. It further puts a restraint upon the Thoughts and Desires, which no other Religion doth; forbids us to be revengful, or to return evil. And therefore far out-doeth the Heathen Divinity, which permitted Revenge in case of Injury, allowed in no case amongst Christians. So that whosoever can pick Rebellion, or cutting of Throats out of these Principles, may as easily prove Adultery lawful from the Seventh Commandment, or Slandering from the Ninth, reconcile Contradictions, and bring Contraries to concur and agree in all Points at one and the same time.

[15.]   And therefore the Delusions of those Atheists, and Imposters in 1642, and afterwards, (since declared, *viz.* by the Parl. in 1660, to be no Protestants, and as certainly no Christians) to whom Christ will one day return but small thanks for occasioning his Doctrine thus to be blasphemed; can be no such convincing Argument, that their Murthers and Depredations, tho falsly pretending Scripture and Inspiration for them, were the genuine result of Christian Principles; until better Proof and Reasons for it be produced, than their own bare Affirmations. And for the Galileans action, it was (like other of the seditious attempts of that Nation, both before and after to assert Liberty) but a Jewish Dream, which Christ himself did to their no small indignation plainly disown, and in that his answer to the Herodians, St. Mat. 16. utterly condemn. And for the Quakers obstinacy (whom yet they here support and encourage against the Ministers) I know no further nor better use can be made of it, than from thence to infer the necessity of Church-Government, and of suppressing false Opinions in Religion, from whence this Obstinacy is occasioned and derived, But not therefore to stifle

and hinder Men from the knowledg of that Profession and Truth, which teacheth the contrary. But our People, who in truth have as little stomach to submit to others, as they believe their Slaves have to submit to them, will scarcely be brought to approve of this Use, or Inference. Tho these Quakers refusal to bear Arms, and to defend their Island, (no not in case of an Invasion) together with their Commission dormant of New Light and Revelation, reserved against some fit time and opportunity of Action (whereby no Man is secure) do often put them upon thoughts of using Violence to that their own dear principle of Libertinism, no less than to the others tender Consciences.

[16.]   Lastly, for Insurrections and Revolts, nothing can be imagined a greater Security against them, than a sincere inward persuasion of the truth of Christianity, with a thorow knowledg of its Principles. Of which the effects have been lately seen in New-England[1], where their Christian-Indians Fidelity was tried to the uttermost; encountred on the one hand by the jealous surmises of their Friends, and on the other by the both invitations and threatnings of their Enemies, if at least we may so term their unconverted Country-men: Yet in despite of all, they remained firm to the English. Who, after that they durst trust them, became very serviceable to our People there, as hath been attested by more than one of their Writers. So powerful are the Bonds of Religion to unite

[1"King Philip's War" of 1676–Ed.]

the minds of Men, tho of most different and even contrary Interests: And when sincere and hearty proving indissolvable, tho under the darkest Eclipse and trial of Adversity. Making Men to forget their own People, and their Fathers House, and joyning them in affection to the most distant Strangers. For these having so fair an opportunity of Revolting, and all the invitements and arguments for it, which Men upon such occasions could wish for; as, the ridding their Country of Foraigners, and the enriching themselves with the Spoils of their well-built and better furnished Houses; their Lands manured and stored with Cattel, and abounding with many other conveniencies, which themselves never were blessed with: And lastly, the Royetlets and several Tribes of that Spacious Continent, all in a manner up in Arms, and unanimous for the rooting them out of it. Yet none of all these considerations could prevail with those Indians, whose minds were thus seasoned with Religion, to falsifie their Faith once plighted to the English. With whom doubtless things might have gone much harder, had they been deserted by them. And they might perchance (all things considered) have been glad to leave their more Inland Stations, and forced to retire and betake themselves to their greater Strengths on the Sea-Coast; there to have remained pent up, and despairing ever to recover their lost Territory, but by the aid of extrinsic force, which would (probably) have cost them more, than they are willing to part with. And to come a little nearer, even to our own Island, where 'tis possible that the late Plot[2] had not been so near taking effect, had the greater, or indeed any considerable, number of the Negro's here been Christians. One thing more I shall add, that the Spanish Indians in America, are not recorded once to have rebelled since their first Reduction under the Spanish Power; nor have the Conquerers themselves been disturbed with any Intestine Broyls, that have been considerable; which is more than we can boast of in our Colonies; tho seated (I speak even of the Eldest of them) not above one third part of the time, that the other have enjoyed theirs. Which effect I can ascribe to nothing more, then to the force and power of Religion.

[17.]   But there is One Instance worth all that can be produced, or said upon this Subject, and that is the Example of the Theban Legion; which I shall present in the words of a Modern Author. [Mr. Dudley Diggs, *of the unlawfulness of Subjects taking up Arms against their Prince, etc....*] "It is, saith he, one of the noblest passages in all the Ecclesiastical History, wherein Christianity did shine forth in its full Lustre, and it affords plentiful Light for our instruction. This band consisted of almost 7000 Men, all Christians. The Emperor Maximimian commands the whole Army to offer Sacrifice to false Gods; they remove their Quarters, that they might avoid, if it were possible, this occasion of discontenting him. He summons them to perform their

[2]Nathaniel Bacon's Rebellion of 1676–Ed.]

part in this devilish Worship. They are forced to return an humble denial, and their resolution not to disobey God, for whose sake they had ever been, and would continue faithful Servants unto him. The Emperour unsatisfied with this Answer, puts them to a Decimation. They submit with much Cheerfulness, and die, praying for their Murtherers. After this sad Spectacle, his Commands are renewed; but prevail nothing upon the Remainder; wherefore they are all Butchered without the least resistance. There was no delay in their Death, except from the weariness of the Executioners. This was truly to confess him, who was led as a Sheep to the slaughter, and like a Lamb opened not his Mouth; and they a Flock of his Fold, are quietly devoured by ravening Wolves. The Commander of this Regiment Mauritius could not contain his joy, when he had seen the first Decimation gallantly suffered. How fearful was I, said he, to his Fellow Souldiers (for armed Men may be tempted to defend themselves), lest any of them upon colour of just resistance for self-preservation in an innocent Cause, should have struggled against this blessed Slaughter, I was watchful, and had Christ's Example in readiness, who commanded his Disciple to put his Sword into the Scabbard. *Salus vestra non periclitatur, nisi armis vestris*; If you use not your Weapons, I have God's own Warrant for your safety.

[18.] "Despair it self could not conquer one single Patience, which yet creates valour in Cowards, and makes them more cour-agious in Extremities, because they are Fearful; since they are likely to endeavour most to preserve Life, who are most terrified with Death.

[19.] "But it may be objected, *Vires deerant,* they were not able to go thorow with the Rebellion. This very Objection, saith he, was made by the Ancients, and answered by themselves to our Hands. Their Speeches witness sufficient strength, if Religion had not tied their Hands. Which had they been other than truth, must have armed their so potent Adversaries with sufficient Arguments against them."

[20.] The same learned Author goes on, and tells us that, "St. Cyprian saith expressly, *Quamvis nimius & copiosus noster fit populus*; Tho we have competent Forces enough, yet we wrestle not with our Oppressors. The Theban Legion was in a posture of resistance, but they durst not lift up those hands, into which the Emperour had put Weapons, against his Personal Commands, tho unjust and bloody. Six thousand six hundred fifty six Men, of such extraordinary Valour, as did not entertain the least fear of Death, might probably have conquered, (and this Cruelty might have encreased their Party, by the defection of Male-contents) at least they must certainly have made some sport for their Lives: They could not have wanted that Comfort, which to some tastes is beyond the pleasure of Life, to die revenged. Besides, had not the Emperour and his Council known them true Christians, and been acquainted with the tameness of that Profession towards the Higher Powers, he would never have hazarded a Rebellion, by making so considerable an Army desperate.

[21.] "And Tertullian, *Cui bello idonei non prompti fuissemus, etiam impares copiis, qui tam libentur trucidamur*; How could they possibly receive a Foil, tho short in number, who so quietly do suffer our Throats to be cut? *Numeri damnum virtus pensaret*, tho we wanted the advantage of number, which you perceive we do not, Courage would supply that defect, And tho fewer, since we contemn our own Lives, we might be Masters of yours. We could undo you, not if we should Rebel, but if we would be Idle; we were lost, if we did not Fight for you. *Vestra omnia implevimus, castra ipsa, etc.* We fill all places in the Empire, and even your Camp would be empty without us Christians. The same Father makes a bold Challenge, and desires them to produce, if they can, but one example of any Christian taking part with Rebels. Their unanimous Confession was, We kiss the Hands that wound us, and the Example of Christ is made our Law. *Inde est quod nemo nostrum, quando apprehenditur, reluctatur, nec se adversus injustam violentiam vestram, quamvis nimius & copiosus noster sit populus, ulciscitur.* For this cause none of us makes resistance, when apprehended, nor revengeth your unjust Violence; for God is able to reward our Patience, and to requite all our Sufferings. *Si injuriam, etc.* If you depend upon God, he will under-

take your Quarrel, and revenge your Wrongs; your Wounds shall save you: and if you fall a Martyr, you shall rise a Saint. What cannot our Sufferings do? They make even God our Debtor; He owes us Heaven for our selves, and Hell for our Enemies, but we breath[e] out our Souls in Prayer, that he may be entreated not to pay this. Here is the Patience and Faith of the Saints; they believed, therefore they suffered such things, etc." Thus far that loyal and ingenious Person, in whom is legible the genuine temper and Spirit of a Christian: Unless it can be supposed that the whole multitude of them, as well their more learned Guides, as the ignorant and simple, were wholly unacquainted with their Profession. And from hence, with what elsewhere hath been said, I may safely presume to conclude, that Christianity which obligeth Men to the strictest Vertue; and that upon such weighty Motives, as no Profession did ever pretend to, is so far from working Mischief to Superiours and Governours, that it rather appears of absolute necessity for the security both of Themselves and their Affairs, that their Subjects be thorowly acquainted with it; As, er'e I come to close up my Discourse, I hope, I shall yet further shew.

II. 1. The first and great danger which concerns their Lives being escaped, I come to examine the two Last Objections, which for their near affinity and resemblance, I shall twist together, and dispatch under one. These do concern their Estates and worldly Interests, things no less dear unto them, but both dearer than Religion; for otherwise such Objections had not been to be answered. Now in the first they affirm, Their Estates will be threatned no less than four several ways; of each of which I shall give this short, but true Account; *viz.* That, the first is Idle and Ridiculous; the second Sordid and Unchristian: The third a mixture of Gentile and Mahumetan Superstition and Irreligion: The fourth Inhumane and Monstrous, a reproach to Mankind, and a dishhonour to the English Government and Nation.

2.   For the first, They affirm their Estates will suffer by the Charges from hence ensuing: As by Baptizing, Marrying, Churching, and Burying their Slaves. All now either totally omitted, or else performed by the Overseers, (in a kind of prophane Merriment, and derision as it were of the Ordinances), or (as in Marriage) by mutual agreement amongst themselves; and (as is used jestingly here to be said, when speaking of the Quakers [like] Marriages) after the Negro fashion. As for Visitation of the Sick, I shall not insert it in the List, because here laid aside in a manner by all, besides the richer English. The other (like those poor desperate Souls in Limbo, that for wont of Money, have no Body to pray them out) being by the remoteness of their Habitations, the frequent badness of the Weather and the Ways, the scarcity of Ministers, an evil, but little felt, tho much fewer, (notwithstanding there are not above five;) and the numerousness of the Inhabitants

(supposed not fewer than one hundred and odd thousands) not possibly to be thought on, unless we should suppose the Ministers always on Horse-back for that very work: And then who should preach (without Book) upon Sundays?

3.   Secondly, They apprehend that this would produce a necessity of enlarging their Churches, and encreasing the number of Parishes and Ministers, of both which there are but too many already, half of the Churches being destitute of Ministers, tho but Eleven in all. And in those Churches that are better supplied, 'tis known that the Prayers and Sermons are usually delivered to little more than the bare Walls only, notwithstanding the multitude of People belonging to each; of whom not a fifth part (I speak only of the English) could be admitted into the most of them, should they all appear. [A County in England of the same extent with this Island, has commonly 100 or more Parishes and Ministers; all, one with an other, not worse provided for Maintenance, tho not a quarter so Populous nor Rich as these here.]

4.   Thirdly, They add the time to be spent in this (needless) work of Religion, which amongst so many labouring Hands must be considerable. Besides their Sunday-work, would be quite lost, as also their increase by the Negro's Polygamy.

5.   Fourthly, They have a strange apprehension and foresight, that their Slaves when admitted Christians, would be apt to

expect better usage (which even Heathens will tell them they ought to have without it) for Food, Clothes, and Rest, and more merciful Correction, moderated according to some Law, (and not left to each Tyrants pleasure) which perchance, may be but reasonable. These, as indeed the former, they sparingly mention, being ashamed to own, and it were to be wished they would also to practice them. Of all which I shall leave others to judg, whether they do not fully answer my short Character and Description of them.

6.   But as bad as these are, the following are worse; wherein like down-right Atheists, they stand up for Libertinism, and object directly against Christianity, blaming the equability and justice of its Terms, the thing that chiefly renders it commendable. [Luc. 1. 9. *Olim vera fides—obit, nunc & ficta perit.* They declare their Sins as Sodom, Isa. 39.] These they complain of, as on the one hand too large, but on the other too straight and narrow, in neither able to content them, being both, they say, inconsistent with Bondage, These Terms are, 1. Privileges. 2. Prohibitions.

[7.]   The privileges are chiefly these three: First, Their Slaves admittance to an Oath, which, being at present Heathens, are scarce currant in a Christian Court; as some of them have been made to understand in England from a certain Judg's reprehending and menacing of them for their brutish neglect herein; tho they were not ignorant of it before. Secondly,

Their equality as to the Communion and Church-Administrations; which, to all are, or ought to be, the same. Thirdly, the inconvenience that may ensue upon their acquaintance with this Precept of our Blessed Saviour; Thou shalt love thy Neighbour as thy self. It may perchance be expected that I should add a fourth, *viz.* A Supposed Right to Freedom, and of being set at Liberty immediately upon their Baptism; which is by some apprehended to be in it self a release from Servitude. To which last, (tho it be needless, they having secured that Interest, as I have understood, by a Law of their own, whose Validity they do not question,) I shall speak something also, after having first replied to the three former.

[8.]   The first whereof is their admission to an Oath, wherein they seem again to have forgotten, the thing I am interceding and suing for on their behalf, *viz.* That they may be made Christians; which, as is before shewed, is certainly of it self a sufficient remedy and security against all temptations to Perjury. A Crime, which according to the true Principles thereof, is next to irremissible: And for which the Ancient Canons did enjoyn Penance to the Offender during his Life.

[9.]   And yet should we suppose the worst, I cannot imagine the danger to be greater than it was in former Ages, when both Slaves and Villains were freely admitted, without this scruple, to give Evidence; even as in Poland, and elsewhere, 'tis not to be doubted, but they still are. Nor do I conceive that St. Paul thought his Christian Slaves Oath more to be suspected than other Mens, whilst they no less stuck to the Principles of Christianity. And in truth, at the same rate, all the World may be no less suspected: it being possible that all Men may prove deceitful and wicked, tho not in the least probable.

[10.]   That their Oath may be useful, we even now find, where their bare word or testimony given without it, is often found very serviceable, tho not admitted for a sufficient proof. The want whereof is many times no small impediment to the course of Justice. And for Subornations, the thing chiefly objected; for my part, as I see not but they might (especially being made Christians) be as well trusted as most others, so should any such thing happen, it will be presumed that the wise Judges will be no less Eagle-sighted, and able to descry such practices in these, than in the English.

[11.]   As for the second, it is hard to find out what they intend by it, unless it should be that the Negro's would thereby be apt to think more proudly of themselves, and less worthily of their Masters; which yet cannot be gathered from Christianity, nor indeed can ever happen, if St. Paul's rule be well applied; And they that have believing Masters, let them not despise them, because they are Brethren, but rather do them [the better] service, because they are Believers, 1 Tim. 6. So that this Authority of the Master is so far from being hereby

diminished, that it is rather confirmed, and a stricter observance for that cause charged upon the Servants Conscience. Nor do we find that Abraham, Job, etc. were the less esteemed by their Bondmen, for their being initiated into Religion, by the same Ceremonies with themselves; neither do we find or suspect this in our English Servants, or Dependents. That Woman also whose Negro . . . I baptized, had not more cause to complain that he thereafter failed in his Duty and Fidelity, tho she quarrel'd at it. Nor yet two others in Virginia (the former being in Carolina) whom I likewise Baptized, were ever taxed by their Masters, as less diligent after Baptism, than they were before. Nor lastly, did the Hebrew or Christian Masters, nor I believe hardly any other Sect, ever ascribe to Religion the disorders of their Servants as the cause thereof, if at any time they found themselves disrespected by them. Except only the Romans Saturnalia, wherein the Slaves were permitted to retaliate their Masters cruelties; which extravagancy Christianity doth not in the least allow of. And for the third, they may remember, that if Christ hath taught, That we should love our Neighbours as our selves, his Apostle hath from his Mouth also, no less enjoyned Servants obedience to their Masters; which two Precepts do no more thwart either the other, than that of the same Apostle, commanding, To render to every Man his due, and Masters to allow their Servants that which is just and equal, doth destroy their just Right and Authority over them. And this, if we were to deal with Men that had any sense of Christianity, or Religion, (which the Objection doth most evidently shew that they have not) might prove satisfactory to them; but as the case stands, 'tis not to be hoped will much avail to their Conviction.

12.   And as to that which some would in the fourth place object, touching their release from servitude upon Baptism, tho I do not see that they here do retain any apprehensions thereof, their Law (of which I have only heard mention here, but do know that there is such both in Virginia and Mary-land) having carefully barred all such Pleas; yet were there no such Law enacted, I cannot understand that a necessity for such a release does arise from any Principles of Christianity, nor of Religion in general. For if we look into the Old Testament, we find that Circumcision (to the Faithful then the same with Baptism now) did not release Abraham's three hundred and eighteen Slaves, nor those afterwards belonging to his Posterity, any more than their partaking of the Passover, Exod. 12, did of which yet no hired Servant was to eat. And the Gibeonites were perpetual Bondmen and Vassals, notwithstanding their admittance to the Temple, and to Religion. And then to come to Christianity and the New Testament, Onesimus, who is stiled [Δοῦλος (doulos), a Slave] (to Philemon) as (that word importing no less) is generally agreed, was not made a Freeman by his being Baptized; which St. Paul's returning him to his Master, a Christian also, and his interceeding for him, doth manifest. Whom tho he bespeaks as a Convert, yet lets him know that his Obligation to his Master was still the same. And tho he professeth that he might be much bold in Christ to enjoyn Philemon that which was convenient, yet that he chose rather to entreat him by Love: And what was that? Not that he might be set at liberty, as being now a Christian, and even a Brother; but that, forgetting wherein he had offended, being now a Penitent and a Convert, he would receive him again. Nor against this do we find Onesimus urging his Privilege, nor refusing to carry the Letter with his own hand. A manifest sign that there was then no such understood, or heard of. And in 1 Cor. 7.21, 22. where the same St. Paul asserts the privilege of Christian Servants, he withal tells them their Duty, giving them to know, that they were to abide in the same Calling, wherein they were when first converted, or called; not but that if they could procure their liberty, they should rather use it. And if any shall demand what then is that liberty of a Christian, which St. Paul elsewhere asserts and urgeth? I answer, That I know no more by it, than a liberty from the yoke of Judaism, from Sabbaths, Circumcision, and such like Ordinances and Levitical Ceremonies. As also a release from our former slavery to our Lusts, which is the greatest liberty and happiness, if considered and understood. And lastly, An admission to serve Christ, our most perfect Freedom, and to partake of the Privileges and Promises of the Gospel, and thereby to obtain an Adoption to the glorious liberty of the Sons of God in Heaven. Which certainly

are far greater Immunities, than a bare release from temporal Servitude can possibly amount to. For Christ's Kingdom being not of this World, his Religion was never designed to deprive any Man of his civil Rights, but rather did confirm them all to us. And to shew that Bondage is not inconsistent with Christianity, we see it practiced by other Christian Nations in these parts without the least prejudice to them: Even as not one hundred Years since in England, Villanage, a kind of Slavery, was in force, and still is in other Countries; and some do say, in our own too.

13.   And whereas 'tis further Objected, That certain Canons and Imperial Edicts (neither of them admitted here) and the Municipal Laws of some Countries ('tis possible of England it self) heretofore enacted or decreed for the honour of Christianity, or to strengthen its Party against the Heathen, do oppose this continuation of our Slaves in Bondage. I answer, First, That these Laws being designed for the good of Servants, and the promoting of Christianity, there is now no reason they should be continued, when experimentally found, through the hardness of Mens Hearts, so great impediments thereto; and even to be turned against them, for the benefits of whose Bodies and Souls they were intended. But, Secondly, I add, that this (tho true) doth not trouble my Assertion, because we do not find that these Laws do flow from any necessity thereof, concluded in the Principles of Christianity; as being meerly voluntary, and the effects only of the good Na-

ture and Piety of their first Christian Contrivers; and to which a Christian (as such) is no more bound, than to sell all his Goods, and give them to the Poor: Which yet may be a good work, and very commendable, in those that shall aspire after such perfection.

14.   But yet further, if any shall make it a matter of Conscience to continue Christians in Servitude; it would concern those that entertain that scruple (which I fear few do) to remember how much more against a good Conscience it is, either through Sloth, or for a petty Profit, to keep Men, that have Souls to be saved, destitute of the means thereto, and consequently to occasion their Damnation; than simply to retain them under Servitude, abstracted from that other Irreligion. Which tho perhaps less commendable in Christians, is far short of the Impiety of keeping them Slaves to Hell, and to our selves too. And here also, supposing the worst, it ought by Christians to be considered how much the loss of a Servant is less than of a Soul, (yea of many) for whom Christ died, no less than for their Masters and who cannot expect to be saved, if the other, through their occasion, perishes. But letting this scruple pass, (to salve which there never will be here any occasion) I think it clear enough that Christianity doth not lessen any obligations of Servants to their lawful Masters: And therefore that if any positive Laws to the contrary do as yet stand in their way, I should be apt to recommend the Bermudian caution of Indentures for 99 years Service, to our

Peoples imitation, in the interim till those Laws (I say, if any such there be) might by Authority be fairly removed.

III. 1.   And thus our dangers from the Privileges being cleared, I proceed to do the like by the Prohibitions, *viz*. Of their Polygamy, their Sunday-Labour; frequent repudiating and changing their wives, usual amongst most Heathens. As also their Idolatrous Dances and Revels, permitted and practiced by them (so often as they can steal any time from their Work) even upon that Day, whose Morality (to the danger of straining it to the height of a Jewish Sabbath) hath been so much for these many Years, insisted on amongst the English; with other such Recreations and Customs, by them brought out of Africa, and here connived at, because either gainful to their Owners, (such as the first) or grateful to the poor Slave (such as the latter) without prejudice to their Masters Business. None of which yet are heard of amongst the Virginia Negro's, tho alike Gentiles with these: And there not laid aside or forbidden, but forgotten by disuse.

2.   Now might not this cause one to stand still and to admire, how such things should come to be, I do not say, justified, but even permitted, or endured by Christians: Who, as before they were not ashamed to begrudge the poor Wretches thus spending their strength and days in their Service, even a miserable Subsistence, for they expect no more: So here they alledge things palpably wicked, as a pretence for a worse and more dangerous Frugality, if I may so call it, *viz*. The Starving of their Souls. Contenting themselves to give a free course to Turkish and Heathenish Licentiousness, and even to all Irreligion and Atheism, for a wretched false gain; but in the mean time blindly overlooking the many greater Advantages, which are the undoubted fruit of true Christianity.

3.   For can it be believed that the small trouble of Christenings, to be had without Fees; as also of Catechizing, Marrying, Churching and Burying of them (the consenting to which will one Day, like Nehemiah's good deeds for Jerusalem, or Tobit's charity for the Dead, be our greatest comfort;) can equal, or any way be compared with the solid benefit and satisfaction arising from the unquestionable Fidelity and Integrity of a vertuous Servant? [Think upon me, O my God, for good according to all that I have done for this People, Neh. 5] Can a few hours Sunday-Work (for I plead not for the other Holy-days) be alike beneficial to us, as the same spent in learing them their Duty, or as the blessing of God upon us for it in the ensuing Week? Can starving, or working them to Death, (for it cannot be denied but that these are too frequent) be equally profitable with keeping them alive for our future Service? Or can we believe it alike expedient; or conducive to our Interest, to be put each Year to purchase and train up Raw, Ignorant, and unhandy Barbarians, with preserving for our occasions, the tried

and more experienced, by good usage of them? 'Tis true, you may alledge the temptation and certainty of the present Profit, with the uncertainty of future Contingencies, the possibility of their outliving those hardships, and of their dying also under better usage; yet surely this is but a brutish Plea, and at best not a little favouring of their Providence, who devour all at one Meal, as uncertain whether ever they should live to enjoy another.

[4.]   As for the charge of Instructing them, if they think it too much to undertake themselves, (which the holy Patriarchs did not) they cannot but know the same person who attends this work upon Sundays, or Saturdays Afternoon, (which last was formerly allowed to both Slaves and Servants, when this Island was less Wealthy and Populous, than now it is) may be further useful in the rest of the Week; particularly in teaching their own, and the neighbouring Youth, (or possibly in keeping their Accounts, etc.) which would prevent a greater Charge, together with the hazard of transporting them to Europe for Education: Not omitting that so much (beyond the dangers of the Sea, and of different Climes) worse mischief of their being betimes Debauched; scarce to be avoided at so great a distance from their Parents care and inspection, as in many Instances is too apparent. And this also might be a means in some measure to put a stop to that Barbarism, which through the want of Schools, do threaten the irrecoverable Ruine of all our Hopes in them.

[5.]   As for the danger of our Slaves release from Servitude thereby, to what I have said before, I shall only add, That if they suspect the Validity of their own Laws, the contrary to which I have always found; no doubt but his Majesty, and the Honourable Houses of Parliament, will have their Ears open to their just Fears and Complaints, thus arising from a pious sense of their Duty, and the safety of their Peoples Souls, no less than of their own; so as to fortifie their Interest with as good Laws and Fences, as themselves shall in Reason propose, or their Omnipotencie (pardon the expression, Rulers can do much within their proper Spheres) can create, or give life to. Nor let that over-proud fear of thereby acknowledging (what they cannot possibly avoid,) their dependence upon England, nor that of rendring the rest of their Laws, with their Legislative Power (which, I confess, some would fain extend beyond its due bounds) questionable, be any impediment thereto; since neither the one nor the other are more secured without it: And these two being known to be different things in Law, *viz.* To corroborate an old, and create a new Title.

6.   And for the charge of dividing and lessning the Parishes, (very necessary if but for the English alone) and the encreasing the number both of Churches and Ministers (tho this doth not absolutely follow; the foregoing Expedient being admitted, nor perhaps without it;) All the danger which from thence is like to arise, is, that thereby we are like to be made bet-

ter Christians, and by such a convenience enabled more duly to serve God; a benefit well worth the purchasing at so small an Expence. Tho Christians in such a case should first reflect upon the Prophets reply to King Amaziah, 2 Chron. 25.9. The Lord is able to give thee much more than this. And the old Jewish Aphorism, *Decima ut dives fias,* answering to our English Adage, that Meat and Mass, (others have rendred it, Prayer and Provender) do never hinder Work, do confirm that in the Sum total, Nothing is lost by our attending upon God's Service and Religion.

7.   Hereby also, besides the Integrity and Long-livedness of their Slaves (which would abundantly recompence the loss of other less commendable Profits and Advantages), their gettings would not be so clogg'd with those troublesome gripes, and Stings of Conscience, which first or last are the certain Appendices of unlawful and bloody Gain; nor with that Curse denounced by the Prophet, Hab. 2.6,7,8. for such Unmercifulness and Impiety. Nor would their Estates be so subject to that Moth and Canker, which some observing Persons (not over addicted to Priests, nor to Religion, 'tis well known, but) even from amongst themselves, have (so forcible are Right words, Job. 6.25.) been brought to confess, as being most Notorious: Who at the same time could not find out any cause whereto to ascribe those apparent effects, besides that of oppressing these People. For as an Achan, or a Saul may trouble Israel, so even

very Gibeonites may bless the Inheritance of the Lord. And so all would be enjoyed with greater Security: And that which now is unstable as Water, and a Curse rather than a Blessing, would be a durable and firm Possession; not as now for the most part to the immediate Heirs only, but even to the succession of many Generations: for as one very well observes, "Interest is best preserved by Justice and Equity, which will entitle it to that blessing from God, which he hath promised in his Word, and which are naturally apt to be instrumental to Providence in producing that good, which he hath promised."

8.   And as each private Man, so also the public will be made more happy. Religion, saith one, causeth good Orders, and good Orders do create Peace and Concord, which is a Peoples greatest strength. A Fool, if he tread in the ways of Holiness and Religion cannot err, according to the Prophet Isaiah 35.8. There shall be an Highway and a Way, and it shall be called the Way of HOLINESS; the wayfering Men, the Fools, shall not err therein. And on the other side, Baalam hired to procure the ruine of Israel, could not devise a more pernicious Counsel, than to make Israel sin. Livie in his fifth Book, rehearseth a speech of Camillus, to the Romans, wherein he appeals to their own Experience, whether ever they had better Luck, than when they carefully served God, or worse than when they neglected it. So Horace also in his 1.3.Ode 6. And Cicero ascribes all the good fortune of the same People (and no less doth St. Augustine in his Book,

De Civitate Dei:) to their Piety and
Devotion. *Nec numero Hispanos,
nec robore Gallos, nec calliditate
Poenos, nec artibus Graecos; nec
deniq; hoc ipso hujus gentis & ter-
rae domestico nativoq; sensu Ita-
los ipsos & Latinos; sed Pietate ac
Religione, atq, hac una sapietia
quod deorum immoralium Nu-
mine omnia regi gubernariq; pros-
peximus, omnes gentes Nationesq;
superavimus;* That is, We [Ro-
mans] neither outnumbered the
Spaniards, nor were stronger than
the Gauls nor outwitted the Car-
thaginians, nor were more learned
than the Greeks, nor surpassed the
Italians and Latines, our predeces-
sors in their natural Capacities:
But by our Religion, Piety, and by
this one only point of WISDOM,
that we believed all things to be
directed by the appointment of
Heaven, we have been able to worst
all other Nations. Xenophon tells
us, That the great Cyrus laid not
the foundation of his Persian Mon-
archie so much by his Valour and
Wisdom, as a Religious Worship of
Heaven, and a liberality even to
profuseness in the service thereof.
This also was that which did ag-
grandize Alexander the founder
of the Macedonian Empire. And
hence it was, saith one, That the
Romans made not an unworthy
choice of a Commander, or Officer,
for many Years; the way there to
be preferred, being by Religion.
Therefore this became the grand
Emulation of the People, Souldiers,
Captains, and Senatours. And
Comines was persuaded, that here-
of did spring the greatness of the
Venetian Seigniory. From thence Mat-
chiavel admonisheth those Princes
and Republic's, that would keep

themselves from Ruine, above all
things to preserve the Rights of
their Religion uncorrupt, and to
maintain it always venerable. And
he further adds, That there is no
surer sign of a Countries destruction, than to see in it a contempt
of Divine Worship.

9.   Before I can conclude
this part, I must crave leave to recite another memorable passage
out of Livie's first Book of his Roman History, as conceiving it per-
tinent to the Point I am upon: It
being touching the effects of Religion upon Rome's first Planters, for
that also was a Colonie. Whom in
the first place, he bespeaks to have
been a People rude and savage: But
to abate whose fierceness, and to
render them more tame and man-
suete; Numa their second King, en-
deavours by good Laws and Orders,
to reduce them to Civility, thereby
as it were to reedifie that City,
whose Foundation had before been
laid by Force and Arms. Howbeit
this being too little to accomplish
his purpose, (a thing worthy to be
taken Notice of;) He in the next
place, deviseth to bring them to
some sense of Religion, and the
fear of God; *Rem omnium primam
ad multitudinem efficacissimam
ratus*; judging this above all most
operative upon the generality of
Men. Whereby, as it follows, their
Minds possessed with an awe of Religion; A solemn promise and the
respect of an Oath, did, without
further Laws or Penalties, govern
the City. Nor was the blessing from
abroad attending their Devotion,
less remarkable. For, saith our Author, This Piety observed in them,
did so affect their Neighbours: *Ut.*

civitatem totam in cultum versam Deorum violari ducerent nesas: That they judged it Sacrilegious to vex or molest a People, so addicted to the Service of God. I shall leave our People to make the Application, without adding any thing more thereto, than what our Lord Christ replied to the Inquisitive Lawyer, St. Luke 10.37 *Vade & tu fac similiter,* Go, and do thou likewise.

Ezek. 8.17.

"Then said he unto me,—Is it a light thing—that they commit the Abominations, which they commit here? For they have filled the Land with Violence, and have returned to provoke me to anger: And lo they are [ὡς μυκτηρίζοντες (*hos mukterizontes*)] like them that make Sport or Mock."

CHAPTER TWO

THE AGE OF REASON
AND THE AMERICAN COLONIES
(1688–1740)

With the Glorious Revolution and the accession of William and Mary in 1688 the English were for the first time able to establish a consistent policy toward their colonies in the New World. Now that their own religious controversy was settled—in the Revolution the English ejected a James II intent on returning their nation to Roman Catholicism, reaffirmed a state church with episcopal polity and the 1662 Book of Common Prayer, and granted limited toleration to other Protestants—the English had a standard by which to measure colonial religion. They found that the Church of England was established firmly only in Virginia and that even there it was in need of supervision and reform. The bishop of London, the archbishops, the Parliament, and the new monarchs, therefore, instituted a three-pronged program for the colonies: 1. Where it was possible, they extended the establishment of the Church of England to other colonies. North and South Carolina, Maryland, and, when founded, Georgia, would become Anglican. 2. Where the non-Anglicans were too firmly in control, Anglicans organized individual congregations. Thomas Bray (1656–1730) greatly aided this effort by forming the Society for the Propagation of the Gospel in Foreign Parts (SPG) in 1701. In the years prior to the American Revolution this missionary organization would provide support for a large percentage of clergy in colonies without establishment. 3. The bishop of London appointed commissaries, representatives with authority to discipline clergy in the colonies. James Blair (1656–1743) was chosen as the first colonial commissary in 1689. Sent to Virginia, he would stress clerical discipline, campaign for higher clergy salaries, and found the first colonial Anglican college, William and Mary, in 1693.

The following selection is from Thomas Bray's *Catechism* (third edition, London, 1703; pages 39–53). Bray was the first commissary to Maryland. He spent little time in the colony, but proved very effective in organizing for missions while in England. In addition to founding the SPG, he organized the Society for the Promotion of Christian Knowledge (SPCK), which published Christian literature and established a series of colonial libraries.

Bray's *Catechism* was one of the works distributed in the colonies by the SPCK. In it Bray outlined his understanding of covenant theology, a modification of the doctrine of predestination that had been pioneered around 1600 by such puritan Anglicans as William Perkins and William Ames. Puritans used covenant theology to make the mystery of election more comprehensible. They believed God chose whom he wished for salvation, but then offered them a reasonable covenant; if they lived with faith and repentance, God guaranteed salvation. Thus far Bray was only following Perkins and Ames. He went beyond them, however, to suggest that apostolic succession was a necessary element of this covenant. God only authorized ministers ordained in apostolic succession to preach his covenant and to celebrate the sacraments. While those who were members of denominations lacking apostolic succession were not necessarily damned, they could not count on the assurances of the covenant. They were left to God's "uncovenanted mercies."

Reasonable English men and women in the Moderate Enlightenment that followed the Glorious Revolution were attracted to Bray's argument. At a time when Isaac Newton, Robert Boyle, and other English scientists were uncovering the laws of nature, it was assuring to believe in a reasonable God, who dealt with his creatures according to clear rules. This argument also proved attractive to colonial Anglicans. In the South it provided a rationale for expanding the establishment of the Anglican church. In New England and the middle colonies where Anglicans were often a lower income minority the assurance of participation in a covenant that excluded the more prosperous and often unsympathetic Congregationalists and Presbyterians had a certain attraction. It also proved an effective evangelizing tool. In 1722, for example, Timothy Cutler (1683 or 1684–1765), rector of Yale College, along with Samuel Johnson (1696–1772), a tutor, and a recent graduate, all renounced their congregational orders and sought Anglican ordination.

This covenant argument was less successful with native Americans and blacks. While individual SPG missionaries devoted their lives ministering to them, no black or Indian candidate was ordained to the Anglican priesthood during the entire colonial period. Apostolic orders—the centerpiece of Bray's argument—remained a white institution. Under such circumstances, black and native Americans might be introduced to the Christian faith by Episcopal missionaries, but they seldom had any appreciation for the distinctive nature of the denomination's ministry.

The covenant–apostolic order argument would remain a staple of Episcopal apologetic until the middle of the nineteenth century, when the Roman Catholic church swelled with Irish immigration and replaced the Episcopal church as the largest American denomination with apostolic orders.

THOMAS BRAY
(1697)

Catechetical Lectures
On the Preliminary Questions and Answers
of the Church-Catechism.

[The Fifth Lecture:
Wherein I was made a Member of Christ.]

The Preliminary Questions and Answers of your Catechism, do give you a general Account of all the Terms and Conditions of the Covenant of Grace, both of the Priviledges made over to us by God, and of the Conditions to be perform'd by us. And these Words,

Wherein I was made a Member of Christ, expressing the First of those invaluable Priviledges made over unto us, in this Covenant, on God's Part; I shall therefore endeavour, as well as I can, to explain and open to you, what they do import.

Christ is in Scripture often styl'd, The Head of the Church, as particularly Col. 1.8. And he is the Head of the Body, the Church, it is there said; and we are also styl'd, Members of this Body, the Church. Thus Eph. 5.30. We are Members of his Body, of his Flesh, and of his Bones; so that to be a Member of Christ, is to be a Member, or Part of that body, of which he is the Head, or to be a Member of Christ's Church: And to make it appear to you, how happy a Thing it is to be a Member of Christ's Church,

First, I will shew you, What kind of Body the Church of Christ is.

Secondly, What it is to be a Member of it. And then

Thirdly, What exceeding great and invaluable Priviledges do belong to a Member of Christ's Church.

[I.] And First, let us see, What kind of Body that is which is call'd the Church of Christ. And tho' it does not belong to this Part of your Catechism, to give you a full account, of all that is necessary to be known, concerning Christ's Church, which may more properly be refer'd to that Article of our Creed, I believe the Holy Catholick Church: However, since the high Priviledge and Dignity of any Member, as a Member, cannot be sufficiently understood, nor valued, without knowing the Nature and Excellency of that

Body, of which it is a Member; I do therefore think my self obliged, in order to let you into a th[o]rough Understanding of what is meant by A Member of Christ's Church, and of the greatness of that Priviledge, to speak something largely, in this Place, concerning the Nature and Constitution of the Church it self; and I shall therefore define it, and also Explain, and prove each Part of the Definition, I shall give of it, as follows:

The Church of Christ, is the universal Society of Christians, consisting both of Lawful Governours and Pastors, and also of the People of God committed to their Charge; and who are call'd forth out of the wicked World, by the Preaching of the Gospel, to a holy Profession and Calling; Namely, To Repentance from dead Works, to the Knowledge, Belief, and Service of the One True God, Father, Son and Holy Ghost, and to the Enjoyment of those inestimable Priviledges of the Gospel, viz. Most reasonable and excellent Laws to Conduct 'em to Heaven, Divine Grace and Assistance to Enable 'em to obey those Laws, Pardon of Sins, upon Repentance, for the Violation of 'em, and eternal Life and Happiness upon sincere Obedience to 'em. And who, to the End of being Incorporated into one Society, and of having God, to be their God, and they themselves his People, have Enter'd into Covenant with him, at Baptism, and do often Renew the same in the Lord's Supper, and are Incorporated thereby into one Body, subdivided, indeed, into several particular Bodies, and Churches, for the convenience of Government and Worship, but holding Communion with one another, in One and the same necessary and fundamental Points of Christianity, necessary to constitute the Church, under Jesus Christ, their supreme Head.

(1) And First, The Church of Christ is the Society of Christians, consisting both of Lawful Governours and Pastors, and of the People of God committed to their Charge. The Church of Christ is not a Confus'd, an Undigested, Headless Multitude, but a Regular and Well-order'd Society. Hence, it is so often in the New Testament call'd, The Kingdom of God, as Matth. 21.31. The Kingdom of Christ, as Rev. 11.15. and The Kingdom of Heaven, Matth. 11.12. and the Members of it, Children of the Kingdom, Matth. 13.38. And Eph. 2.19, 20, 21. The Members therefore are styl'd, Fellow-Citizens, Members of a Household, and Parts of a Temple, all which Expressions speak the Church of Christ to be a Regular Society of Men, combin'd and knit together by Laws, derived from some supreme Head and Governour. A Society, I say, wherein some are Superiours, some are Inferiours, some Governours, some Governed, and who altogether make up a well-compacted Body of Men. This last cited place out of the Ephesians, speaks the Thing out: Now therefore, saith he to those, who are call'd into the Church, ye are no more Strangers and Forreigners, but Fellow-Citizens with the Saints, and of the Houshold of God, and are built upon the Foundation of the Apostles and Prophets, that is, Governours and Teachers, Jesus Christ being the chief Corner-Stone, in whom all the Building,

fitly framed together, groweth up into an Holy Temple in the Lord. Here, in this Description of the Church, you have Jesus Christ the chief Corner-stone, or Head of the Building, and Body; the Apostles and Prophets Foundation-stones, next unto him, and all the rest of Christians, Fellow-Citizens, depending upon Jesus Christ, their Supreme Head, and others his subordinate Governours, and Teachers, next under him, and the Whole represented as a well-compacted Building. Or, to make it yet more clear to you, Eph. 4.11, 12. it is said, that He gave some, Apostles: and some, Prophets: and some, Evangelists: and some, Pastors and Teachers, for the work of the Ministry, for the Edifying of the Body of Christ. So that upon the whole Matter, you see, that the Church of Christ is a well-order'd Society of Men.

And I do withal say, that in the Constitution of Christ's Church it is requir'd, that the Governours and Pastors thereof be Lawful Ones, that is, such as Christ has Commission'd to those Offices, because if they usurp the sacred Offices of the Church, without being lawfully Ordain'd to the same, by the Successors of Christ and his Apostles, there will be very great danger of a Nullity in all their Ministerial Acts and Offices. You must all needs understand this, That those, who shall pretend to act in any Office, by the King's Authority, without a true Commission, the King will be so far from reckoning himself oblig'd, to Confirm what they shall pretend to do in his Name, that he will punish the Presumption of such Officers, and

ministry may be called if it is in Apostolic Succession

those that adhere to 'em. And what reason have those to expect better Treatment from the King of Heaven, who shall either take upon themselves the Ministry, or receive an Ordination to it from those Hands, who have no Power to confer it, or shall Adhere to Such Usurping Ministers? To put the case as Favourably, as possibly we can, it does not appear, that God is under any Promise, or Engagement to hear the Prayers, that such Ministers shall put for the People, to convey the Graces of his Holy Spirit, by the Sacraments they shall Administer, or to Ratify the Pardon of those Penitents, whom they shall Absolve; whereas he has assured the Church, with respect to his lawful Ministers, that whatsoever of this Nature they shall do on Earth, shall be Establish'd in Heaven, Matth. 16.19. And we are farther told by St. Paul, Heb. 5.4. That under the Old Law, No man took the Honour of the Priesthood unto himself, but those who were called of God, as was Aaron. And as to the Ministers of the Gospel, St. Paul does sharply demand, Rom. 10.15. How any shall Preach the Gospel, except they be sent? So that it does extreamly concern all Christian People, that the Governours and Pastors of the Church be lawful Ones, such as are Sent, Ordain'd, and Commission'd thereunto.

And now, if you would be well satisfy'd, who are certainly Sent, Ordain'd and Commission'd to Govern and Teach in the Church; it is beyond all doubt, that Bishops are lawful Governours in the Church of Christ, and that those, who are Ordain'd by their Hands, have Commission to Preach the Gospel, and Administer the Sacraments, because they do undoubtedly derive their Power by an uninterrupted Succession from Christ and his Apostles; for our Saviour, when he sent forth his Disciples into the World, to Preach the Gospel, and to gather a Church, he told 'em, Mat. 28.20. He would be with them, or stand by 'em in giving Authority and Success to their Ministry, to the end of the world; and yet for certain, for 1500 Years he did Authorize no other, than those Episcopally Ordain'd, as the Histories of all Ages of the Church do testify; so that it concerns you, who have not that Necessity to plead for not Enjoying Bishops, and an Episcopal Clergy, as our Sister Churches Beyond-Sea think they have; It concerns you, I say, as you would be secure of being within the Pale of a right Constituted Gospel-Church, not to separate your selves from this, wherein you are undoubtedly under a true Gospel Ministry. But to proceed

Secondly, The Church of Christ ② is the Universal Society of Christians. The Christian Church is not now confin'd to one particular Place, or Nation, as the Jewish was; but is Catholick and Universal, spread over all the Face of the Earth, and taking in all Nations of Men, as well those, who were Gentiles, as those, who were Jews: For Christ is our Peace, and hath made both One, and hath broken down the middle Wall of Partition between us, Eph. 2.14. The Synagogue of the Jews consisted of one Nation, and the more solemn Parts of their Publick Worship, were confin'd to one Place, as you will see,

Deut. 12.5, 6. So that it was rightly said, Joh. 4.20. Tho' the Woman of Samaria did Schismatically question it, That Jerusalem was the place wherein men ought to worship; For the Temple was the only place in which the Sacrifices could be Offer'd, and wherein the Priests could perform their daily Ministration; so that the Church, under the Law, was an Inclosure divided from all the World besides. But our Saviour, at the opening of the Christian Church, assures the Woman, who demanded of him, Whether in that Mountain, near to Samaria, whereon they both stood, or in Jerusalem, were the place where men ought to worship, he assures her, The hour cometh when neither in that Mountain, nor yet at Jerusalem, they should worship the Father; that is, not there only, nor any where in so carnal a manner, Joh. 4.20, 21, 22, 23. But as St. Peter tells us, now under the Gospel, In every Nation, he that feareth God, and worketh Righteousness, is accepted of him, Act. 10.35. And therefore our Saviour, when he sent forth his Disciples into the World, to Preach the Gospel, and to gather a Church, he commanded them, Mar. 16.15. saying, Go ye into all the World, and preach the Gospel to every Creature. From whence we find them, in Revelations 5.9. Crying unto the Lamb, Thou wast slain, and hast redeemed us unto God by thy Blood, out of every Kindred, and Tongue, and People, and Nation. So, that whereas concerning the Jewish Church it was, that God declar'd formerly, Exod. 19.5, 6. That in keeping his Covenant, they should be a peculiar Treasure unto him,

above all People, a Kingdom of Priests, and a holy Nation. Now under the Gospel it is declar'd, 1 Pet. 2.9. with respect to Persons of all Nations, who shall come within the Christian Church, that they are a Chosen Generation, a Royal Priesthood, an holy Nation, a peculiar People, that they should shew forth the Praises of him, who hath call'd them out of Darkness, into his marvellous Light: But then, I say, the Church of Christ, tho' it takes in Persons of all Nations, yet it is still to be a Holy Nation, a peculiar People. For tho' it be spread over all the World, yet

Thirdly, It consists only of such, who are Called forth out of the wicked World, by the Preaching of the Gospel, to a Holy Profession and Calling. It is not either Jews, or Gentiles, whilst they continue such, that are of the Church of Christ; but it consists of those, who are Call'd out from amongst both. The Church is a selected People, separated from the Profane part of the World, to be a Chosen Generation, a Royal Priesthood, a Holy Nation, a Peculiar People. To understand which, you must know, that the World, at the time of our Saviour's coming into it, was grown to a sad pass, and was miserably Estrang'd from God. The world, indeed, soon after the Creation, began to fall off from God, and to take part with the Devil: But by the time that our Saviour came into the Flesh, the Apostle declares, Rom. 3.11, 12. concerning as well Jews, as Gentiles, that there was none that understood, there was none that sought after God; that they were all gone out of the way, they were all become unprofitable, that there was none that did good, no not one. Particularly, as to the Gentiles, they were charg'd, Rom. 11.23, 24, 28, 29. to have Changed the Glory of the incorruptible God, into an Image made like to corruptible Man, and to Birds, and four-footed Beasts, and creeping things, and were thereupon given up to Uncleanness, and vile Affections; and as they did not like to retain God in their Knowledge, they were given up to a reprobate Mind, being filled with all Unrighteousness, Fornication, Wickedness, &c. And as to the Jews, they had in a manner wholly voided the Force of God's Laws, by their false Interpretations, as you will see in our Saviour's Sermon on the Mount, which cost him so much Pains to clear the Text from their false Glosses, and to shew them the full Extent of their Duty, contain'd in the Law. This was the State of both Jews and Gentiles, at that time: And therefore did Christ come to Call out such, as would obey his Calls, to Call 'em out, I say, out of the wicked World, to a Holy Profession and Calling; for which reason he is said to have Saved us, and called us with an Holy Calling, 2 Tim. 1.9. and in a great many Places of Scripture, Christians are therefore styl'd, the Called; and Joh. 17.6. they are said to be such, whom the Father had given our Saviour out of the world, and tho' they are in the world, ver. 11. that is, Live in the World, yet they are not of the world, ver. 16.

True it is, It is not every Member of the visible Church, that does effectually obey this Holy Calling, and in his Life and Conversation, shews himself not to be of the

World; and therefore it is, that the Kingdom of Heaven, that is, the Church, is liken'd Mat. 13.24. to a Field, in which Wheat and Tares grow up together until the Harvest; and to a Net that was cast into the Sea, and gather'd of every Kind: But however, tho' too many of those, of whom the Church is compos'd, are in their own Persons Ungodly, yet, I say,

Fourthly, They are Called by the Preaching of the Gospel, to a Holy Profession and Calling, as Namely, to Repentance from Dead Works; for so our Saviour says, He came to Call the sinners to Repentance, Matth. 9.13. And thus also his Apostles Preacht unto Men, that they should turn from the Vanities of Idol-worship, unto the Living God, which made Heaven, and Earth, and the Sea, and all things therein, Acts 14.15. which is an Instance of Repentance, that the Gentile World were particularly Call'd to.

And then as to the Knowledge and Belief of the only True God, and Jesus Christ; the distinguishing Character given of the Church of Christ, Joh. 17.2. is, that they are such, whom the Father hath given him (or given him out of the world, as it is ver. 6.) that they might have Eternal Life; and this, he tells us, ver. 3. is Eternal Life; or the way by which we can only come by Eternal Life, That we know the only True God, and Jesus Christ, whom he hath sent. The Gentiles they knew not the only True God, but Own'd and Worship'd many Gods, and did Sacrifice to Devils, I Cor. 10.20. And as for the Jews, tho' they Believ'd, indeed, in the only True God, yet they Acknowledg'd not his Son Jesus Christ, whom he had sent, to be also the True God, as he is call'd, I Joh. 5.20. And now both these Enemies to Truth, our Saviour calls the world, Joh. 17. and in Opposition to both tells us, ver. 3. that This is Life Eternal, to know the only True God, and Jesus Christ, whom he hath sent. So that the Church of Christ are such, who are peculiarly Separated from the World, to the Knowledge and Belief of the Only True God.

And they are such also, who have been Baptized into the Knowledge, Belief, and Service of Three Persons, Father, Son, and Holy Ghost, in that One Godhead, Mat. 28.19. And particularly they are such as are Baptized into the Name of Jesus, Acts 19.5. that is, into the Belief, That Jesus is the Christ, or Mediatour between God and Man, for this is the great Fundamental Doctrine of Christianity, as the Apostle tells us, I Cor. 3.11. assuring us, that Other Foundation can no man lay, than that Jesus is the Christ, or Mediatour between God and Man, for this is the great Fundamental Doctrine of Christianity, as the Apostle tells us, I Cor. 3.11. assuring us, that Other Foundation can no man lay, than that Jesus is the Christ. And he, that denyeth that Jesus is the Christ, is the great Liar, and an Anti-Christ, I Joh. 2.22. But, whosoever believeth, that Jesus is the Christ, is Born of God, I Joh. 5.1. that is, is Adopted into the Christian Church and Family.

Fifthly, And as Christians are a Society of Persons, call'd out of the World to Repentance, Faith, and Gospel-Obedience; so to the Enjoyment of those Inestimable Priviledges of the Gospel, viz. 1. Most Reasonable and Excellent Laws, given by a most Great and Gracious Governour, to Conduct 'em to Heaven, Laws writ in their Minds, and in their Hearts, Heb. 8.10. that is, Laws, which are for the most part, the very Dictates of natural Reason. 2. They are such, as are Priviledg'd with having great Measures of Divine Grace, and Assistance to enable 'em to Obey those Laws, for, whereas the Law was given by Moses, Grace and Truth came by Jesus Christ, Joh. 1.17. and is the Priviledge of the Church of Christ under the Gospel. 3. They are such, who have Assurance of Pardon of Sins, upon their Repentance for the Transgression of those Laws, for, with respect to those of the Christian Church, God is pleas'd to say, Heb. 8.12. I will be merciful to their Unrighteousness, and their Sins and Iniquities will I remember no more. And lastly, As to the Eternal Life and Happiness, Christ does assure us, Joh 17.2. that The Father has given him power over all Flesh, that he should give Eternal Life to as many as are given him, [or are] given him out of the World, ver. 6. that is, that he has a Power of conferring the Rewards in Heaven, to as many as come within the Pale of the Church, if they do withal live in Obedience to its Laws and Constitutions. Thus is the Church of Christ a Society of Men, call'd forth of the World, as to a most Holy Profession and Calling, so to the Enjoyment of most singular Priviledges.

Sixthly, And they are such, Who to the End of being Incorporated into One Society, and of having God, to be their God, and they themselves his People, have Enter'd into Covenant with him. It is the Royal Charter granted by the King, to the Members of a Corporation, or City, whereby they have certain Priviledges granted them from the King, and wherein they are Tied to discharge certain Duties to him, and to One another, that makes 'em, of a confus'd Multitude, to become a Corporation, or regulated Society. And those who stand out, and will not accept of those Priviledges, nor oblige themselves to their several Duties, shall not be reputed of that Corporation, nor receive any Advantages from it. And so it is here with that Society, which is call'd the Church of Christ. It is the Covenant of Grace, granted us by the King of Heaven, wherein we have the most inestimable Priviledges, those contain'd in the Gospel, graciously Ensur'd unto us, and most reasonable Duties both to God and Man, required of us, that do embody and join us into one Spiritual Society, the Church; and those who will not Enter into such a Covenant with God, are Aliens from the Commonwealth of Israel, and Strangers from the Covenants of Promise, having no hope, and without God in the world, Eph. 2.12. But those who have join'd themselves in Covenant with Him, are No more Strangers and Forreigners, but Fellow-Citizens with the Saints, and of the Household of God, ver. 19.

And as by being United in one Covenant, Christians are Incorporated into one Society; so by the same Means it comes to pass also, that they have God to be their God, peculiarly, and they become his People. Thus Heb. 8.10. This is the Covenant that I will make with the house of Israel after those days, that is, in the time of the Gospel, I will be to them a God, and they shall be to me a People. It is the Nature of all Covenants, to Unite the Parties Covenanting together, and to give to each Party an Interest in the other. I enter'd into Covenant with thee, and thou becamest mine, Ezek. 16.8. So that by having Enter'd into Covenant with God, we are Entitled to his particular Protection and Care over us, and we give to him thereby a new and stronger Claim to our Obedience.

Seventhly, And Christians are thus Enter'd into Covenant with God, and thereby made Members of Christ's Church in their Baptism: For as all the Members of a Corporation, are not usually made Members of that Society, without some certain Solemnities; so it pleas'd God, that no One Should be Enter'd into Christ's Church, and be made a Partaker of the Priviledges of it, without that outward Rite of Baptism; for so we find, that when our Saviour sent his Apostles to Found, and Build the Church, they receiv'd, as a Commission to call forth out of the World, a Church, by the Preaching of the Gospel: So an Appointment to Incorporate all Men therein, by Baptism; Go and teach all Nations, Baptizing them in the Name of the Father, of the Son, and of the Holy Ghost, Matth. 28.19. And hence, 1 Cor. 12.13. it is said, That we are all Baptiz'd into one Body, or admitted by Baptism into one Church.

[handwritten marginalia: Euch. = Renewal of Bapt. Covenant / = Important event / you have sinned since Bap., @ Euch you've restored.]

Eighthly, And they are appointed to Renew the same, by Feasting often together at the Lord's Supper. This was anciently, and is still the usual Method of Uniting more closely together the Members of any Society or Corporation, their Feasting often together at one common Table; and for this Reason, amongst others it is, that the Sacrament of the Lord's Supper is Appointed in the Church of Christ: So the I Cor. 10.17. it is said, That we being many are one Bread, and one Body, for we are all Partakers of that one Bread.

Ninthly, And now upon all these foremention'd Accounts, the Church of Christ is One Body. Thus Eph. 4.4, 5, 6. There is one Body, and one Spirit, even as ye are all called in one Hope of your Calling, one Lord, one Faith, one Baptism, one God and Father of all, who is above all, and through all, and in you all; where you see, that because all Christians are call'd out of the World, into one Hope of their Calling, or to the Enjoyment of the same Priviledges, to one Faith, or to Believe one God, Father, Son, and Holy Ghost, exprest here by one Spirit, one Lord, one God, and Father of all; and because Incorporated by one Baptism, or by the Use of the same Sacraments, that therefore they are one Body. The Covenant of Grace, that great Charter, whereby we are Incorporated into one Society, is One and the same amongst all Christians, containing the same Duties to be perform'd by all, and promising to every one that performs those Conditions, the same Priviledges. And all Men are every where admitted and continued in it by the same

Sacramental Solemnities, and therefore the Church founded upon, and Incorporated by that Covenant, must needs by One.

Tenthly, This One Body or Society, the Church, true it is, is Subdivided into several particular Bodies, or Churches, both for the convenience of Discipline and Government, and also for the convenience of Divine Worship. For the convenience of Government it was anciently divided into Diocesan Churches, wherein, because no one Man is able to Govern so vast a Body, as is the whole Church of God, each Bishop had his particular Flock, arising out of one City, and the Parts adjoyning, to Oversee and to Govern. Hence we read, Rev. 2. and 3. chap. of the Church of Ephesus, the Church of Smyrna, the Church of Pergamos, the Church of Thyatira, the Church of Sardis, the Church of Philadelphia, and the Church of Laodicea, all which were so many Cities in the Lesser Asia; and the Bishops of those Churches are styl'd, the Angels of those Churches, in those Second and Third Chapters of Revelations. And the Elders, or Bishops of these Churches, probably it was, that St. Paul sent for, to meet him at Miletus, Act. 20.17. and to whom he gave that solemn Charge, ver. 21.28. To take heed unto themselves, and to all the Flock, over the which the Holy Ghost had made them Overseers, to feed the Church of God, that is, to Govern and Teach the Church of Christ, which he had Purchased with his own Blood.

And as for the Convenience of Government, the Church of Christ was anciently divided into Diocesan Churches, in which Constitution of the Church, each City has its Bishop to govern and direct the Affairs of the Church: So for the Convenience of Divine Worship, and because all the Members of a City, and the Parts adjoyning, could not meet together in the same Place, was each Bishop's See farther divided, into particular Congregations and Assemblies, under the Care of its respective Pastors: Hence as to the Church of Corinth we gather, that, as it was but one Church, in regard it had but one Bishop, or Governour, for St. Paul directs his Epistle thus, Unto the Church of God which is at Corinth, I Cor. 1.2. yet in that one Episcopal Church, being there were several Congregations met together, for the Worship of God, we read, I Cor. 14.34. of Churches in the Plural Number, and this particular Order of the Apostle, about the Decency of Divine Service, in those particular Churches, or Congregations; Namely, that Women should keep Silence in the Churches.[1] Thus, true it is, the Church, which is but one Body, is Subdivided into several particular Bodies, or Churches; both for the conve-

---

[1] Bray's insistence here that St. Paul's injunction applied to "those particular Churches, or Congregations" in Corinth may reflect a long-standing debate between Anglicans and Puritans on the status of women. Puritans, both within the Church of England before the Restoration and outside of it as separate denominations afterwards, argued that women could not baptize in emergency and were not to speak in churches. "Balanced Anglicans," such as Richard Hooker, no doubt mindful of the important role of Elizabeth I in the Church of England, defended the right of women to baptize in emergency. See *Ecclesiastical Polity*, book v, chapter lxii. —Ed.

nience of Discipline and Government, and also for the convenience of Divine Worship: But however those several particular Churches were United into one Body, by one Covenant; for the Church of Corinth, the Church of Ephesus, Smyrna, &c. were are all called to the same Holy Profession and Calling, to the same Faith in God, and to the same Priviledges of Grace, Pardon, and Happiness, as the whole Church, and were admitted into that same Covenant, by the same Sacraments, as the whole Catholick Church was; by which means They kept the unity of the Spirit, in the bond of Peace, Eph 4.3. And each of those particular Congregations, also in the Church of Corinth, for Instance, were United also to the Church of God, in that City, by holding no other than the Doctrine Establish'd in that Church: And by being United thereby to that particular Part of Christ's Church, they were United also to the whole Body of Christ, and made up but one Body, For as the Body is one, and hath many Members, and all the Members of that one Body being many, are one Body; so also is Christ, or the Christian Church, for by one Spirit, we are all Baptized into one Body, whether we be Jews or Gentiles, whether we be Bond or Free; and have been all made to drink into one Spirit, I Cor. 12.12, 13. So that the Church of Christ, you see, tho' divided into many Branches, or Members, is but one Body in the whole, because United in, and by One and the same Covenant of Grace: And also in the

Eleventh Place, Because all the several particular Churches are to Hold Communion with each other.

Now as to that Communion, which the Members of Christ's Church held with one another in the Apostle's Times; (and sure their's must be a Pattern of Church-Communion) we are told, Act. 2.42, that it consisted in this, That They continued stedfastly in the Apostles Doctrine, and Fellowship, and in breaking of Bread, and in Prayers. They continued stedfastly in the Apostles Doctrine, that is, they continued constantly, and also steddily, without swerving aside by Separation, in Hearing the Apostles Teach. They continued also stedfastly in Breaking of Bread, and in Prayers, that is, they Join'd constantly and frequently in the same Prayers and Sacraments. And lastly, They continued stedfastly in the same Fellowship, by which is principally meant in the Original, both here, and in several other Places of the Scripture, that Communication of charitable Assistances, that all the Members did afford each other, according to their several Wants and Necessities: For whether any Sister-Church were under Persecutions, or any particular Christians did labour with Want, the other Members of the Body did Communicate to the Relief of either. And the Apostle did also appoint that to be done in the Christian Assemblies, when they met together to Communicate in Hearing, Prayers, and Sacraments, ordering, that The first day of the Week, which was the Day of their Publick Assemblies, every one should lay by him in store, as God had prospered him, to this Purpose, I Cor. 16.2. So that if One Member suffered, all the Members suffered with it, and there was no Schism in the Body, but the Members had the same care one of another, I Cor. 12.25, 26.

In a word: Such was the Communion, which the Members of the Church held with each other, in those Days, which made it one Church, that there was no such thing as any separate Meetings, from those of the Apostles, and their lawful Successors, the Bishops and Pastors of the Flock, set up under the Pretence of better Edification, and for more pure Administrations of Ordinances. No, no sooner did any attempt to make such a Schism, but he was accounted a Gangreen'd Member, and cut off from the Body for so doing. And so much was mutual Kindness and Charity to be the distinguishing Character of Christ's Church, that our Saviour declar'd, Joh. 13.35. That by this should all men know his Disciples, that they had love one for another.

And now Lastly, It only remains, to compleat this my Explication of Christ's Church, to shew you, That this whole Society of Men, call'd forth out of the World, to such Duties and Priviledges, as has been spoke, is to be United into one Body, as has been declar'd, under Jesus Christ its Supreme Head. Every Society of Men must have some supreme Head to keep it, both in Being, and Order; and Christ is so much, to all Intents and Purposes, the Head of the Church, that there is no respect, in which any thing is the Head of the Body, in which Christ is not, in like manner, the Head of the Church. And First, There is the Political Head in every Kingdom, which is the Prince, that gives Laws to his

People, and Heads and Protects them against their Enemies. And such a Head is Christ in that Spiritual Kingdom, the Church of God, Whom the Father having Raised from the Dead, did put all things under his Feet, and gave him to be Head over all things to the Church, which is his Body, Eph. 1.20, 21, 22, 23. And therefore pursuant to this Power, which was Given him in Heaven, and in Earth, to give Laws to Mankind, did he Commission his Disciples, and send them forth into the World, to Proclaim his Laws, to Teach all Nations, Baptizing them in the name of the Father, and of the Son, and of the Holy Ghost; Teaching them to observe all things whatsoever he had Commanded them; assuring them withal, that Lo he would be with them always, even unto the End of the World, Matth. 28.18, 19, 20. that is, That he would be ever with 'em, to Head and Protect 'em against their Adversaries.

Secondly, There is also a Domestick Head, viz, the Husband, in respect of the Wife; and so likewise is Christ the Head of the Church, and he is the Saviour of the Body, Eph. 5.23. And, indeed, the Holy Spirit does love to Represent him as such a Head, as also by the Title of a Shepherd over the Flock, to signify the Gentleness of his Laws, tending all for the Good of those he Governs.

And Thirdly, There is the Natural Head of the Body, which is the Foundation of Life and Spirit, from whence it is deriv'd into all the Parts of the Body, to enable and enliven all the Members thereof, to discharge their several Offices and Duties: And in Allusion to this, is Christ, said to be the Mystical Head of the Church, from whom all the Body, by Joynts and Bands, having Nourishment ministred, increaseth with the Increase of God, Col. 2.19.

And thus I have at length sufficiently, in order to my Design of Explaining this Article, Wherein I was made a Member of Christ, shew'd you, What kind of Body the Church of Christ is. And, by the By, from what has been said, it does appear, That the Church of Christ is a Spiritual Kingdom, put up in the World by God, on purpose to reduce Man to his due Allegiance to his Maker, and to destroy the Dominion of Satan, which he had so long Usurpt over Mankind. It is a Kingdom, as it consists of inferior Governours and Subjects, combin'd together, by special Laws of Allegiance, to the Sovereign King of Kings, and Lord of Lords, and by Priviledges granted, by that Supreme Head and Governour, to such his Subjects; and therefore it is so often, in the Scripture, call'd a Kingdom: But you see withal, it is a Spiritual Kingdom, by the Nature and Design of which, God is to Rule in the Hearts and Spirits of Men, and therefore it is, all over the New Testament, call'd the Kingdom of God, the Kingdom of Christ; For Christ does Reign and Rule therein by his Gospel, as the Laws of that Kingdom, over the Spirits of Men; and those are the People, or Subjects of this Kingdom, who own him for their King, and his Gospel for the Laws of this Kingdom, and who do give themselves up wholly, both Body, Soul and Spirit to be Governed by those Laws.

And the Church is also often call'd in the Holy Scripture, the Kingdom of Heaven, for indeed it is not a Kingdom of this World, supported with outward State, and armed Forces, in order to promote, and to secure from those who would Invade 'em, our temporal Interests; If my Kingdom were of this World, then would my Servants fight, that I should not be deliver'd to the Jews, Joh. 18.36. but it is a Kingdom, or Society of Men, associated together, and Lifted to Fight under Christ, the Great Captain of our Salvation, against much more formidable Enemies, than any Earthly Potentates; Even against Principalities and Powers, against the Rulers of the Darkness of this World, against spiritual Wickedness in high Places, Eph. 6.12. that is, against the Devil, and his wicked Angels, who would despoil us of our Heavenly Inheritance. Lifted, I say, to fight under Jesus Christ, the Great Captain of our Salvation, for so he is call'd Heb. 2.10. and to our Comfort, who are to fight under him, he has already Spoiled these Principalities and Powers, and has made a shew of them openly upon the Cross, triumphing over them in it, Col. 2.15. So that our Work is in a great measure already done under his Conduct, for he himself has divested the Devils of much of their Power, he has thrown 'em out of their Temples, silenc'd their Oracles, and does daily, by his Assistances, enable us to Foil 'em. So that the Church of Christ, you see, is a Spiritual Kingdom.

But yet notwithstanding, that this Society, the Church, is a Spiritual Kingdom, both as its Laws are Spiritual, reaching to the Government of the Inward Man; and also, as it is a Body Lifted under a Spiritual King, to fight against Spiritual Enemies: Yet however, from what has been said, it does appear, that the Church, or Kingdom of Christ, is a Visible Society of Men, consisting of such who make an Outward and Visible Profession of Allegiance to Christ, having visibly, by an Outward Sacrament, Enter'd into Covenant with him, and being such as do visibly Communicate together in his Holy Ordinances. And therefore it is not only of such who by an inward, real, and true Faith are United to Christ, that the Church and Kingdom of God, in this World, does consist, but of all those outward Professors of Christianity, who, by the Sacrament of Baptism, have Enter'd into Covenant with God, Such indeed as besides an outward Covenanting, (which is certainly necessary) are Renew'd withal to the Image of God in Knowledge, Righteousness, and true Holiness, are the only Persons of which the Invisible Church, as it is call'd, does consist in this World, these perhaps being meant by the Little Flock, Luk. 12.32. and of such only will the whole Church, in the World to come, be made up, being, of The many that are Called, the few that are Chosen, Matth. 20.16. But if we consider the Church of Christ in its fully Latitude, and in that imperfect State wherein it now is, on this side [of] Heaven; many Hypocrites and bad Men, as well as truly sincere and good Christians, do belong to it, for the Church of Christ, here on Earth, is compar'd, Matth. 13.24, 25. to a Field, which contains

Wheat and Tares growing up together, and to a Net, ver. 47. wherein there are Fish, both good and bad. Such you see is the Nature and Temper of that Body of Christ, his Church; concerning which I thought it requisite to give you a more than ordinary full account, even in this place, before we come to the Article, I believe the Holy Catholick Church, because that otherwise it cannot be so well apprehended.

[II.] Secondly, What it is to be a Member of Christ's Church; which now the way being so far clear'd, I shall in few words shew you. And from what has been said it does easily now appear, that a true Member of the Church of Christ, is one who belongs to that Society of Christians which consists of Lawful Governours and Pastors, and of the People of God committed to their Charge, the one Ministring in Holy Things, and the other Partaking thereof at their Hands. He is not a Member of that narrow and enclos'd Society of Worshipers, the Jewish Synagogue, who by their peculiar Rites and Ways of Worship, were confin'd to one Nation and Place, no more than he is one of the Gentile World at large; but he is One, who either himself was call'd, or is descended of those who were call'd, from out of the wicked World of Jews and Gentiles, to a Holy Profession and Calling, viz. To the Belief of the One True God, Father, Son and Holy Ghost; as also to Repentance from dead Works, to Faith and Repentance, so to enjoy the Priviledges of the Gospel, and the Rewards of such Faith and Repentance; namely, Most Reasonable and Excellent Laws and Ordinances, to conduct him to Heaven, with a plentiful measure of Divine Grace and Assistance also, convey'd by those Ordinances, to enable him to Obey those Laws; and he is One, who to the End of being of that Society of Men, the Christian Church, and of having God a Friend to him, and he himself a Servant of God's, has solemnly Enter'd into Covenant with God in his Baptism, and continues often to Renew the same in the Lord's Supper, because the Divine Goodness does in both Vouchsafe to make over and ensure to him those exceeding Great and Invaluable Priviledges, and most singular Benefits, as well as he on the other side, does solemnly Engage to yield himself up to the Service and Obedience of God. Farther yet, a Member of Christ's Church is one, who is not only United to the Catholick Church in and by one Covenant, that is, in the Profession of the same Faith and Repentance, and in the Enjoyment of the same Priviledges, and in the use of the same Sacraments. But also he maintains this Union therewith, by Communicating with that particular Part of the Catholick Church where he lives, and whereof he is a Member in particular; by communicating, I say, therewith in Hearing, together with the rest of the Body, the same Doctrine, in Joyning in the same Common-Prayers, and receiving the same Holy Sacraments; and Lastly, in Receiving from and Administring mutual Assistances to the Members of that Body, where-ever dispers'd, or however distress'd over the Face of the whole World, as there shall be occasion. And Lastly, a Member of Christ's Church is One, who belongs to that universal Society of Men, call'd out of the World, to such Duties and Priviledges, as has been spoke, and is united into one Body, by the same means, as has been declar'd, under Jesus Christ its Supreme Head. And if you consider him as a Member of the Kingdom of Christ, he is one who is Delivered by God from the power of Darkness, and is translated into the Kingdom of his dear Son, Col. 1.13. that is, he is one of those, who is deliver'd by the Gospel, from under the Tyranny of Satan, under which the whole World was held Captive, and is made a Subject to the Gracious Government of the Son of God. From what has been said, it does plainly appear, I think, that such, and such a One only, is a true Member of Christ's Church.

And in the Sence of your Catechism, which teaches all to Answer, That in their Baptism they are made Members of Christ; every Person who has been admitted into the Church by Baptism, is a Member of Christ, and shall continue such till he is cut off by the just Sentence of those Governours in the Church, who have the Power of the Keys, to Receive in, or Shut out; or till he cuts off himself from that mystical Body, by a causeless Schism and Separation from any of its found Parts.

Every Baptized Person, I say, is a Member of the Visible Church. So the Apostle expresly speaks, Gal. 3.27. assuring us, that As many as have been Baptized into Christ, that is, the Christian Church, have put on Christ, or have put on that Relation to Christ that Members have to the Body. True it is, amongst those, that are Incorporated by Baptism into the Church, many do prove but very unsound and unfruitful Members; such as, tho' they are admitted into that Holy Society, in order to their Edification, and through Conversion, by the means of those Holy Ordinances, which Christ has appointed in his Church, do yet continue to be very bad Men, both in their Principles and Practices. Hence it is said, Matth. 22.10. that of those who were called into the Wedding, that is, the Church, by the Servants or Officers of the Bridegroom, that is, Christ, there are as well Bad as Good. Yet as appears from that, and many the like Parables of our Saviour, concerning the Materials and Constitution of his Church, even such bad Men, when once Baptized into it, are Members of it.

And shall continue to be Members of it, till such time as they are cut off by the just Sentence of those who have the Power of the Keys, to Receive in, or Shut out. For this you are to know, that Christ has given his Apostles, and their Successors in the Government of the Church, a Church Authority, consisting in Receiving in, or Shutting out of the Church. To Receive into the Church, is to Admit such as make a Profession of Christianity; to Admit 'em, I say, by the Sacrament of Baptism, to all the outward Acts of Communion. To shut, or cast out of the Church, is by Excommunication to Exclude unworthy Persons from that Priviledge of Church-Communion, to deny 'em the Liberty to Pray, or Receive the

Sacrament, or perform any Religious Office in the Publick Assemblies of the Church. And now accordingly has Christ appointed the Bishops and Governours of his Church, to be as Shepherds to Oversee the Flock, as you will find, Act. 20.28. and has given 'em The Keys of the Kingdom of Heaven, Matth. 16.19. that is, Authority, as to Admit into the Church, by Baptism, all who make a Profession of Christianity; so to Expel out of it, by Excommunication, all those scabbed Members thereof, who contrary to such their Holy Profession, either by their pestilent Heresies, or by their scandalous Lives, are Unworthy of it, and in danger to Infect it. If they Preach, or anywise propagate any pestilent Heresy, contrary to the Fundamental Truths of Christianity, let their Persons be never so acceptable, upon the account of some shining Vertues of Charity, or their Doctrines never so Plausible, as pretending to Reason, they ought not to be spared. Tho' we, or an Angel from Heaven, preach any other Gospel unto you, than that which we have preached unto you, let him be Accursed; that is, Excommunicated, and cut off from Church-Communion, Gal. 1.8. So far was this Blessed Apostle, so Zealous for the Glory of his Saviour, from sparing others, that he would not have himself be suffer'd to continue in the Communion of the Church, were it possible he should be guilty of propagating Heresy: And so likewise is any Person, guilty of a notorious and scandalous Ill Life. Why then also are the Governours of Christ's Church commanded, To put away from 'em that wicked person, I Cor. 5.13? And all the Members of the mystical Body, are so far bound to take notice of such an Excommunication, as to disown and discard such a Person, and to have no Society with him, so I Cor. 5.11. If any Man that is called a Brother, be a Fornicator, or Covetous, or an Idolater, or a Railer, or a Drunkard, or an Extortioner, with such a one, after Excommunication, they were not to Eat. In such Cases as these, indeed, an Evil Member becomes no Member, and is to be to the rest as a Heathen Man, and a Publican, that is, One that is out of the Church, Matth. 18.17.

And so likewise is he, who cuts himself off from that mystical Body the Church, by a causeless Schism, and Separation from any of its sound Parts. I say, any of its sound Parts, for where-ever there is a true Church, if there be nothing in its Doctrine nor Worship that is sinful, every Person is bound to Continue stedfastly in the Doctrine, Prayers, and Sacraments, and Fellowship of that Church, as in the Apostle's times they did, Act. 2.42. and to reject the Communion of all other Parties and Sects of Christians, or otherwise he will cut off himself from the Church, and will cease to be a real Member of it, as the Finger ceases to be of the Body, when it is cut off from the Arm. Thus in either of these Cases, indeed, shall a Person discontinue to be a Member of Christ's Church; when either he is Cut off, by the just Sentence of those Governours in the Church, who have the Power of the Keys, to Receive in, or Shut out, or when he Cuts himself off by a causeless Separation and Schism, from any of its sound Parts.

But otherwise, all Persons who have Enter'd into Covenant with God, and have been Admitted into it by Baptism, are Members of Christ's Church, (as has been already sufficiently prov'd, and need not again be repeated:) And so shall Partake of those exceeding great Priviledges, which belong to the Members of it; which what, and how great they are, I come next to declare unto you.

CHAPTER THREE

THE GREAT AWAKENING
(1740–1776)

By the middle of the eighteenth century some Anglicans began to complain that the reasonable faith preached by their coreligionists since the time of the Glorious Revolution was too intellectual and did little to reach the heart. In 1739–40 Englishman George Whitefield (1714–70) made his first preaching tour of the colonies. He brought with him a simple message that had attracted large crowds in England: God had changed his life, and God would change the lives of others who turned to Him. Congregationalist Jonathan Edwards (1703–58) and other colonial clergy had preached a similar message before Whitefield's coming. Together they helped promote a great religious awakening in the colonies.

Though an Anglican, Whitefield preached in churches of any denomination that would welcome him. When no invitation was issued, he preached outdoors. The awakening that he helped to spread proved at times divisive—Congregationalists and Presbyterians divided into "old" and "new" factions, depending on their response to the "new" message—but it left a permanent mark on all of American Christianity.

United by ties to England rather than by any colonial hierarchy, Anglicans did not divide over the awakening in the same way as Congregationalists and Presbyterians. Their communications with England did, however, reveal a diversity of opinion. The parishioners of St. Paul's in Philadelphia would "only look to Mr. Whitefield to send them a minister." In contrast, Yale convert Timothy Cutler wrote a detailed description of George Whitefield's first visit to New England, advising that "we must caution our People against" his doctrines.[1]

The doctrinal issue that so worried Cutler was Whitefield's disregard for the covenant–apostolic order argument. For Whitefield the church's legitimacy depended not on its apostolic link with the past, but on its ability to promote personal conversion in the present. Yet logically the apostolic succession and personal conversion were not mutually exclusive. Anglicans in the colonies sought to reconcile them in one of two ways: by making their church the primary agent of awakening, or by seeking to promote piety in ways that were peculiar to the Anglican church. Charles Pettigrew (1744–1807) of North Carolina, whose father had been converted by Whitefield's preaching, and Devereux Jarratt (1733–1801) of Virginia, whose sermon follows, both took the first approach. A majority of the New England clergy took the second. Their search for uniquely Anglican sources of piety led them to call for a colonial episcopate and to stress the advantages of a fixed liturgy. Their appeal would attract many Protestants wearied by the liturgical excesses of the awakening liturgics.

The first selection is one of Devereux Jarratt's early sermons. Jarratt had traveled from Virginia to England for ordination in 1762. While there he had heard Whitefield preach. When he returned to the colonies in the following year to become the rector of Bath Parish, he began to emulate Whitefield's style. Leaving behind any concern for the dictates of natural religion, he stressed the importance of personal conversion. Many were touched by Jarratt's preaching and in the years before the Revolution he spoke not only to increasing crowds in his own congregation, but also to numerous gatherings in other parishes.

Martha Laurens Ramsay (1759–1811) wrote the second selection, "A Self Dedication and Solemn Covenant with God," in 1773. Mrs. Ramsay was the daughter of South Carolina patriot Henry Laurens. At the time she wrote her covenant, she was a fourteen-year-old parishioner of St. Philip's in Charleston. In the years that followed she demonstrated both a lively intellect—learning, for example, both Greek and Latin so that she could prepare her sons for college—and a continuing personal piety. While in England

---

[1]William Stevens Perry, *Historical Collections Relating to the American Colonial Church*, 3 vols. (Hartford, 1870; reprint ed., New York: AMS Press, 1969), 1:348, 2:414.

from 1775 to 1778, she became acquainted with Whitefield sup-
porter Selina Countess of Huntington (1707–91). After her marriage to Dr. David Ramsay in Charleston in 1787, she directed
much of her efforts to the spiritual and physical care of her eleven
children. Struck by her deep faith, Dr. Ramsay had her memoirs
published after her death.

Her covenant, which she did not share with others during her
lifetime, was the product of an eager adolescent spirit. It con-
trasted strongly with the formal covenant of Bray's *Catechism*.
Though Mrs. Ramsay recognized the importance of the institutional church—she reaffirmed her covenant by receiving communion—it was the awakened personal sense, rather than the
nature of the ordained ministry that was central for her.[2]

Jarratt and Ramsay acknowledged their debt to Whitefield and
the Awakening. Those who were lukewarm or antagonistic to
Whitefield may not have admitted it, but they were also strongly
influenced by the Awakening. They emphasized personal faith.
They placed greater importance on preaching, often replacing two-
foci church designs (altar and pulpit on different walls) with central pulpits that towered over the congregation. They discovered
the emotive power of music in public worship. Before the Awakening they sang only metrical arrangements of psalms; in the de-
cades after it, they would sing an increasing number of hymns that
testified to personal faith.

The text of Jarratt's sermon is taken from *Sermons on Various
and Important Subjects, in Practical Divinity, Adapted to the
Plainest Capacities, and Suited to the Family and Closet* (Philadelphia: Johnston & Justice, 1793–94), pp. 63–84. David Ramsay
printed his wife's covenant as an appendix to his *Memoir of the
Life of Martha Laurens Ramsay*, fourth edition (Boston: Samuel T.
Armstrong, 1814), pp. 54–62.

---

[2]Joanna Bowen Gillespie, a fellow at the Institute of Early American History and Culture,
is preparing a biographical account of Mrs. Ramsay's life. For additional information on
Awakening religious accounts by American women, see Dr. Gillespie's "'The Clear Leadings
of Providence': Pious Memoirs and the Problems of Self-Realization for Women in the Early
Nineteenth Century," *Journal of the Early Republic* 5 (Summer 1985), pp. 197–221.

DEVEREUX JARRATT
(c. 1763)

The Miserable State of Man, by Nature;
and the way of Recovery, by Faith in Jesus Christ.

But the Scripture hath concluded all under sin,
that the promise by faith of Jesus Christ might
be given to them that believe. [Galatians, iii. 22.]

Saint Paul was indeed a wise master-builder; and well knew how to lay a sure foundation for men to build their hopes for eternity.—He was well acquainted with the fallen and miserable state of mankind;—that none but Christ could save them;—and that, from the pride of their hearts, they never would be induced rightly to apply to the Redeemer for salvation, until they are made deeply sensible of their guilt, danger and helplessness.—He had been divinely and experimentally taught this truth, and that the whole system of redemption, through Jesus Christ, was founded on the fall and ruin of the human race, and their utter inability to save themselves, or regain the divine *favour* and *image, which* they had lost, by their apostacy. He also knew, at the same time, how prone all men are to depend on their own power and good deeds to recommend themselves to the favour of God;—and to seek justification, in his sight, by the works of the law, or by the merit of their own righteousness.

Now, as it is of the greatest importance, for men to be undeceived, in these respects, the apostle wrote two whole epistles, pointedly on this subject;—to wit, that to the *Romans,* and this to the *Galatians.*—In these he exposes, in the most striking and alarming colours, the intire depravity, and universal corruption of human nature, in its fallen state;—that Jew and Gentile were all equally depraved and obnoxious;—he thunders out the tremendous curses of the holy law, to which they stood exposed for their multiplied breaches thereof;—and proves, to a demonstration, that they were so far from being able to obtain justification and eternal happiness, by the law of works, which is infinitely holy, just and good, that *the Scripture,* which reveals that law, *hath* clearly shut up, or, *concluded all* men, of every nation and description, *under sin,* as malefactors; under sentence of death;—and assures sinners that the law was not given, or published, with an intent, that they should seek and obtain

[44]

pardon and life thereby, this being impossible after it was once broken,—but to give the knowledge of sin,—shew the danger of it, and thus convince them of their ruined and helpless state, in themselves, and thereby evince the necessity of a Mediator, and constrain the guilty to fly to Jesus Christ, as their only refuge and deliverer.—And it is in this respect, I apprehend, that the law is said to be our *schoolmaster, to bring us to Jesus Christ, that we may be justified by the faith of Christ.* And that there is no other door of hope, but in this way, is proved by a variety of arguments; and one of great weight is contained in the words of the next. "But the Scripture hath concluded all under sin, that the promise by faith of Jesus Christ might be given to them that believe."

To bring sinners to Jesus Christ, as their only refuge from the storms of divine wrath and vengeance, due to their transgressions, is a principal design, not only of Saint Paul's writings, and of revelation in general, but also, of our preaching and your hearing: and this prime object, I would ever keep in view, in my ministry among you, the dear people of my charge—But as I am fully convinced, that none will ever prize the physician, until they feel their soul's disease, and are earnestly wishing for health, I intend, in the prosecution of this subject,

I. To speak something of the miserable and wretched state of man, implied in these words, *The Scipture hath concluded all under sin.*

II. Point out the connection of the text, by showing how the scrip-ture, by concluding, or shutting up, all under sin, is subservient to the attainment of life and salvation, by faith in Jesus Christ.

III. Make some application.

I. I am to speak something of the miserable and wretched state of man, implied in these words, *the Scripture hath concluded, etc.*

The miserable and wretched state of mankind consists, in their original and actual sin, whereby they have attainted all their blood, and are become condemned malefactors, in the sight of God.

The total depravity and corruption of the human race might be clearly evinced from the general history of the world, and the conduct of mankind towards their Creator, in all ages. But as this would lead me into a detail of matters, too tedious and lengthy for a popular discourse, I shall therefore, in proof of this particular, chiefly confine myself to the *sacred writings,* which is the fountain of intelligence, and the standard of our faith and practice. Testimonies from *these* are very express and decided, on this head; and so numerous, that I shall content myself with producing only a few, which will abundantly suffice for the present purpose.

With the testimony of *Moses,* recorded in the vi. chap. of Genesis, 5th verse, I shall begin. "And God saw that the wickedness of man was great in the earth, and that every imagination of the thoughts of his heart, was only evil continually."—The apostate nature of man is the source of all wickedness: hence it is that all his thoughts are perverse, and every rising imagination pregnant with evil, without intermission. What a lively picture is this of the fallen spirit of man?—David bears testimony to the same melancholy truth, when he says, "I was shapen in iniquity, and in sin did my mother conceive me."—As if he had said, "My nature is altogether corrupt, and utterly vitiated with sin, and from *this root* have those foul offences sprung, which I now deplore with streaming eyes and a broken heart." The Old Testament abounds with testimonies of this sort, as may be seen in one view, in St. Paul's gloomy picture of human nature, Rom. iii. 10–18;—and which he tells us is drawn from an Old Testament original. "As it is written," says he, "there is none righteous, no not one: there is none that understandeth, and that seeketh after God. They are all gone out of the way,—there is none that doeth good, no not one," etc.—Of moral rectitude, which is the glory of the rational nature, we are stripped and deprived, by our fall from God; so that every mouth must be stopped, and all the world of mankind stand guilty before *him.*—Nor are the lines less strong and expressive, whereby the same truth is laid before us, Eph. ii. 1–3. "And you hath he quickened who were dead in trespasses and sins; wherein, in times past, ye walked according to the course of this world, according to the prince of the power of the air, the spirit that now worketh in the children of disobedience. Among whom also we all had our conversation in times past, in the lusts of the flesh, and of the mind; and were, by nature, children of wrath even as others."—*Children of wrath!*—how strong and gloomy the expression!—Heirs of the curse denounced against sin and all moral turpitude and disobedience,—and unable to help ourselves, as being by nature *dead* in trespasses and sins: *dead* to God;—*dead* in law, as being under the curse and condemnatory sentence of the broken covenant;—and dead in state,—incapable of spiritual sensations and actions, till we are quickened by divine grace, and aided by divine power.—How manifestly does this whole passage mark and describe our guilty and helpless state, and the dangerous consequences of sinning against the holy and just God?—

But man's guilt, misery and condemnation, and his utter inability to help himself, are so clearly and repeatedly pointed out in the bible, that every one of you must discover these things, who will not obstinately shut your eyes against the light. O that God may give you to see and feel them in a proper manner.

As an additional proof, or evidence of original sin, and of human guilt and wretchedness, I might call your attention to the innumerable miseries and calamities, which now, and in all ages have pervaded the earth. No age, no station has been exempted. In cries, in pains, in sickness, and in death, the infant of days plentifully shares with manhood, and hoary hairs. Now, as it is not agreeable to the justice and goodness of God, to afflict innocence; guilt must necessarily be supposed.

I might also appeal to your own hearts and consciences for the truth of this case. Look into your own hearts and lives. Are your hearts right with God? And are your tempers humble, filial and dutiful towards him? Do not you find in yourselves a strange disaffection and backwardness to the service of God, and the duties of religion; while you are all alive to the world,—fond of its vanities, riches, honours and pleasures;—and eager in the gratification of sinful desires, passions, and appetites? May not your conscience bear witness against you, that this is the case with you? And do not your own hearts condemn, and pronounce you guilty of ten thousand breaches of that righteous law, which denounces every one accursed, who has not continued *in all things written in the book of the law to do them*?—Say then, O man, do not these things prove, beyond all controversy, both the original depravity and corruption, as well as the guilt of multiplied actual transgressions against that eternal majesty, whose justice will by no means clear the guilty?—You know, my brethren you are guilty of many violations of the moral law;—You have again and again left undone those things, which you ought to have done; and done those things which you ought not to have done. And if even your own partial hearts and blinded minds condemn you,—alas! how do you expect to stand acquitted at the awful bar of Jehovah, who knows your hearts, and all your God-provoking and heaven-daring practices!—And now, O ye Christless, impenitent, and uncovered sinners, I beg of you in the name of heaven's eternal King, consider the miserable and wretched state your precious souls are in, at this present time: and say, is it safe,—is it wise for you to continue therein, for a single day longer?—And if not, pray what are you thinking to do? How do you expect to obtain a pardon, or make an atonement for your guilt?—Do you think of doing this, by your repentance, tears, reformation, future obedience, or any thing you can either do, or suffer? Be assured, O vain man, that none of these things nor all of them together, can give you boldness and acceptance in the presence of God, in the day, that he shall judge the secrets of all hearts, by Jesus Christ. No, nor will all these things together cancel your debt to Divine Justice, or atone for the least sin. For these are but works of that law, which hath concluded all under sin and guilt, and condemnation,—and by the deeds of which, shall no flesh living be justified.

But here you might probably ask,—"of what use then is the law?—or why was it published to mankind, if life and salvation are not to be obtained by the observance of it?" I answer, in the apostle's words, that, *the law was added because of transgression*; and by the law is the *knowledge of sin*: and in this respect it answers a very valuable purpose, as I shall now proceed to shew, under the

II. Head: where I am to point out the connection of the text by shewing how the law, by concluding, or shutting up, all under sin, is subservient to the attainment of life and salvation by faith in Jesus Christ.

In pointing out the connection of the text, it is to be observed, that the scope of the apostle's design, in the preceding part of the epistle in general, and of this chapter in particular, was to prove that justification and eternal life could not possibly be obtained by the law of works, even the most perfect edition of it. In the 19th verse, he intimates that some might object to this representation of the matter, and say, "If we cannot be justified and saved by an observance of the precepts of the law, what is the use of it, or wherefore, or to what purpose serveth the law?"—I have already noticed the answer to this question, that it *was added,* because of transgressions;—that is, it was promulgated, on mount Sinai, a considerable time after the gracious promise made to Abraham, that *in his seed all the nations of the earth should be blessed.* And the intent of its promulgation was, *because of transgressions*; that is, to convict the Jews and others of the guilt of their crimes committed against God, and thus to induce them to seek, with the greatest degree of earnestness, to obtain pardon and life, by faith in Jesus Christ. And to shew that the law was not given in wrath, but in mercy, and to subserve the gracious designs of the gospel, it is added that *it was ordained by angels in the hand of a mediator*: that is, it was promulgated, by the ministration of angels, and deposited in the hand of Moses, who was appointed, by God, to mediate between him, and the people of Israel.—The depositing of the law in a Mediator's hands shewed that it was given, in mercy, and to answer a gracious purpose;—for had it been given, in wrath, it would have been lodged, no doubt in the hands of an executioner.

But as the law was published after the promise was given to Abraham; some might think that the law had superseded the promise, and rendered it of no effect: and so it might be asked, Is the law then against the promises of God? Does the law infringe, or disannul the promises?—To which the apostle answers, *God forbid.* So far from this, that on the contrary it was intended to subserve the promise, by leading the hearts and thoughts of those, who are under it, and observe its strictness and broad extent, to a more benign and gracious dispensation. *For if there had been any law given, which could have given life,* or by which any sinner could possibly be saved, then verily this Mosaick law would have been it,—as being the most excellent and perfect edition of the law. But, this was so far from being the case, that *the Scripture,* in revealing this law, *hath concluded all under sin*; plainly shewn that Jews and Gentiles are guilty and helpless, as well as condemned malefactors:—and it was wisely and mercifully ordered,—that men, being convicted of their guilt and misery, by the law, might be constrained to quit all hope and dependence on it and to look for deliverance from their lost and helpless condition, from some other quarter;—even from that promise of righteousness and life, which can only be obtained by faith in Jesus Christ. Thus you see the connectin of the text, and how the seeming severity of the law was mercifully intended to subserve the promise, and promote the salvation of sinners through Jesus Christ.—

The state of the case is briefly thus. When God made man, he entered into a *covenant of works* with him,—the condition of which was perfect obedience, on pain of death.—Man broke this covenant, whereby he forfeited the favour of God, and every blessing, and incurred the threatened penalty.— But after the covenant of works was broken, by Adam, God was pleased to enter into a covenant of grace with fallen man, which was calculated to deliver him out of that state of sin and misery, to which his apostacy had reduced him, and to bring him into a state of favour and salvation, by a Redeemer.

This covenant, with the blessings it contains, was first published to Abraham, and in him to us, and to all, who will plead an interest in it, and the benefits of it, on the gracious terms, on which they are offered.—But men, being insensible of their guilt and danger, and also proud and self-sufficient, disregard these offers, and make light of Christ and the gospel. Therefore God published his holy and terrible law, by Moses, in thunder and fire, which made the mountain to quake, and even Moses to tremble.—In doing this, he pursued the same merciful design: because he knew, that till mankind were convinced of their guilt and danger, by means of the law they had broken, they never would prize the gospel, or fly to the Lord Jesus Christ for help and deliverance; and plead that pardon and salvation which, in

Christ, are promised to all that believe. Thus, or to this purpose, *hath the Scripture concluded* all under sin; made it manifest that all are so, that the promise by faith of Jesus Christ, may be given to and gladly accepted by, all that believe.—

Pride being the reigning sin in man, the law was given to humble and convince him of his guilt and miserable state, and compel him, as it were, by happy necessity, to fly to the *gospel method* of salvation: *this* being the only way, by which fallen sinners can possibly escape the wrath of God, which is revealed from heaven, against all ungodliness and unrighteousness of men. *It is the only way*;—for the law demands nothing less than perfect, perpetual, and unsinning obedience, to all its precepts, on pain of death. It admits of no failure in thought, word, or deed. It declares what is due from the creature to the Creator, and insists upon full payment, even to the last mite. The law shews no mercy, makes no promise of pardon to the guilty, —but for the first offence, for ever excludes from all hopes of mercy.—It denounces condemnation *and wrath, tribulation and anguish against every soul* of man *that doth evil.* Hear its awful language, O yet guilty sinners, and tremble, "Cursed is every one, that continueth not in all things written in the book of the law, to do them." *All things,* without exception, and that at all times, seasons and places,—from the first moment of existence, to the utmost point of duration; and all this to the highest degree of perfection.—By any deviation from the strictness and spirituality of the law, whether small or great;—whether by omitting what is commanded, or committing what is forbidden, we forfeit the favour of God, and become liable to the strokes of eternal Justice.—*Do this, and live,—transgress and die,* is the uniform cry of the law of works.

From the consideration of these things, we may readily discover how the law, by concluding all under sin, subserves the gracious purposes of the gospel, and tends to lead mankind to the Saviour. Because it makes a discovery of sin, and as at the same time it continues to demand nothing less than perfect obedience, it shews sinners that they are *helpless,* as well as *guilty.* For, I presume, none will pretend to plead innocence; and the law will admit of no plea for guilt;—it is not only silent about forgiveness, but in the most express and awful words, thunders out the sentence of death and damnation against all the workers of iniquity without exception. Thus every sinner is *shut up under sin,* bound hand and foot;—his mouth is stopped, and nothing remains for him, but to continue in misery, and under the curse of the law for ever; or else to take the alarm, and fly to the promise of life, which is by the faith of Jesus Christ: or, in other words, appeal from the law to the gospel, from the covenant of works to the covenant of grace, and claim the benefit of that indemnity, which Christ hath purchased with his precious blood, and freely offers to *all;*—to *all,* who condemning themselves, and renouncing all trust in their own righteousness,

flee to him, as their only refuge and rock of salvation. I now proceed to make some

III.

APPLICATION

A very natural inference from the doctrine is, that while sinners are insensible of the evil and danger of sin, and of their own lost and helpless state;—and as long as they go about to make excuses for sin, and lessen its guilt, or seek to recommend themselves to God, by the works of their own hands,—they are out of the way of salvation, and exclude themselves from *the promise of life* in Christ Jesus, which is *given,* and must be received, as a matter of free, unmerited favour,—and not in consideration of our own merits or deservings.— But the *soul,* that, having seen his guilt and misery in the glass of the law,—is humbled and self-condemned, acknowledging his guilt, and groaning beneath its enormous load,—*this soul,* lies in the very road of mercy, and is in a fair way of obtaining salvation and everlasting happiness, by faith in our Lord Jesus Christ.—For if it be the great end of the law to convince of sin, and to bring down the haughtiness of man, that he may feelingly acknowledge his guilt and wretchness, and thus be constrained to fly to Christ, the only Saviour;—then, the law having had this salutary effect, that man is not far from the kingdom of heaven. Let him only wait diligently upon the Lord in the use of the means of grace, and cry for the gift of faith, and the God of mercy will hear him, in the day of trouble and distress, and enable him to believe, that, being justified by faith, he shall enjoy peace with God, through Jesus Christ our Lord.

Be persuaded then, my dear brethren, to humble yourselves before your offended Sovereign, that you may be exalted in due time. And that you may be constrained so to do, consider the miserable state your souls are in, while you have no interest in the promise, which is by the faith of Jesus Christ. My brethren, you have all sinned, and by sin exposed yourselves to the curse of the divine law, and to all the racking tortures of everlasting burnings:—by sin you have sustained the loss of heaven, and all its blooming and unfading joys;—and death stands ready at your doors to rend you from earth and all the joys and comforts of this fleeting world.— Then, stripped of all good, and destitute of every blessing,—you must languish and pine away, in remediless want and wretchedness, through an endless duration, without ease or hope.—Reflect, O reflect, but a moment, ye impenitent, Christless sinners,—that if you do not now escape the tremendous curse of that broken law, to which, at this moment, you stand exposed, you must for ever feel the twinging agonies of remorseful conscience,—you will be cut off by the sword of justice, and swept away by the besom of destruction.— Swept away into the doleful regions of horror and despair, there to spend a long, long eternity in inextinguishable flames, in remediless, intolerable torments;—to live in the wretched society of malignant devils and damned souls,—mu-

tually promoting, and mutually joining in the general ROAR of torture, desperation, mourning, and woe.—This is undoubtedly, your just,—your unavoidable doom, unless you take the alarm, given by the law, and instantly fly to, and by faith obtain an interest in the only Saviour of a lost and guilty world.—And will you still loiter and delay, while exposed to so much danger, and the load of sin, heaped up for so many years, lies so heavy upon you, and is ready to crush you down to bottomless perdition.—

Perhaps one and another may be ready to say, "I am convinced that I am a grievous sinner,—condemned for my transgressions, and that there is no salvation for me, by the constitution of the law of works:—but you tell us that God has constituted a new covenant of grace, wherein pardon and salvation are offered to sinners, and that these are to be obtained by faith in Jesus Christ.—But how shall I obtain a living faith; or how am I to be interested in the benefits, which Christ has purchased and promised to believers."—I answer, God has been pleased to appoint means for the attainment of *this,* and it is only in the vigorous use of these means, that we can expect to attain.—'Tis our bounden duty to read, hear, watch and pray. And though these things do not merit or deserve the *blessing,* yet it is only in the diligent use of them, that we have any reason to expect it. Faith cometh by hearing; and it is by the use of means, that it pleases God to make a sinner deeply sensible of guilt and condemnation, and of his utter inability to justify himself.—

personal conversion regined

But when a sinner is really humbled under a sense of sin, and, despairing of all relief in himself, renounces all hopes in his own righteousness, and trusts only and intirely in the free grace of God in Jesus Christ;—when he places his whole dependence upon Christ's righteousness, that is, on what he has *done* and *suffered*; and most earnestly pleads, that God would deal with him intirely upon that footing,—then the man believes, and the promise, which is by faith, is given to him;—for the righteousness of Christ is made over to him, that God no longer views him as under condemnation, by the law, but as a justified believer, who has, in Christ, a righteousness equal to all the demands of the law, or covenant of works. Hereupon he is pronounced righteous, or just; a title to heaven is given to him, and every blessing necessary to make him holy here, and happy hereafter.—This, I believe is the gospel method of salvation, and to induce sinners to accept this free and full salvation, the scripture hath concluded all under sin.—Now as it is certain that every man and woman, in this large assembly, has either accepted this blessed promise of salvation, by faith, or has not:—and that whosoever has, is in a happy state,—and whosoever has not, is still under the curse; it highly becomes us to examine, whether we have actually taken refuge in Christ, and so are under grace; or whether we be still under the law; and so subjected to its curse.

Be assured of this, that every man is still under the law, and exposed to all its terrors, who has not personally fled to the gospel for refuge, and received and rested on Jesus Christ, by the humble faith of a guilty, helpless, self-condemned, penitent sinner.—We cannot be freed from the law, till we are brought off from all dependence upon the law and constrained to choose Christ, as the Lord our righteousness, and the Lord our strength.—And who among you have done this?—Who of you have been deeply convicted of sin and condemnation, by the law; so that your mouth has been stopped, all your excuses for sin silenced, and you lay at mercy, as guilty, wretched and undone before God?—Where is the man, where is the woman, in this assembly, that has been wounded by the law, and made so sensible of your helplessness, that you have despaired of ever recommending yourself to the favour of God, by all that you could do? And have you actually renounced all hope and trust in yourself and cast yourself at the foot of the cross, crying *undone, undone, unclean, unclean*? Have you, in such circumstances, given up yourself to the Saviour, that you might be justified by his merit, and sanctified by his Spirit? And have you the marks of one who is not under the law? If you are not under the law, you are under grace:—and if you are under grace, then sin has not dominion over you. These few marks must suffice, for you to examine yourselves by at present. But I would have you particularly to remember this one thing;—that if you are under the power of sin, or allow yourselves in the practice of it,—whether in swearing, lying, drunkeness, whoredom, and such like;—or in the omission of the well known duties of religion,—it is a plain evidence that you are yet under the curse of the law, and not under the grace of the gospel.—

Let me then, dear immortal souls,—beseech you, who are yet under the curse,—once more to consider your danger: and, for the Lord Jesus Christ's sake, and for your soul's sake, rest not in your present condition;—a condition so full of peril and danger, that if death should find you in it, you are engulphed in the flaming dungeon of hell to all eternity.—O beg of God that he would search and try you, and make you thoroughly acquainted with your real condition:—that, finding yourselves wretched, and miserable, and poor and blind and naked, you may repair, without delay, to that all-sufficient Saviour, whose blood cleanseth from all sin, and who is made of God, to all that believe, wisdom, and righteousness, sanctification and redemption.—

But such of you, my brethren, as have been constrained to fly to the promise by faith of Jesus Christ, and have taken refuge, from the curse of the law, in the grace of the gospel; your state is blessed and happy indeed. The law of the spirit of life in Christ Jesus hath made you free from the law of sin and death. You are no longer under the curse and condemnatory sentence of that law, which hath concluded all under sin and death,—for there is *no condemnation to them who are in Christ Jesus, and walk not after the flesh but after the Spirit.* And let it be your study and endeavour always thus to walk, and to please God,—abounding in works of holiness, and in labours of love. "Give all diligence to add to your faith virtue—to virtue knowledge—to knowledge temperance—to temperance patience—to patience godliness—to godliness brotherly kindness, and to brotherly kindness charity. For if these things be in you, and abound, they make you, that ye shall neither be barren nor unfruitful in the knowledge of our Lord Jesus Christ." And hereby, "an entrance shall be ministered unto you abundantly, into the everlasting kingdom of our Lord and Saviour Jesus Christ."—You have been slain by the law, and are dead to all expectations of justification by the deeds of the law, that you may live unto God, a life of peace and holy obedience. Hold on your way, rejoicing in the Lord, and in the power of his might. Enter more and more into the Spirit of the gospel, and the depths of holiness, so will you increase in happiness, and ripen daily for the celestial kingdom. To which happy place, may God of his infinite mercy bring us all for Christ Jesus' sake. Amen.

Martha Laurens Ramsay
(1773)

Appendix No. II.

RELIGIOUS EXERCISES.
Thursday, Dec. 25, 1773.
BEING THIS DAY FOURTEEN YEARS AND
SEVEN WEEKS OLD.

I do this day, after full consideration, and serious deliberation, and after earnest prayer for the assistance of Divine Grace, resolve to surrender and devote my youth, my strength, my soul, with all I have, and all I am, to the service of that great and good God, who has preserved and kept me all my life until now, and who in infinite compassion has given me to see the folly of my ways, and by faith to lay hold on a dear Redeemer, and obtain peace to my soul through his precious blood.

Martha Laurens.

A SELF DEDICATION AND SOLEMN COVENANT WITH GOD.

Eternal and unchangeable Jehovah! Thou great Creator of heaven and earth! And adorable Lord of angels and men, I desire, with the deepest humiliation and abasement of soul to fall down at this time in thine awful presence, and earnestly pray that thou wilt penetrate my very heart and soul with a suitable sense of thine unutterable and inconceivable glories! Trembling may justly lay hold upon me when I, a sinful worm, presume to lift up my head to thee, presume to appear in thy majestic presence, on such an occasion as this.

Who am I, Oh Lord God, or what is my house? What is my nature or descent, my character and desert, that I should speak of this, and desire that I may be one party in a covenant, where thou, the King of kings and Lord of lords, art the other. I blush and am confounded, even to mention it before thee. But, Oh Lord, great as is thy majesty, so also is thy mercy. If thou wilt hold converse with any of thy creatures, thy superlatively exalted nature, must stoop, must stoop infinitely low; and I know that in and through Jesus the Son of thy love, thou condescendest to visit sinful mortals, and to allow their approach to thee, and their covenant intercourse with thee. Nay, I know that the scheme and plan is thine own, and that thou hast graciously sent to propose it to us; as none untaught by thee would have been able to form it, or inclined to embrace it even when actually proposed. To thee, therefore, do I now come, invited by the name of thy Son, and trusting in his righteousness and grace; laying myself at thy feet with shame and confusion of face, and smiting upon my breast, I say with the humble publican, "God be merciful to me a sinner." I acknowledge, Lord, I have been a great transgressor. My sins have reached unto heaven, and mine iniquities are lifted up unto the skies. The irregular propensities of my corrupt and degenerate nature have, in ten thousand aggravated instances, wrought to bring forth fruit unto death. And if thou shouldst be strict to mark mine offences, I must be silent under a load of guilt, and immediately sink into destruction. But thou hast graciously called me to return unto thee, though I have been a wandering sheep, a prodigal daughter, a backsliding child. Behold therefore, O Lord, I come unto thee. I come, convinced not only of my sin but of my folly. I come from my very heart ashamed of myself, and with sincerity and humility confess that I have erred exceedingly. I am confounded with the remembrance of these things; but be thou merciful to my unrighteousness, and do not remember against me my sins and my transgressions. Permit me, Oh Lord! to bring back unto thee those powers and faculties, which I have ungratefully and sacrilegiously alienated from thy service, and receive, I beseech thee, thy poor perverted creature, who is now convinced of the right thou hast to her, and desires nothing in the whole earth so much as to be truly thine! Blessed God! it is with the utmost solemnity that I make this surrender of myself to thee. Hear, Oh heavens! and give ear, O earth! I avouch the Lord to be my God. I avouch and declare myself this day, to be one of his covenant people. Hear, Oh thou God of heaven! and record it in the book of thy remembrance, that henceforth I am thine, entirely thine. I would not merely consecrate unto thee some of my powers, or some of my possessions, or give thee a certain proportion of my services, or all I am capable of for a limited time; but I would be wholly thine, and thine for ever. From this day do I solemnly renounce all the former lords which have had dominion over me; every sin and every lust, and bid in thy name an eternal defiance to the powers of Hell, which have most unjustly usurped the empire over my soul, and to all the corruptions which their fatal temptations have introduced into it. The whole frame of my nature, all the faculties of my mind, all the members of my body, would I present before thee this day, as a living sacrifice holy and acceptable unto God, which I know to be my most reasonable service. To thee I consecrate all my worldly possessions; in thy service I desire to spend all the remainder of my time upon earth, and beg thou wouldst instruct and influence me so that, whether my abode here be longer or shorter, every year and month, day and hour, may be used in such a manner as shall most effectually promote thine honor, and subserve the scheme of thy wise and gracious providence; and I earnestly pray that whatever influence thou givest me over others, in any of the superior relations of life in which I may stand, or in consequence of any peculiar regard which might be paid me, thou wouldst give me strength and courage to exert myself to the utmost for thy glory. Resolving, not only that I will do it myself, but that all others, so far as I can rationally and properly influence them, shall serve the Lord. In this course, Oh blessed God! would I steadily persevere to the very end of my life, earnestly praying, that every future day of it may supply the deficiencies and correct the irregularities of the former, and that I may, by divine grace, be enabled, not only to hold on in that happy way, but daily to grow more active in it.

Nor do I only consecrate all that I am and have to thy service, but I also most humbly resign and submit to thy heavenly will, myself and all that I can call mine. I leave, Oh Lord, to thy management and direction all I possess and all I wish; and set every enjoyment and every interest before thee, to be disposed of, as thou pleasest. Continue, or remove what thou hast given me; bestow or refuse, what I imagine I want, as thou, Lord shalt see good; and though I dare not say I will never repine, yet I hope I may venture to say, that I will labor not only to submit but to acquiesce; not only to bear what thou doest in thy most afflictive dispensations; but to consent to it, and to praise thee for it, contentedly resolving, in all that thou appointest, my will into thine, and looking on myself as nothing, and on thee, Oh God! as the great eternal all, whose word ought to determine every thing, and whose government ought to be the joy of the whole rational creation.

Use me, Oh Lord, I beseech thee, as the instrument of thy glory, and honor me so far, as either by doing or suffering what thou shalt appoint, to bring some revenue of praise to thee, and of benefit to the world in which I dwell; and may it please thee, Oh my Creator! from this day forward, to number me among thy peculiar people, that I may no more be a stranger and foreigner, but a fellow-citizen with the saints, and of the household of God. Receive, Oh heavenly Father! thy returning prodigal. Wash me in the blood of thy dear Son; clothe me with his perfect righteousness, and sanctify me throughout by the power of thy Spirit! Destroy; I beseech thee, more and more the power of sin in my heart! Transform me more into thine own image, and fashion me to the resemblance of Jesus, whom henceforward I would acknowledge as my teacher, and my sacrifice, my intercessor, and my Lord! Communicate to me, I beseech thee, all needful influences of thy purifying, thy cheering, and thy comforting Spirit; and lift up the light of thy countenance upon me, which will put the sublimest joy and gladness into my soul.

Dispose my affairs, Oh God! in a manner which may be most subservient to thy glory and my own truest happiness; and when I have done and borne thy will upon earth, call me from hence at what time, and in what manner thou pleasest; only grant that in my dying moments, and the near view *vision of dying*

of eternity, I may remember these my engagements to thee, and may employ my latest breath to thy service; and do thou, Oh Lord, when thou seest the agonies of dissolving nature upon me, remember this covenant too, even though I should then be incapable of recollecting it. Look down, Oh my heavenly Father, with a pitying eye upon thy languishing, dying child; place thine everlasting arms underneath me for my support; put strength and confidence into my departing spirit, and receive it to the embraces of thy everlasting love! Welcome it to the abodes of them that sleep in Jesus; to wait with them that glorious day, when the last of thy promises to thy covenant people shall be fulfilled in their triumphant resurrection and that abundant entrance, which shall be administered to them into that everlasting kingdom, of which thou hast assured them in thy covenant, and in the hope of which, I now lay hold of it, desiring to live and to die as with my hand on that hope!

And when I am thus numbered among the dead, and all the interests of mortality are over with me for ever, if this solemn memorial should chance to fall into the hands of any surviving friends, may it be the means of making serious impressions on their mind. May they read it not only as my language, but as their own; and learn to fear the Lord my God, and with me to put their trust under the shadow of his wings for time and for eternity; and may they also learn to adore with me that grace which inclines our heart to enter

after death, may my writings inspire others

into the covenant, and condescends to admit us into it, when so inclined; ascribing with me and with all the children of God, to the Father, to the Son and to the Holy Ghost, that glory, honor, and praise, which is so justly due to each divine person for the part he bears in this illustrious work. Amen.

> Lord I am thine, forever thine,
> My soul doth cleave to thee;
> My dearest Lord, be ever mine,
> I'll have no love but thee.

Henceforth I am not mine but God's forever.

Martha Laurens.

I had fallen, shamefully fallen, and broken the solemn covenant engagements in so dreadful a manner, that none but he who is holy and true, who hath the key of all hearts, who openeth and no man shutteth, could ever have restored me, but through the unbounded and astonishing measures of his grace; I was awakened to a sense of my vileness and ingratitude; made to feel more bitter pangs than ever; and after much struggling and many intreaties from my compassionate Redeemer I renewed my *H. E.* violated vows in the most solemn manner, not only privately, but publicly, by giving up myself to him in the ordinance of the Holy Supper, before near three hundred persons at St. Werbrough's, December *Kmer* 25, 1775.

Solemnly again, April 7, 1776, *Easter* and more solemnly and with more *Perkins* affecting circumstances than ever, May, 26, 1776.

CHAPTER FOUR

REVOLUTION AND REORGANIZATION
(1776–1800)

In 1776 Anglicans in the colonies had to subordinate their preoccupation with the Great Awakening to a far more pressing concern. American colonists were at war with England. A significant portion of Anglican clergy and laity decided that in good conscience they could not support the Revolution. Did not Anglican clergy swear loyalty to the British crown at the time of ordination? Did not the prayer book contain prayers for George III?

The percentage of Tories was highest in those areas—New England and the middle colonies—in which the church was not established. Many clergy in these areas received salaries from the Society for the Propagation of the Gospel (SPG) in England; because of the SPG charter, these salaries would halt if the Revolution were successful. Moreover, unlike the established colonies, the colonial legislatures in these states had no direct authority over Anglican congregations and could not direct clergy to read prayers for the patriots in the place of those for the king in the Book of Common Prayer.

Of the three largest colonial denominations (Congregational, Presbyterian, and Anglican) the Anglican church suffered most from the Revolution. Anglicans who refused to alter the prayers for the king were looked upon as traitors. One SPG missionary in Pennsylvania wrote that those who attended worship were primarily women; men feared arrest if discovered using the prayer book.[1] Even in areas where the majority of Anglicans were patriots,

[1] Classified Digest of the Records of the Society for the Propagation of the Gospel in Foreign Parts, 1701–1892, fourth edition (London: published at the Society's Office, 1894), p. 40.

the Revolution brought hardship. In Virginia, for example, the legislature suspended salaries for clergy, abolished the chair of religion at William and Mary, and eventually seized some church property.

When the Revolution ended with the Treaty of Paris (1783), a remnant of Anglicans set to work in reorganizing their denomination. William White (1748–1836), a Philadelphia priest who was a chaplain to the Continental Congress, provided a needed catalyst with the publication of his *Case of the Episcopal Churches* (editions in 1782 and 1783). White believed that Episcopalians (a name already suggested by Anglicans in Maryland) could organize in their new setting by combining a traditional doctrine with a democratized church order. They shared the religious principles of the Church of England, but they could organize their church government in a very different way. White proposed a voluntary association independent of both the English church and the American state. A representative General Convention would set policy for the church; regional conventions would elect superior clergy (bishops).

Episcopalians in the middle and southern states responded favorably to White's proposal. They met in preliminary sessions in 1783 and 1784 and in General Conventions in 1785 and 1786. In 1787 they sent White and Samuel Provoost (1742–1815) of New York to England for consecration.

Two very different groups objected to White's proposal: New England clergymen and members of methodist societies. The first group was centered in Connecticut. The Anglican clergy there had long used the covenant–apostolic order argument; they were unenthusiastic about organizing prior to obtaining a bishop. They elected two candidates to the episcopate. The second of these, Samuel Seabury (1729–96), agreed to go to England to seek consecration. When the English did not agree—though Parliament provided for the ordination of priests for America in 1784, it was uncertain about the reception of a bishop elected in secret without lay participation, and did not approve ordination of bishops for America until 1786—Seabury traveled to Scotland, where he was consecrated on November 14, 1784. After his return, Seabury organized his diocese around a clergy convocation. For five years there would be two competing Episcopal churches: White's middle and southern states group and Seabury's New England church. In 1789, however, the two groups merged. White made a number of concessions to Seabury. A house of bishops was added to the previously unicameral convention, and states were permitted to omit lay persons from their delegations; but the broad outlines of his democratic American church remained. Nonetheless, many Episcopalians in the years prior to the Civil War would share Seabury's suspicion about the merits of American democracy. They accepted democracy in their own church, because there was no reasonable alternative. They objected to the loss of ties to the English church and the English king, and in some cases refused to vote.

The second group that objected to White's *Case* was centered in Maryland. Leaders of the methodist movement, which had spread as a result of the Great Awakening, saw little advantage in remaining linked to the dispirited Anglican church. When John Wesley found that he was unable to obtain consecration of bishops to preside over methodist societies in the United States, he appointed Francis Asbury and Thomas Coke as superintendents. On Christmas Eve of 1784, they organized as the Methodist Episcopal church. Unlike White or Seabury, the Methodists were anxious to make substantial changes in doctrine. By streamlining worship, simplifying qualifications for ordination, and adopting a revivalist theology, they created an effective evangelical denomination that would grow to become the largest Protestant church of the nineteenth century.

The formation of a separate Methodist Episcopal church created a difficult decision for Anglicans who had hoped to make their church a primary agent of renewal. They were forced to decide how important the apostolic succession was to their vision of the faith. Jarratt and Pettigrew remained with the Episcopal church. Others decided for Methodism. Some persons wavered, moving from one denomination to another.

One significant group that ultimately decided for the Episcopal church was the black membership of St. George's Methodist Episcopal Church of Philadelphia. When Absalom Jones (1746–1818), Richard Allen (1760–1831), and other black members were denied an equal voice in parish affairs, they walked out rather than accepting second-class status. The majority of the members became St. Thomas' Episcopal Church for which Bishop White ordained Jones a deacon in 1795 and a priest in 1804. He was the first American black ordained by a hierarchical denomination. Allen remained in the Methodist church (in which he was ordained a deacon in 1799 and an elder in 1816) until 1816 when he joined with other black Methodists to form the African Methodist Episcopal church.

The text of William White's *The Case of the Episcopal Churches in the United States Considered* is taken from volume two of William Stevens Perry's *Journals of General Conventions of the Protestant Episcopal Church* (Claremont, N.H.: The Claremont Manufacturing Company, 1874), pp. 420–36.

WILLIAM WHITE   *needs footnote to explain what*
(1782)   *"Episcopal"*

Case of the Episcopal Churches

PREFACE

It may be presumed, that the members of the Episcopal Churches, some from conviction, and others from the influence of ancient habits, entertain a preference for their own communion; and that accordingly they are not a little anxious, to see some speedy and decisive measures adopted for its continuance. The author believes, therefore, that his undertaking needs no apology to the public; and that those for whom it is designed will give him credit for his good intentions.

Nothing is farther from his wishes, than the reviving of such controversies as have been found destructive of good neighbourhood and the christian temper; especially as he conceives them to be unconnected with the peculiar situation of the churches in question. He has for this reason, avoided the discussion of subjects, on which Episcopalians differ from their fellow christians; and even of those, concerning which a latitude of sentiment has prevailed among themselves.

He thinks his design is subservient to the general cause of religion and virtue; for a numerous society, losing the benefit of the stated ordinances within itself, cannot but severely feel the effect of such a change, on the piety and morals of its members. In this point of view, all good men must lament that cessation of public worship, which has happened to many of the Episcopal churches, and threatens to become universal.

The present work he also believes to be connected with the civil happiness of the community. A prejudice has prevailed with many, that the Episcopal churches cannot otherwise exist than under the dominion of Great Britain. A church government that would contain the constituent principles of the Church of England, and yet be independent of foreign jurisdiction or influence, would remove that anxiety which at present hangs heavy on the minds of many sincere persons.

Such is the natural tendency of this performance. If it should fail of effect on account of the insufficiency of the author, it may nevertheless be of advantage, by drawing to the subject the attention of others, better qualified for the undertaking.

CHAPTER I.

To form an idea of the situation of the Episcopal[1] Churches in the present crisis, we must observe the change their religious system has undergone in the late revolution.

On whatever principles the independence of the United States may be supposed to rest; whether merely on establishments which have very probable appearances of being permanent, or on withdraw-

ing the protection of the former sovereign, or (as the author of these sheets believes) on the inherent right of the community to resist and effectually to exclude unconstitutional and oppressive claims, there result from it the reciprocal duties of protection and allegiance, enforced by the most powerful sanctions of natural and revealed religion.

It may reasonably be presumed, that, in general, the members of the Episcopal Churches are friendly to the principles, on which the present governments were formed; a fact particularly obvious in the southern states, where the Episcopalians, who are a majority of the citizens, have engaged and persevered in the war, with as much ardour and constancy as their neighbours. Many even of those whose sentiments were at first unfavourable to the revolution, now wish for its final establishment, as a most happy event; some from an earnest desire of peace, and others from the undistinguished oppressions and ravages of the British armies. Such persons accordingly acknowledge allegiance, and pay obedience to the sovereignty of the states.

Inconsistent with the duties resulting from this allegiance, would be their subjection to any spiritual jurisdiction connected with the temporal authority of a foreign state. Such a dependence is contrary to the fundamental principles of civil society, and therefore cannot be required by the Scriptures; which, being accommodated to the civil policy of the world at large, neither interfered with the constitution of states as found estab-

---

[1] The general term "Episcopal" is usually applied, among us, to the churches professing the religious principles of the Church of England. It is thought by the author to be sufficiently descriptive, because the other Episcopal Churches in America are known by names peculiar to themselves.

lished at the time of their promulgation, nor handed down to succeeding ages any injunctions of such a tendency.

To apply these observations to the case of the Episcopal Churches in the United States. They have been heretofore subject to the ecclesiastical authority of the Bishop of London. This authority was derived under a commission from the crown; which, though destitute of legal operation, found a general acquiescence on the part of the churches; being exercised no farther than to the necessary purposes of ordaining and licensing ministers. Hereby a connection was formed, between the spiritual authority in England and the Episcopal Churches in America, the latter constituting a part of the Bishop of London's diocese.

But this connection is dissolved by the revolution. Had it been matter of right, it would have ceased with the authority of the crown; being founded on consent, and the ground changed, it cannot be allowed of in future, consistently with the duties resulting from our allegiance.[2] Even suppose the Bishop of London hereafter exempted, by act of Parliament, from the necessity of exacting the oaths, a dependence on his lordship and his successors in that See, would be liable to the reproach of foreign influence, and render Episcopalians less qualified than those of other communions, to be entrusted by their country; neither (as may

be presumed) will it be claimed after the acknowledgement of the civil independence, being contrary to a principle clearly implied in many of the institutions of the Church of England, particularly in the 34th article of religion; which asserts, that "every particular or national church hath authority to ordain, change, and abolish ceremonies or rites of the church, ordained only by man's authority, so that all things be done to edifying." Though the Episcopal Churches in these states will not be national or legal establishments, the same principle applies, being the danger of foreign jurisdiction.

The ecclesiastical power over the greater number of the churches, formerly subsisting in some legislative bodies on this continent, is also abrogated by the revolution. In the southern states, where the Episcopal Churches were maintained by law, the assemblies might well have been supposed empowered, in conjunction with the other branches of legislation, to regulate their external government; but now, when the establishments are overturned, it would ill become those bodies, composed of men of various denominations (however respectable collectively and as individuals) to enact laws for the Episcopal Churches, which will no doubt, in common with others, claim and exercise the privilege of governing themselves.

All former jurisdiction over the churches being thus withdrawn, and the chain which held them together broken, it would seem, that their future continuance can be provided for only by voluntary as-

[2]Were the British colonies independent of their parent kingdom, the Episcopalians in this country would be a society independent of the national church. Dr. Chandler's Appeal farther defended. Page 113.

sociations for union and good government. It is therefore of the utmost consequence to discover and ascertain the principles, on which such associations should be framed.

CHAPTER II.

Whoever should consider the subject before us as merely speculative and propose the suggestions of his own judgment or fancy, without attention to the sentiments, habits, and circumstances of the people interested would probably have little weight, and would unquestionably not be useful. In the present investigation, therefore, it will be proper to keep in view the particular situation of the churches in question.

In most cases where spiritual jurisdiction has been established or defined, such has been the connection between church and state, that it was scarcely possible to adopt measures, which did not show some traces of accommodation to political views; but this may be avoided in the present instance, where all denominations of Christians are on a level, and no church is farther known to the public, than as a voluntary association of individuals, for a lawful and useful purpose. The effect of this should be the avoiding of whatever may give the churches the appearance of being subservient to party, or tend to unite their members on questions of a civil nature. This is unquestionably agreeable to the simplicity of the gospel; it is conceived to be also, under the present circumstances, agreeable to good policy; for whatever church shall

aim at such subjects, unless on account of an invasion of their religious privileges, will be suspected by all others, as aiming at the exclusive government of the country.

In the parent church, though whatever regards religion may be enacted by the clergy in convocation, it must afterwards have the sanction of all other orders of men, comprehended in the parliament. It will be necessary to deviate from the practice (though not from the principles) of that church, by convening the clergy and laity in one body. The former will no doubt have an influence proportioned to the opinion entertained of their piety and learning; but will never (it is presumed) wish to usurp an exclusive right of regulation; a sentiment which cannot more properly be expressed than in the following words of that great defender of the church of England Mr. Hooker: "The most natural and religious course of making laws, is that the matter of them be taken from the judgment of the wisest in those things which they are to concern. In matters of God, to set down a form of prayer, a solemn confession of the articles of the christian faith and ceremonies meet for the exercise of our religion, it were unnatural not to think the pastors and bishops of our souls, a great deal more fit than men of secular trades and callings—howbeit, when all that the wisdom of all sorts can do is done for the devising of laws in the church, it is the general consent of all that giveth them the form and vigour of laws."[3] And in another

[3] Ecclesiastical Polity. Page 432.

place "but were it so that the clergy might give laws to all the rest, forasmuch as every estate doth desire to enlarge the bounds of their own liberties, it is easy to see how injurious this would prove to men of other conditions."[4] *bishop*

The power of electing a superior order of ministers ought to be in the clergy and laity together, they being both interested in the choice. In England, the bishops are appointed by the civil authority; which was an usurpation of the crown at the Norman conquest, but since confirmed by acts of parliament. The primitive churches were generally supplied by popular elections; even in the city of Rome, the privilege of electing the bishop continued with the people to the tenth or eleventh century; and near those times there are resolves of councils, that none should be promoted to ecclesiastical dignities, but by election of the clergy and people. It cannot be denied, that this right vested in numerous bodies occasioned great disorders; which it is expected will be avoided, when the people shall exercise the right by representation.

Deprivation of the superior order of clergy should also be in the church at large. In England, it has been sometimes done by the civil authority; particularly in the instances of Queen Mary's Roman Catholic bishops by Queen Elizabeth, and of the non-juring bishops at the revolution; which last occasioned a separation from the national church, Sancroft and the others being still considered by their advocates as bishops of their

respective sees, and Tillotson and his associates reprobated by them as schismatics. So far is the civil policy of England from permitting an entire separation of ecclesiastical authority, that in Queen Ann's reign, when Bishop Watson was deprived for immorality, it was allowed, that as a peer he might have objected to the archbishop's jurisdiction, provided he had pleaded his privilege in time. It is well known, that the interference of the civil authority in such instances as the preceding has been considered by many as inconsistent with ecclesiastical principles; an objection which will be avoided, when deprivation can only be under regulations enacted by a fair representation of the churches, and by an authority entirely ecclesiastical. It is presumed, that none will so far mistake the principles of the church of England, as to talk of the impossibility of depriving a bishop.

In England, dioceses having been formed before parishes, a church supposes one common flock, subject to a bishop and sundry collegiate presbyters; without the idea of its being necessarily divided into smaller communities, connected with their respective parochial clergy; the latter having been introduced some considerable time after the conversion of the nation to the christian faith. One natural consequence of this distinction, will be to retain in each church every power that need not be delegated for the good of the whole. Another, will be an equality of the churches; and not, as in England, the subjection of all parish

[4]Ibid. Page 437.

churches to their respective cathedrals.

The last circumstance to be here mentioned, is the impossibility that the churches should provide a support for that superior order of clergy, to which their acknowledged principles point; of consequence, the duty assigned to that order ought not materially to interfere with their employments, in the station of parochial clergy; the superintendence of each will therefore be confined to a small district; a favorite idea with all moderate Episcopalians.

It is proposed to offer the outlines of a frame of church government, founded on the preceding sentiments.

CHAPTER III.

The author offers the following sketch of a frame of government, though he is far from thinking it complete; to make it so even according to his own ideas, would carry him beyond the compass intended in this essay.

As the churches in question extend over an immense space of country, it can never be expected, that representatives from each church should assemble in one place; it will be more convenient for them to associate in small districts, from which representatives may be sent to three different bodies, the continent being supposed divided into that number of larger districts. From these may be elected a body representing the whole.

In each smaller district, there should be elected a general vestry or convention, consisting of a convenient number (the minister to be one) from the vestry or congregation of each church, or of every two or more churches, according to their respective ability of supporting a minister. They should elect a clergyman their permanent president; who, in conjunction with other clergymen to be also appointed by the body, may exercise such powers as are purely spiritual, particularly that of admitting to the ministry; the presiding clergyman, and others to be liable to be deprived for just causes, by a fair process, and under reasonable laws; meetings to be held as often as occasion may require.

The assemblies in the three larger districts may consist of a convenient number of members, sent from each of the smaller districts severally within their bounds, equally composed of clergy and laity, and voted for by those orders promiscuously; the presiding clergyman to be always one, and these bodies to meet once in every year.

The continental representative body may consist of a convenient number from each of the larger districts, formed equally of clergy and laity, and among the clergy, formed equally of presiding ministers and others; to meet statedly once in three years. The use of this and the preceding representative bodies is to make such regulations, and receive appeals in such matters only, as shall be judged necessary for their continuing one religious communion.

These are (what was promised) no more than outlines; which it will not be proper to dismiss, without a few observations on the degree of power to be exercised, in matters of faith, worship, and government.

For the doctrinal part, it would perhaps be sufficient to demand of all admitted to the ministry, or engaged in ecclesiastical legislation, the questions contained in the book of ordination; which extend no farther than an acknowledgment of the scriptures, as a rule of faith and life; yet some general sanction may be given to the thirty-nine articles of religion, so as to adopt their leading sense;[5] which is here proposed rather as a chain of union, than for exacting entire uniformity of sentiment. If the last be considered as a desirable object, the articles have undeniably been found insufficient for the purpose; which is not here said from an opinion that such was the intention of the compilers, but rather with a conviction that they designedly left room for a considerable latitude of sentiment; if to the above there be objected the danger of a public opposition between ministers, this obvious answer may be made; that the strictest tests ever devised cannot

[5]Suppose, for instance, a form RESEMBLING that which Dr. Ferdinando Warner, a late ecclesiastical Historian of the Episcopal church, says (book 16) was proposed in the reign of Charles II. by the Lord Keeper Bridgman, Bishop Wilkins and Chief Justice Hale, "to serve instead of all former subscriptions." The form was this, "I do hereby profess and declare, that I approve the doctrine, worship and government established in the church of England, as containing all things necessary to salvation, and that I will not endeavour by myself or any other, directly or indirectly, to bring in any doctrine contrary to that which is so established; and I do hereby promise that I will continue in the church of England, and will not do anything to disturb the peace thereof."

be so effectual to prevent such conduct, as the regulation contained in the 53d canon; which considers it as indecent and punishable, independently of the merits of the doctrines litigated.

As to divine worship, there must no doubt be somewhere the power of making necessary and convenient alterations in the service of the church. But it ought to be used with great moderation; otherwise the communion will become divided into an infinite number of smaller ones, all differing from one another and from that in England; from whence we may expect considerable numbers to migrate hereafter to this country; who if they find too wide a deviation from the ancient practice, will probably form an independent communion of their own. Whatever may in other respects be determined on this head, it is presumed the Episcopalians are generally attached to that characteristic of their communion, which prescribes a settled form of prayer.

On the subject of government, whether civil or ecclesiastical, there is great truth and beauty in the following observation of the present Bishop of St. Asaph, "the great art of governing consists in not governing too much." Perhaps it would be sufficient, if an immoral life were followed by exclusion from the sacrament and ecclesiastical employment; deprivation from church benefices following of course. The above is not to be understood as excluding the enforcing such rules, as are necessary to preserve decency and order. As to excommunication or an entire separation from the church, however necessary it was in the primitive ages, when christianity itself, being not generally known, and misrepresented as a sanction for lewdness, treason and clandestine murders, must have been essentially wounded by the immoralities of any of its professors; there is great room to doubt of their being the same use in it at present, when the vices of a professing christian are universally known to be opposite to the precepts of his religion. Such are the tyranny and hypocrisy too frequently arising from the exercise of this power, that it may be thought safest to leave men to those great sanctions of duty, the will of God and a future retribution; attended as they will generally be with a sense of shame, dissuading from actions so notoriously scandalous, as to be a foundation for church censures.

In the preceding pages, the idea of superintending ministers has been introduced; but not a word has been said of the succession supposed necessary to constitute the Episcopal character; and this has been on purpose postponed, as demanding a more minute discussion.

CHAPTER IV.

On the subject of Episcopacy, the general opinion of the churches in question is of peculiar consequence; yet it can be collected only from circumstances; to assist in ascertaining it, the two following facts are stated.

Wherever these churches have been erected, the ecclesiastical government of the church of England has been adhered to; they have depended on the English bishops for ordination of their clergy, and on no occasion expressed a dissatisfaction with Episcopacy. This, considering the liberty they enjoyed in common with others, of forming their churches on whatever plan they liked best, is a presumptive proof of their preferring the Episcopal government; especially as it subjected them under the former connection to many inconveniences, such as sending to the distance of three thousand miles for ordination, the scandal sometimes brought on the church by the ordination of low and vicious persons,[6] the difficulty of getting rid of immoral ministers, and that several of the clergy formed attachments of which this country has been always jealous, and which have at last proved extremely prejudicial to her interests.

On the other hand, there cannot be produced an instance of laymen in America, unless in the very infancy of the settlements, soliciting the introduction of a bishop;[7] it was probably by a great majority of them thought an hazardous experiment. How far the prerogative of the king as head of the church might be construed to extend over the colonies, whether a bishop would bring with him that part of the law which respects ecclesiastical matters, and whether the civil powers vested in bishops in England would accompany that order to America, were questions which for aught they knew would include

[6]Generally by deceptions on the Bishop of London.
[7]If there has been any, it must have been from so few, as rather to corroborate than weaken the sentiment conveyed.

principles and produce consequences, dangerous and destructive to their civil rights.[8]

From these two facts it may fairly be inferred, that the Episcopalians on this continent will wish to institute among themselves an Episcopal government, as soon as it shall appear practicable, and that this government will not be attended with the danger of tyranny, either temporal or spiritual.

But it is generally understood, that the succession cannot at present be obtained. From the parent church most unquestionably it cannot; whether from any is presumed to be more than we can at present be informed. But the proposal to constitute a frame of government, the execution of which shall depend on the pleasure of persons unknown, differing from us in language, habits, and perhaps in religious principles, has too ludicrous an appearance to deserve consideration; the peculiar circumstances of the war in which our country is engaged preclude us

from procuring the succession in those quarters to which alone application could consistently be made; the danger of offending the British government constraining (perhaps) a refusal of what, it would of course be indelicate to ask. (Now, on the other hand, to depart from Episcopacy, would be giving up a leading characteristic of the communion; which, however indifferently considered as to divine appointment, might be productive of all the evils generally attending changes of this sort. On the other hand, by delaying to adopt measures for the continuance of the ministry, the very existence of the churches is hazarded, and duties of positive and indispensable obligation are neglected.)

The conduct meant to be recommended, as founded on the preceding sentiments, is to include in the proposed frame of government a general approbation of Episcopacy, and a declaration of an intention to procure the succession, as soon as conveniently may be; but in the mean time to carry the plan into effect without waiting for the succession.

The first part of this proposal is conceived to be founded on the plain dictates of propriety, prudence, and moderation; for if the undertaking proceed on acknowledged principles, there will be far less shock to ancient habits, and less cause of intestine divisions, than if new principles are to be sought for and established. To illustrate this by an allusion; had our old governments been so adjusted to the genius of the people and their present circumstances, as at

---

[8]Whether the above appendages would have accompanied an English bishop to America, the author is no judge. That they were generally feared by the Episcopalian laity, he thinks the only way of accounting for the cold reception they gave (a fact universally known) to every proposal for the introduction of a bishop. Those who pleaded for the measure on a plan purely spiritual, thought he would not be invested, by the laws of England, with such powers; but in case it had proved otherwise, they proposed the limiting him by act of parliament. What the people would have thought of measures, which must have required an act of that body to render them harmless, no person formerly acquainted with their temper and sentiments need be told; and whether they judged right or not, recent events have abundantly shown.

the revolution to have required no farther change than what necessarily arose from the extinction of royal authority, it is obvious, that many pernicious controversies would have been prevented. Such, however, except in a few instances, was not the happiness of the colonies. But it is precisely the situation of the Episcopal churches in their religious concerns; none of their constituent principles being thereby changed, but what were founded on the authority of the king.

In the minds of some, the idea of Episcopacy will be connected with that of immoderate power; to which it may be answered, that power becomes dangerous, not from the precedency of one man, but from his being independent. Had Rome been governed by a presbytery instead of a bishop; and had that presbytery been invested with the independent riches and dominion of the papal see; it is easy to conceive, of their acquiring as much power over the christian world, as was ever known in a Gregory or a Paul.

It may be further objected, that Episcopacy is anti-republican; and therefore opposed to those ideas which all good citizens ought to promote, for securing the peace and happiness of the community. But this supposed relation between Episcopacy and monarchy arises from confounding English Episcopacy with the subject at large. In the early ages of the church, it was customary to debate and determine in a general concourse of all christians in the same city; among whom the Bishop was no more than president. Matters were indeed too often conducted tumultuously, and after a manner which no prudent and peaceable man would wish to see imitated; but the churches were not the less Episcopal on that account. Very few systems of religious discipline on this continent are equally republican with that proposed in the preceding pages. The adage of King James I. "No Bishop no King," and "No King no Bishop," ought only to be understood concerning that degree of Episcopal power, together with its civil appendages, of which he certainly meant it.

But it will be also said, that the very name of "Bishop" is offensive; if so, change it for another; let the superior clergymen be a president, a superintendent, or in plain English, and, according to the literal translation of the original, an overseer. However, if names are to be reprobated, because the powers annexed to them have been abused, there are few appropriated to either civil or ecclesiastical distinctions, which would retain their places in our catalogue.

The other part of the proposal was an immediate execution of the plan, without waiting for the Episcopal succession. This is founded on the presumption, that the worship of God and the instruction and reformation of the people are the principal objects of ecclesiastical discipline: if so, to relinquish them from a scrupulous adherence to Episcopacy, is sacrificing the substance to the ceremony.

It will be said, we ought to continue as we are, with the hope of obtaining it hereafter. But are the acknowledged ordinances of Christ's holy religion to be sus-

don't wait for Apostolic Succession

pended for years, perhaps as long as the present generation shall continue, out of delicacy to a disputed point, and that relating only to externals? It is submitted, how far such ideas encourage the suspicion of want of attachment to any particular church, except so far as is subservient to some civil system. All the obligations of conformity to the divine ordinances, all the arguments which prove the connexion between public worship and the morals of a people, combine to urge the adopting some speedy measures, to provide for the public ministry in those churches; if such as have been above recommended should be adopted, and the Episcopal succession afterwards obtained, any supposed imperfections of the intermediate ordinations might, if it were judged proper, be supplied without acknowledging their nullity, by a *conditional* ordination resembling that of *conditional baptism* in the liturgy; the above was an expedient proposed by Archbishop Tillotson, Bishops Patrick, Stillingfleet, and others, at the revolution, and had been actually practised in Ireland by Archbishop Bramhall.[9]

But it will be said, the dropping the succession even for a time would be a departure from the principles of the Church of England. This prejudice is too common not to deserve particular attention.

CHAPTER V.

It would be to the greatest degree surprising, if the Church of England, acknowledged by all Protestant churches to lay a sufficient stress on the essential doctrines and duties of the gospel, should be found so immoderately attached to a matter of external order, as must in some cases be ruinous to her communion. But, far from this, it will not be difficult to prove, that a temporary departure from Episcopacy in the present instance would be warranted by her doctrines, by her practice, and by the principles on which Episcopal government is asserted.

Whatever that church holds must be included in the "thirty-nine articles of religion;" which *No* were evidently intended for a comprehensive system of necessary doctrine. But what say these articles on the present subject? Simply, that "the book of consecration of archbishops and bishops and the ordering of priests and deacons, doth contain all things necessary thereunto; neither hath it any thing that of itself is superstitious and ungodly."[10] The canons speak the same sense censuring those who shall "affirm that the government of the Church of England by archbishops, bishops, &c. is antichristian, or repugnant to the word of God."[11] And those who shall "affirm that the form and manner of making and consecrating bishops, priests, and deacons, containeth any thing in it that is repugnant to the word of God, or that they who are thus made bishops, &c. are not lawfully made, &c."[12]

How can such moderation of sentiment and expression be justi-

---

[9]Nichol's Defence of the Church of England, Introduction.

[10]Article 36.
[11]Canon 7.
[12]Canon 8.

fied, if the Episcopal succession be so binding, as to allow no deviation in a case of extreme necessity? Had the church of England decreed concerning baptism and the Lord's supper, only that they were "not repugnant to the word of God," and that her offices for those sacraments were "not superstitious and ungodly," would she not be censured by almost all christendom, as renouncing the obligation of those sacraments? Equally improper would be the application of such moderate expressions to Episcopacy if (as some imagine) she considers it to be as much binding as baptism and the Lord's supper.

The book of consecration and ordination carries the idea no farther, except that the preface as altered at the restoration (for it was not so in the old preface) affirms that "from the apostle's times there have been these orders in Christ's church, bishops, priests and deacons." But there is an evident difference between this and the asserting the unlawfulness of deviating from that practice in an instance, extraordinary and unprovided for.

Next to the doctrine of the church, let us enquire, whether her practice will furnish us with a precedent to justify the liberty we plead.

Many of the English protestants, during the persecution by Queen Mary, took refuge in foreign countries, particularly in Germany and Geneva. When protestantism revived at the auspicious accession of Queen Elizabeth, and at the same time a cloud was gathering on the continent in consequence of the emperor's victories over the princes of the Smacaldic league, many of the exiles returned to their native land; some of whom, during their absence, had been ordained according to the customs of the countries where they had resided; these were admitted without re-ordination to preach and hold benefices; one of them[13] was promoted to a deanry; but at the same time, as several of them were endeavouring to make innovations in the established church, it was provided in a law (13th Elizabeth 12.) that "whoever shall pretend to be a priest or minister of God's holy word, by reason of any other form of institution, consecration or ordering, than the form set forth by act of parliament, before the feast of the nativity of Christ next ensuing, shall in the presence of the bishop —— declare his assent and subscribe to all the articles of religion agreed on, &c."[14] Here existed an extraordinary occasion, not provided for in the institutions for common use; the exigency of the case seems to have been considered; and there followed a tol-

---

[13]Whittingham.

[14]Bishop Burnet says (History of his own times, anno 1661) that until the act of uniformity, passed soon after the restoration, "those who came to England from the foreign churches had not been required to be ordained among us." If so, the argument founded on practice extends farther than it has been here urged. The act of Elizabeth, however, had no operation beyond the Christmas next ensuing; neither indeed did it pronounce that a good ordination which would have been otherwise defective; but its being meant to comprehend those who were AT THAT TIME invested with foreign non-episcopalian ordination, is evident from their being actually allowed to preach and hold benefices, on the condition of their subscribing the thirty-nine articles.

eration, if not implied approbation, of a departure in that instance from Episcopal ordination. There cannot be expected another example, because no similar instance of necessity has happened; unless that at the restoration be considered as such; but, it is presumed, no stress will be laid on the omission of the like indulgence at that period; when the minds of the ruling Episcopalians, irritated by recent sufferings, were less intent on conciliation than on retaliation.[15]

Let us next take a view of the grounds on which the authority of Episcopacy is asserted.

The advocates for this form maintain, that there having been an Episcopal power originally lodged by Jesus Christ with his apostles, and by them exercised generally in person, but sometimes by delegation (as in the instances of Timothy and Titus) the same was conveyed by them before their decease to one pastor in each church, which generally comprehended all the Christians in a city and a convenient surrounding district. Thus were created the apostolic successors, who, on account of their settled residence are called bishops *by restraint*; whereas the apostles themselves were bishops *at large,* exercising Episcopal power over all the churches, except in the case of St. James, who from the beginning was bishop of Jerusalem. From this time the word "episcopos," used in the New Testament indiscriminately with the word "presbuteros," (particularly in the 20th chapter of the Acts where the same persons are called "episcopoi" and "presbuteroi,") became *appropriated* to the superior order of ministers. That the apostles were thus succeeded by an order of ministers superior to pastors in general, Episcopalians think they prove by the testimonies of the ancient fathers, and from the improbability that so great an innovation (as some conceive it) could have found general and peaceable possession in the second or third century, when Episcopacy is on both sides acknowledged to have been prevalent.[16] The argument is here concisely stated, but (as is believed) impartially, the manner in which the subject is handled by Mr. Hooker and Bishop Hoadly being particularly kept in view.

Can any reasonable rule of construction make this amount to more than ancient and apostolic practice? That the apostles adopted any particular form, affords a presumption of its being the best, all circumstances at that time considered; but to make it unalterably binding, it must be shown enjoined in positive precept. Bishop Hoadly clearly points out this distinction in his answer to Dr. Calamy. The latter having considered it as the sense of the Church, in the

---

[15]Bishop Burnet assigns a reason still less excusable: that many great preferments were in the hands of obnoxious persons, who, on account of their services towards the restoration, could not otherwise be ejected, than by making the terms of conformity difficult. History of his own times, anno 1661.

[16]The original of the order of bishops was from the presbyters choosing one from among themselves to be a stated president in their assemblies, in the 2d or 3d century. Smectymnuan divines, as quoted in Neal's history of the Puritans, anno 1640.

preface to the ordinal, that the three orders were of divine appointment, and urged it as a reason for non-conformity; the bishop, with evident propriety, remarks that the service pronounces no such thing; and that therefore Dr. Calamy created a difficulty, where the church had made none: there being "some difference," (says he) "between these two sentences—bishops, priests, and deacons, are three distinct orders in the church by *divine appointment*—and—*from the apostle's time* there have been in Christ's Church bishops, priests, and deacons."[17,18]

Now, if the form of church government rest on no other foundation, than ancient and apostolic *practice*, it is humbly submitted to consideration, whether Episcopalians will not be thought scarcely deserving the name of Christians, should they, rather than consent to a temporary deviation, abandon every ordinance of positive and divine appointment.

Any person, reading what some divines of the Church of England have written against dissenters, would in general widely mistake their meaning, should he apply to the subject before us, the censures he will sometimes meet with, which have in view, not merely the merits of the question, but the duty of conforming to the established church, in all things not contrary to the law of God. Thus Bishop Stillingfleet, who at the restoration had written with great tenderness towards the dissenters, and many years afterwards preached a sermon on a public occasion, containing severe animadversions on their separation; on being accused of inconsistency, replies (in the preface to his treatise on the unlawfulness of separation) that the former was "before the laws were established;" meaning principally the act of uniformity. So also Bishop Hoadly says, the acceptance of re-ordination by the dissenting ministers, would not be a denial of that right, which (as they conceived) presbyters had to ordain; but a confession that their former ordination was "so far null and void, that God did not approve the exercise of that right in opposition to the lawful settled method."[19] Dr. Henry Maurice also, who has written with great learning and reputation in defence of Episcopacy, makes the same distinction; observing that the "dissenters do foreign churches great injustice when they concern them in their quarrel," the ordination of the latter being "not only without, but in opposition to bishops, against all the established laws of

[17]Reasonableness of conformity, part I.

[18]The same distinction is accurately drawn and fully proved by Stillingfleet in "the Irenicum." But as that learned prelate was afterwards dissatisfied with his work (the most probably not with that part of it which would have been to our purpose) it might seem uncandid to cite the authority of his OPINION. Burnet, his cotemporary and friend, says (History of his own times, anno 1661) "to avoid the imputation that book brought on him, he went into the humours of an high sort of people beyond his own sense of things." The book, however, was it seems easier RETRACTED than REFUTED: for though offensive to many of both parties, it was managed (says the same author) with so much learning and skill, that none of either side ever undertook to answer it.

[19]Reply to objections against Episcopal ordination.

this church, &c."[20] Even where the same distinction is not expressed, it is generally implied. Whether the above censures are well or ill founded, is a question that has no connection with our subject; they cannot be thought applicable to the liberty here pleaded.[21]

Again, it cannot be denied, that some writers of the Church of England apply very strong expressions to Episcopacy, calling it a divine appointment, the ordinance of Christ, and the law of God, and pronounce it to be of divine right. Yet, in reason they ought to be understood only as asserting it to be binding, wherever it can conveniently be had: not that law and gospel are to cease rather than Episcopacy. Mr. Hooker, who uses such strong expressions, makes nevertheless a clear distinction between matters of necessity and those of ecclesiastical polity; as may be seen at large in his third and fourth books. Even Archbishop

Whitgift, said by some[22] to have been the first in his high station, under whose patronage such pretentions were annexed to Episcopacy, and whose zeal for that form and the other rights of the church, made him verily believe in the famous conference at Hampton court, that "the king spoke by the spirit of God," is quoted by Bishop Stillingfleet, as asserting that "no kind of government is expressed in the word or can necessarily be concluded from thence."[23] In short, particular expressions which writers use from zeal for that form they endeavour to establish, are not to be given in proof of their opinions, concerning the conduct suited to extraordinary occasions. Many instances to the same purpose might be produced of English divines qualifying such high expressions and guarding against seeming consequences; but this part of the subject shall conclude with the authority of a clergyman of this country, who a few years ago wrote on Episcopal government. He insists on it as of divine right, asserts that "the laws relating to it bind as strongly as the laws which oblige us to receive baptism or the holy eucharist,"[24] and that "if the succession be once broken, not all the men on earth, not all the angels of heaven, without an immediate commission from Christ, can res-

---

[20]Maurice against Clarkson, page 453.
[21]In England, the members of the established church consider the dissenters as blameable in not conforming to it as such, there being nothing required contrary to the law of God. These on the other hand blame the members of the establishment, for not yielding to their conscientious scruples, which thus exclude them from public offices, and subject them to considerable burthens. Such were the principle sources of the animosities which have subsisted between the two parties; and hence arises an argument for charity and mutual forbearance among religious societies in America, with whom the same causes of contention and mutual censure have no place, and with whom of course the same degree of bitterness would be less excusable than in England.

[22]Dr. Warner says (book 14) that "Archbishop Bancroft was the first man who had preached up the divine right of Episcopacy in the church of England." The first occasion of his doing this, is said by others to have been when he was Whitgift's chaplain.
[23]Irenicum, chapter 38.
[24]Dr. Chandler's appeal, page 7.

tore it."[25] Nevertheless, he acknowleges "the necessity of bishops is no more than a general necessity, or in other words, bishops according to the belief of the Church of England, are necessary only where they can be had."[26] He then distinguishes between cases where the necessity is real, and those where Episcopacy had been willingly and expressly rejected, as by the people of Scotland and the English dissenters.

Now if even those who hold Episcopacy to be of divine right, conceive the obligation to it to be not binding when that idea would be destructive of public worship, much more must *they* think so, who indeed venerate and prefer that form as the most ancient and eligible, but without any idea of divine right in the case. This the author believes to be the sentiment of the great body of Episcopalians in America; in which respect they have in their favour *unquestionably* the sense of the Church of England, and, *as he believes,* the opinions of her most distinguished prelates for piety, virtue and abilities.

CHAPTER VI.

It is to be expected, that the far greater number of writers in defence of Episcopal government, confine their observations to the ordinary state of the church, without giving their opinions on supposed cases of necessity. Yet, if it were required to multiply authorities, and writers were consulted

with that view, it is probable that many more than the following might be produced. But, as the lawfulness of deviation, in cases of necessity, is a fair inference from the sentiments of expressly to the purpose (perhaps) all, it will be sufficient if those quoted rank among the most respectable for their authority.

The first mentioned shall be the venerable Hooker. His books on ecclesiastical policy are universally allowed to be a work of masterly judgment, and deep erudition; they are frequently spoken of as containing the most rational and complete defence of the Church of England; and were recommended by king Charles I. (whose attachment to Episcopacy will not be doubted) as the best for fixing the principles of his children, on those questions which had distracted the nation. This accomplished writer, after asserting with great zeal the authority of Episcopal government, makes the following exception; "when the *exigence of necessity* doth constrain to leave the usual ways of the church, which otherwise we would willingly keep; when the church must needs have some ordained and neither hath nor can have possibly a bishop to ordain; in case of *such necessity* the law of God hath oftentimes and may give place: and therefore we are not, simply and without exception, to urge a lineal descent of power from the apostles, by continued succession in every effectual ordination."[27]

The same great man, speaking in another place of some churches

---

[25]Ibid, page 4.
[26]Chandler's appeal defended, page 68.

[27]Ecclesiastical Polity, Book 7, Section 14.

not Episcopal, says, "this their defect and imperfection, I had rather lament in such a case than exaggerate; considering that men oftentimes, without any fault of their own, may be driven to want that kind of polity or regiment, which is best; and to content themselves with that which either the irremediable error of former times, or the *necessity of the present* hath cast upon them."[28]

Had Mr. Hooker been asked to define *"the exigence of necessity,"* could he have imagined any more urgent than the case in question? Or had he been enquired of concerning the *"necessities of present times,"* could he have mentioned any in the cases to which he alludes (those of Scotland and Geneva,) so strongly pleading for the liberty he allows, as those now existing in America?

The name of Bishop Hoadly will probably be as long remembered, as any on the list of British worthies; and will never be mentioned without veneration of the strength of his abilities, the liberality of his sentiments, and his enlightened zeal for civil liberty. He has written in defence of Episcopal government, with more argument and better temper than is commonly to be met with in controversial writings. This amiable prelate expresses himself as follows, "as to the credit of the reformed churches abroad we think it no presumption, as we censure them not, who *in a case of necessity* went out of the ordinary method, so to expect they will not censure us for not approving such irregu-

larities, where there is *no such necessity* for them.[29] In another place he says, "for my own part I cannot argue that Episcopacy is *essential* to a christian church, because it is of apostolical institution; and on the other hand, I do argue, that we are obliged to the utmost of our knowledge, to conform ourselves to the apostolical model, unless in such where the imitation is *impracticable* or would manifestly do more hurt than good to the church of Christ; neither of which can possibly be affirmed in the *ordinary* state of the church."[30]

What necessity was there of the "reformed churches abroad" equal to ours? Is not an immediate imitation of the ancient usage *"impracticable?"* Would not such a plan as has been proposed be conforming (as far as circumstances allow) to our ideas of "the apostolic model?"

The character of Archbishop Usher for extensive learning and fervent piety is generally known; and is distinguished both by his great moderation on the subject of Episcopacy, and by the service it has received from his indefatigable researches. In a letter to Dr. Bernard he writes thus, "in places where bishops *cannot be had,* the ordination of presbyters stands valid."[31] What part of the christian world could the learned primate have named, of which it could have been so properly said as it may be of ours, that "ordination by bishops *cannot be had?*"

[28]Ibid, Book 3, Section 11.

[29]Reasonableness of conformity, part I.
[30]Defence of Episcopal ordination, conclusion.
[31]Quoted from Neale's History.

The great reformer and martyr Archbishop Cranmer was one of the first characters of the age in which he lived, for learning, piety, and virtue; and is supposed to have done more than any other towards compiling the liturgy of the Church of England; "His equal (says Dr. Warner) was never yet seen in the see of Canterbury, and I will take upon me to say, that his superior never will." In the reign of Henry VIII, according to Bishop Burnet,[32] there were proposed by the King, to this great man, in conjunction with other learned divines, certain question[s], among which are the two following, with the Archbishop's answers annexed:

Question. Whether if it fortuned a Prince Christian, to conquer certain dominions of infidels, having none but the temporal learned men with him, it be defended by God's law, that he and they should preach the word of God there or no, and also make and constitute priests there or no?

Answer. It is not against God's law; but contrariwise they ought indeed so to do; and there be histories that witness, that some christian princes and other laymen have done the same.

Question. Whether it be defended by God's law, that if it so fortuned that all the bishops and priests of a region were dead; and that the word of God should remain there unpreached; and the sacrament of baptism and others unministered; that the King of that region should make bishops and priests to supply the same or no?

[32]History of the reformation, anno 1540. Stillingfleet, with less appearance of authenticity, says it was in the reign of Edward VI.

Answer. It is not forbidden by God's law.

The above may be offered as the opinions of not only Cranmer, but also of most of the eminent bishops and other clergy of that period; for whoever will atttend to all the questions with the several answers as recorded by Burnet,[33] will find, that although the Archbishop seems singular in his sentiments as to the original institution of bishops and priests, they generally agree with him on the supposed occasions of necessity. On the former subject, the learned historian believes, that Cranmer soon afterwards changed his opinion: but the reason assigned for that belief, if it be well founded,[34] does not extend to the purpose for which his authority is here cited.

Now every circumstance in the cases supposed makes the principle apply, with the greater force, to that now under consideration. If a

[33]History of the reformation, appendix to vol. I.
[34]The reason is Cranmer's signing the book called "the erudition of a christian man." This book has led some to believe that the archbishop's principles on church government were unsettled at the time of its publication. That it contradicts itself on that subject, is certain; but this was owing not to Cranmer's inconsistency, but that of the king. In the answers of the former as given by Burnet, his sentiments seem fully fixed, and (perhaps) are reconcileable with the Episcopal plan, according to the distinction taken between the APPROPRIATED and LARGER meanings of the word "Bishop." As to "the erudition," Guthrie says (history of England, vol. 3, page 597.) "the writings were modelled by the King, as he wanted them to appear before the parliament and public;" and Dr. Warner says (book II) "it is more probably a declaration of the King's religion, than of any other man's in the kingdom."

christian King may on an emergency constitute a bishop, much more may the whole body of the churches interested; especially when they interfere not thereby with the civil magistrate. If a Prince would be justifiable in taking such a step, rather than have recourse to the spiritual authority of some neighbouring and allied kingdom, much more would we, who labour under peculiar political difficulties. If it were commendable on the mere hope of converting infidels to the christian faith, it would be more so, for the purpose of maintaining the principles of christian knowledge and practice, among those who are already of the number of its professors. If a prince ought to do this from concern for the spiritual welfare of his subjects, much rather ought we, for that of ourselves and our children.

On the credit of the preceding names, the author rests this the last part of his subject; and if his sentiments should meet with an unfavorable reception, he will find no small consolation from being in a company so respectable.

Perhaps, however, there would be little room for difference of sentiment among the well informed, if the matter were generally taken up with seriousness and moderation, and were to rest on religious principles alone. But unhappily there are some, in whose ideas the existence of their church is so connected with that of the civil government of Britain, as to preclude their concurrence in any system, formed on a presumed final separation of the two countries. Prejudices of this sort will admit of no conviction but such as may

arise from future events; and are therefore no farther considered in this performance, than with a sincere sorrow, that any persons, professing to be of the communion of the church of England, should so far mistake the principles of that church, as to imagine them widely different from what form the religion of the scriptures; which, as Bishop Sherlock observes, "stand clear of all disputes about the rights of princes and subjects; so that such disputes must be left to be decided by principles of natural equity and the constitution of the country."[35]

As for those who are convinced that the "United States," have risen to an independent rank among the nations or who even think that such may probably be the event of the war, they are loudly called on to adopt measures for the continuance of their churches, as they regard the public worship of God, the foundation of which is immutable; as they esteem the benefit of the sacraments, which were instituted by the supreme bishop of the church; and as they are bound to

[35]Vol. 4. Discourse 13th.

The indefeasible right of Kings is pretended to be founded on certain passages of scripture. The author takes the liberty of referring to the very sensible sermon above quoted, for an easy and natural explanation of the passages alluded to; whereby they are vindicated from a sense which makes the Gospel an engine of despotism and oppression, and which, however sincerely believed by some, is with others a mere trick of state. Although Bishop Sherlock's reputation in the church of England is generally known, it may be proper to mention, that his sermons are among the books formerly sent out by the honourable "Society for propagating the gospel," to be distributed by their missionaries.

obey the scriptures, which enjoin us "not to forsake the assembling of ourselves together, as the manner of some is."

More especially is this their duty, if they entertain a peculiar preference for the principles and worship of their own communion, from a persuasion of their superior excellence. That the church of England is a creature of the state, an engine of civil policy, and no otherwise to be maintained than by human laws, has been said by some, as a reason for their dissenting from her. If the same prejudice has been with others a reason for conformity, it is to be hoped they are comparatively few, and that the great majority of Episcopalians, believing that their faith and worship are rational and scriptual, have no doubt of their being supported, independent of state establishments; nay, it is presumed there are many, who, while they sincerely love their fellow christians of every denomination, knowing (as one of their prayers expresses) that the "body of Christ" comprehends "the blessed company of all faithful people," are more especially attached to their own mode of worship, *perhaps* from education, but *as they conceive*, from its being most agreeable to reason and scripture, and its most nearly resembling the pattern of the purest ages of the church. On the consciences of such, above all others, may be pressed the obligation of adopting speedy and decisive measures, to prevent their being scattered "like sheep without a shepherd," and to continue the use of that form of divine service, which they believe to be "worshipping the Lord in the beauty of holiness."

CHAPTER FIVE

RATIONAL ORTHODOXY

(1800–1844)

By 1800 much of the excitement over the American Revolution had passed. Troubled by the outcome of the French and Haitian revolutions, Americans grew suspicious of egalitarian ideals. The campaign to eliminate slavery that had brought abolition to New England, New York, New Jersey, and Pennsylvania, and a liberalization of slave legislation in many of the remaining states stalled. The dividing line between free and slave states would remain unchanged until the Civil War. New Jersey, which had allowed women to vote in its first constitution, limited the franchise to men. America was growing conservative.

In his *Case of the Episcopal Churches* Bishop White had defined an Episcopalian as one who professed the religious principles of the Church of England. With a new church structure in place White and others were now able to shift their attention from changing institutions to sketching the content of these principles. White himself convinced the General Convention of 1801 to adopt the Thirty-nine Articles for the American church, prepared a reading list for ordination candidates, wrote an account of the early conventions, and published a work on predestination.

White did much to establish a consensus in the church on such issues as predestination, baptism, and eschatology. In one important area—apologetics—he was not able to bring concord, however. By the second decade of the century two competing schools of interpretation vied for leadership in the church. High church Episcopalians believed that now that the church had resident bishops the covenant–apostolic orders argument was particularly effective. Evangelical Episcopalians, centered in the Washington, D.C. area, believed that the exclusive argument had no place in the new republic. They recalled the hope of Devereux Jarratt and other Episcopalians of the Great Awakening who had tried to make the church an effective tool for personal conversion and emphasized the similarity of Episcopalians and other Protestants.

Two selections follow from this period. Both are by high church leaders, but neither deals with the disputed covenant–apostolic argument. John Henry Hobart (1775–1830) was a strong-willed clergyman originally from Pennsylvania. He studied with Bishop White and married the daughter of Thomas Bradbury Chandler, a clergyman who had been one of the leading proponents of a colonial episcopate. After election as assistant bishop of New York in 1811, Hobart became the most prominent high church leader. The sermon that follows, an 1816 funeral oration for his predecessor as diocesan bishop, was typical of his abrupt style. Drawing on the early work of such Anglican authors as John Pearson (1613?–86)—Hobart followed White's lead in looking to seventeenth-century English authors for statements of Anglican theology—Hobart stated the proper Episcopal position on death and resurrection: the soul of the departed waited in an intermediate state until the final judgment.

William R. Whittingham (1805–79), a General Seminary professor who would later become the bishop of Maryland, first preached his "Defense of the Worship, Doctrine, and Discipline of the Church" in 1829. He presented what amounted to a standard Episcopal response to nineteenth-century revivalism. While Episcopalians were hesitant to use the word "regeneration" to refer to an adult affirmation of faith (the prayer book used the word "regeneration" to refer to the change of relationship between the individual and God that occurred at baptism), they nonetheless believed in the necessity of such a change of heart (known as renewal or renovation).

Whittingham, like Hobart, was a high church leader. Such evangelical bishops as William Meade (1789–1862) of Virginia and Charles P. McIlvaine (1799–1873) of Ohio would, however, have agreed with him on renewal and with Hobart on the state of the dead. It was on the important issue of apologetics—were other Protestants within the covenant?—that they parted company.

Hobart, Whittingham, Meade, and McIlvaine could rely upon two new institutions to disseminate proper doctrine throughout the church: the Sunday school (Robert Raikes founded the first English Sunday school in 1780. Bishop White visited the school while in England for consecration and brought the idea back home.) and the theological seminary (In 1822–24 Episcopalians founded their first three seminaries—General, Virginia, and Bexley Hall—following the 1804 example of Congregationalist Andover Seminary.).

The text of Hobart's sermon is taken from the fourth edition (New York: Standford and Swords, 1846, pp. 5–23). Whittingham's address is from his collected sermons (*Fifteen Sermons by William Rollinson Whittingham, Fourth Bishop of Maryland,* New York: D. Appleton and Company, 1880, pp. 142–62).

JOHN HENRY HOBART
(1816)

STATE OF THE DEPARTED.

People of the congregation! the remains of your pastor lie before you—the beloved pastor who so long fed you with the bread of life, and whose accents of persuasion you have so often heard in this sacred place.

My brethren of the Episcopal clergy! we have long mourned the living death of our spiritual father—his sufferings are terminated—he is at rest.

When we contemplate that venerated corpse, it is natural to inquire,

WHAT HAS BECOME OF THE SPIRIT WHICH SO RECENTLY INHABITED IT?

WHAT WILL BECOME OF THAT TABERNACLE OF CLAY WHICH THIS SPIRIT HAS DESERTED?

Christian believers, these are inquiries deeply interesting to you. Soon each of you will be as he whose remains you now behold.

WHAT BECOMES OF THE SPIRIT OF THE BELIEVER WHEN IT LEAVES ITS TABERNACLE OF CLAY?

Does it sink into annihilation? We must subdue all those feelings which constitute the perfection and happiness of our nature, before we can contemplate the extinction of being but with horror. There is not a power of his soul which man does not shudder at the thought of losing—not a virtuous enjoyment which he does not wish to carry with him beyond the grave—not an acquisition that ennobles or adorns him which he would not impress with the seal of eternity. The voice of the Creator speaks in the soul of the being whom he has made, and inspires the hope that he is immortal. But alas! that voice is only faint and feeble. Immortality, an unmerited gift to a fallen creature, must be assured by the express promise of Him who alone can bestow it. The word of the Author of our being must be the pledge that this being shall not be extinguished.

Blessed be God, this word we have—God hath spoken—"The spirit shall return to him who gave it."

This, believer, is thy confidence and thy rejoicing. Thy spirit returns to God—to God all glorious and all good—who so loved thee as to give for thee his only begotten Son; and who in the blood of his Son hath sealed the assurance that thou shalt be ever with him. Canst thou doubt whether in his presence thou shalt be happy? Ah! the happiness reserved for thee by thy God, thine eye hath not seen, thine ear hath not heard, and thy heart cannot conceive. But,

WHEN DOES THE SPIRIT ENTER ON THIS STATE OF COMPLETE FELICITY?

There cannot be a moment's doubt that departed saints do not enter on the *full* fruition of bliss immediately on their release from the body. In what does this fulness of bliss consist? In the union of the purified spirit with the glorified body. But until the voice of the Son of God calls to the corruptible to put on incorruption, and the mortal immortality, that body is confined to the tomb, embraced by corruption, mingled with the dust. Admission to heaven, the place of the vast universe of God, where the vision of his glory, more immediately displayed, shall constitute the eternal felicity of the redeemed, does not take place, according to the sacred writings, until the judgment at the great day; when the body, raised incorruptible and glorious, shall be united to the soul, purified and happy. While the soul is separate from the body, and absent from that heaven which is to be her eternal abode, she cannot have attained the perfection of her bliss.

Will the privileges of believers be greater than those of their divine Head? His glory in heaven consists in the exaltation of his human nature—of his glorified body in union with his perfect spirit. But in the interval between his death and his resurrection, his body was embalmed by his disciples, washed with their tears, and guarded in the sepulchre by his enemies. His spirit, therefore, was not in heaven until he ascended there after his resurrection. "Touch me not," said he to Mary Magdalene, when he had risen from the dead, "for I have not yet ascended to your Father and my Father, to your God and my God."[1] Our blessed Lord, in his human nature, was not in heaven until after his resurrection. And will a privilege be conferred on the members which was not enjoyed by the Head? "This day thou shalt be with me in Paradise," was his language to the penitent thief associated with him at his crucifixion—in Paradise, not in heaven; for the happiness of heaven supposes the happiness of the whole man—of his soul united to his body. But on that day in which the Saviour assured the penitent subject of his mercy that he should be with him in Paradise, the body of the one was consigned to corruption, and the body of the other to the tomb.

WHAT THEN IS THE STATE OF THE SOUL IN THE PERIOD BETWEEN DEATH AND THE RESURRECTION—BETWEEN HER SEPARATION FROM THE BODY AND HER RE-UNION WITH IT—BETWEEN HER RELEASE FROM THIS HER STATE OF EXILE, AND HER ADMISSION TO FINAL AND COMPLETE FELICITY IN HER ETERNAL HOME?

Is she in a state of [un]consciousness? All probability is against the supposition. Consciousness seems

[1] John xx.17.

a necessary attribute of spirit in a disembodied state. The temporary suspension of consciousness in the present life, arises from that union of the soul with the body, which in many cases controls, and changes, and suspends her operations.

But a state of unconsciousness is a state of oblivion, and this must be an object of aversion to the happy spirit. In the present life, indeed, there is often an oblivion of care that corrodes, of adversity that wounds the spirit, or that which, from the connexion of the body with the soul, is necessary to the renewed exertion of its powers, and to renewed enjoyment. But when the soul, with her mortal tabernacle, has shaken off her sins and sorrows, this oblivion cannot be necessary; it must interrupt her enjoyment; it cannot, therefore, be assigned her in a state which, her probation being finished, is a state of reward and of bliss.

But, on this as on every other point connected with our spiritual interests, we are not left to speculation, and to a balance of probabilities. What was the language of our blessed Lord to his penitent companion on the cross?—"This day thou shalt be with me in Paradise." But would this have been the language of consolation, of hope, of triumph, if Paradise be a state of oblivion? Or can we for a moment indulge the idea, that the human soul of the blessed Jesus sunk at death into a state of forgetfulness, which reduced it to a level with the body that was sleeping in the sepulchre? No; his soul was actively engaged—engaged in prosecuting that gracious scheme of redemption which occupied his life, which engrossed his last moments of agony, and which he relinquished not even with death. He "went," says the apostle,[2] "and preached to the spirits in prison," to the spirits in safe keeping, "to the *sometime* disobedient," but finally penitent antediluvians, "in the days of Noah," who, though they were swept off in the deluge of waters, found, through the merits of the Lamb slain from the beginning of the world, a refuge from the flames of Tophet, from the surges of the burning lake. While his body was reposing in the grave, he went in his spirit and "preached," or (as the word signifies) *proclaimed* the glad tidings to the souls of the departed saints, of that victory over death which the Messiah, in whom they trusted, was to achieve; and of that final redemption of the body and resurrection to glory, the *hope* of which constituted their enjoyment in the place of the departed.[3]

[2] 1 Peter iii.19, 20.

[3] The above is the interpretation of this very obscure passage, which is advanced and maintained with great ingenuity, force and erudition, by Bishop Horsley, in his sermon on "Christ's descent into Hell." This interpretation gives no sanction, as Bishop Horsley justly observes, to the doctrine of purgatory. Purgatory is considered as a place of punishment and purification for those who die under the guilt of sins of infirmity, from which they are delivered either when they have been sufficiently purified by suffering purgatorial pain, or by the efficacy of the masses which are said for them. There is no foundation for this doctrine in Scripture. At death the souls of the righteous and of the wicked go to a state, the one of happiness and the other of misery, in the place of the departed; and there is no change in their state except what arises from the complete consummation in body as well as soul, of the happiness of the one in Heaven and the misery of the other in (γέεννα) Hell.

Could God, who is "the God of the living" only, be styled emphatically "the God of Abraham, of Isaac, and of Jacob," if their departed spirits did not live to him in a state of consciousness and enjoyment?[4] Did the holy apostle, who in labors and in sufferings died daily, and who daily was renewed by the hope of the glory prepared for him, look forward to a state of unconsciousness after death, when he desired to "depart and to be with Christ," to be "absent from the body and present with the Lord?"

No, believer, when thy soul departs from the body, she does not

Christ proclaimed to the spirits in prison, in a state of seclusion and separation, or, as the word may be translated, in safe keeping, the glad tidings of his victory over death, of their final resurrection to glory. Were they previously in doubt as to these events—a doubt which must have been incompatible with their happiness? By no means. They died in the faith that the Messiah was to achieve this victory; and in this faith their spirits rejoiced. But Christ, when he descended to them, changed their faith in this event as future, into faith in it as actually accomplished—and he thus confirmed the glorious hopes which they already enjoyed.

But why are they antediluvians, those who were "sometime disobedient," but afterwards became penitent "in the days of Noah," selected as the peculiar objects of the Savior's preaching? "To this I can only answer," (says Bishop Horsley,) "that I think I have observed in some parts of Scripture an anxiety, if the expression may be allowed, to convey distinct intimations that the antediluvian soul is not uninterested in the redemption and the final retribution."

But for full answer on this point, and on many other inquiries connected with this subject, the reader is referred to Bishop Horsley's Sermon on Christ's descent into Hell, published at the end of his new translation of Hosea, and in the volumes of his sermons.

[4] Matt. xxii. 32.

pass into that state of utter forget-fulness, which, even in the present scene of sin and woe, thou dost dread as the greatest evil with which thou canst be visited. Thou wilt go to a place of enjoyment, characterized as the *bosom of Abraham*; because there thou wilt be blessed with the company of this Father of the Faithful, of patriarchs and prophets, who are all waiting their consummation, the redemption of the body. Thou wilt go to *Paradise*—to that place separate and invisible—but where thou shalt be with Christ and be present with the Lord; anticipating in constant desire, in rapturous hope, the resurrection at the last day. Then He who holds the keys of death and hell shall say to thy spirit—Go forth; be clothed upon with an house that is from heaven; enter into the joy of thy Lord; inherit a kingdom prepared for thee from the foundation of the world.

Yes, my fellow-Christians, this is the joyful confidence with which we can meet the interesting inquiry—

WHAT WILL BECOME OF THE BODY WHEN IT IS DESERTED BY THE SPIRIT THAT ANIMATES IT?

What can reason teach us here? She may, indeed, by analogy illustrate and confirm the doctrine of the resurrection when it is revealed; but as an original truth she knew nothing of it. The tomb received, in its dark embrace, the mouldering body; and there was no light that dawned on the night of the grave. "Blessed, then, be the God and Father of our Lord and Saviour Jesus Christ, who hath begotten us to a lively hope by the

resurrection of Jesus Christ from the dead."[5] He is "the first fruits of them that slept"[6]—and at the great harvest at the last day "those who sleep in Jesus will God bring with him."[7] The body, sown in corruption, shall be raised in incorruption—sown in dishonor, it shall be raised in glory—sown in weakness, it shall be raised in power—sown a natural body, it shall be raised a spiritual body. Blessed, blessed be the God and Father of our Lord Jesus Christ, who hath begotten us to this lively hope by the resurrection of Jesus Christ from the dead.

How is all this to be effected? By that mighty power which raised up Christ from the dead. Here we take our stand—on the omnipotence of God—and defy every attack against the doctrine of the resurrection. We laugh to scorn all attempts to wrest from us our hope, through a supposed impossibility of the resurrection, as puny struggles against the omnipotence of God. Did he not at first construct a human form from the dust of the earth? Did he not breathe into a mass of clay the breath of life? And when he again speaks, shall it not be done? Can he not again bring bone to its bone, sinew to its sinew, flesh to its flesh? Fear not, Christian! thy dust may be scattered to the winds of heaven—But thy God is there. It may repose in the lowest abysses of the grave—He is there. It may dwell in the uttermost parts of the sea—Even there his hand shall lead thee, his right hand shall hold thee, and bring thee forth, incorruptible and glo-

[5] 1 Pet. i. 3.
[6] 1 Cor. xv. 20.
[7] 1 Thess. iv. 14.

rious, like unto that body which now receives the homage of the angels around the throne. Fear not, thy Redeemer is almighty; and thou shalt be raised at the last day.

Let us comfort one another with these words—

Our venerable Father has gone. In the bosom of Abraham, in the paradise of God, in the custody of the Lord Jesus, his soul reposes, waiting in peace and joy its "perfect consummation and bliss in God's eternal and everlasting glory." Soon the sentence that sin has brought on the whole human race is to be pronounced on the revered remains before us—"Earth to earth—ashes to ashes—dust to dust."

But he lives with us in the memory of his virtues. Let us recall and cherish them. Let us keep him a little longer with us—not as of late, when languishing under disease he gradually lost that engaging expression which had so eminently characterized him, until he at last sunk in the darkness of death—but let us view him such as you, people of the congregation, beheld him when he appeared among you as your pastor—such as we, my brethren, beheld him when he exercised over us his paternal authority.

I should, indeed, violate that simplicity which in a high degree adorned him, if I were to indulge in the language of inflated panegyric. Simplicity was his distinguishing virtue. He was unaffected—in his tempers, in his actions, in every look and gesture. Simplicity, which throws such a charm over talents, such a lustre over station, and even a celestial loveliness over piety itself, gave its insinuating coloring to the talents, the station, and the piety of our venerable Father. But it was a simplicity accompanied with uniform prudence, and with an accurate knowledge of human nature.

A grace allied to simplicity, was the meekness that adorned him— a meekness which was "not easily provoked"—never made an oppressive display of talents, of learning, or of station—and condescended to the most ignorant and humble, and won their confidence; while associated with dignity, it commanded respect and excited affection in the circles of rank and affluence. And it was a meekness that pursued the dictates of duty with firmness and perseverance.

His piety, arising from a lively faith in the Redeemer whom he served, and whose grace he was commissioned to deliver, warmed as it was by his feelings, was ever under the control of sober judgment. A strong evidence of its sincerity was its entire freedom from every thing like ostentation. It did not proclaim itself at the corners of the streets—it did not make boastful pretensions, or obtrude itself on the public gaze—but it was displayed in every domestic, every social, every public relation. It was not the irregular meteor, glittering for a moment and then sinking in the darkness, from which it was elicited; but the serene and steady light, that shineth more and more unto the perfect day.

He rose to public confidence and respect, and to general esteem, solely by the force of talents and worth. In the retirement of a country village, the place of his nativity, he commenced his literary career, and he prosecuted it in the public seminary of this city, and subsequently in his private studies, until he became the finished scholar and the well furnished divine.

This city was the only scene of his parochial labors. Here he commenced and here he has closed his ministerial life.[8]

[8]Bishop Moore was born October 5, 1748, at Newtown, Long-Island. He went to school in Newtown, and afterwards in New-York, in order to prepare for entering King's (now Columbia) College, where he graduated.

He pursued his studies, after he graduated, at Newtown, under the direction of Dr. Auchmuty, Rector of Trinity Church; and he was engaged some years in teaching Latin and Greek to the sons of several gentlemen in New-York.

He went to England in May, 1774; was ordained Deacon, Friday, June 24, 1774, in the chapel of the Episcopal palace at Fulham, by Richard Terrick, Bishop of London; and Priest, Wednesday, June 29, 1774, in the same place, by the same Bishop.

After his return from England he officiated in Trinity Church and its chapels, and was appointed, with the Rev. Mr. Bowden, (now Dr. Bowden, of Columbia College,) an Assistant Minister of Trinity Church; Dr. Auchmuty being Rector, and afterwards Dr. Inglis, since Bishop of Nova-Scotia.

On the resignation of Bishop Provoost, Dr. Moore was appointed Rector of Trinity Church, December 22, 1800. He was unanimously elected Bishop of the Protestant Episcopal Church in the State of New-York, at a special convention in the city of New-York, September 5, 1801; and was consecrated Bishop at Trenton, New-Jersey, in St. Michael's Church, Friday, September 11, 1801, by the Right Rev. Bishop White, of Pennsylvania, Presiding Bishop; the Right Rev. Bishop Clagget, of Maryland; and the Right Rev. Bishop Jarvis, of Connecticut.

He was attacked by paralysis in February, 1811; and for the last two or three years repeated attacks gradually weakened and disabled him, until he expired, at his residence at Greenwich, near New-York, on Tuesday evening, the 27th of February, 1816, in the 60th year of his age. The duties of the Episcopal office in this diocese have

People of the congregation! you have seen him, regular and fervent, yet modest and humble, in performing the services of the sanctuary. You cannot have forgotten that voice of sweetness and of melody, yet of gravity and solemnity, with which he excited while he chastened your devotions; nor that evangelical eloquence which, gentle as the dew of Hermon, insinuated itself into your hearts.

His love for the Church was the paramount principle that animated him. He entered on her service in the time of trouble. Steady in his principles, yet mild and prudent in advocating them, while he never sacrificed consistency, he never provoked resentment. In proportion as adversity pressed upon the Church was the firmness of the affection with which he clung to her. And he lived until he saw her, in no inconsiderable degree by his counsel and exertions, raised from the dust, and putting on the garments of glory and beauty.

It was this affection for the Church which animated his Episcopal labors—which led him to leave that family whom he so tenderly loved, and that retirement which was to dear to him, and where he found while he conferred enjoyment, and to seek in remote parts of the diocese for the sheep of Christ's fold. I know that his memory lives where I have traced the fruits of his labors.

My brethren of the Episcopal clergy! I need not tell you how

_____

been discharged by the author of this address as Assistant Bishop, since his consecration, in May, 1811. [1816. And after the decease of Bishop Moore he became the sole Bishop of the diocese.]

much prudence, gentleness and affection, distinguished his Episcopal relation to you.

We are not without many recent monitions of that summons which we shall all receive—Give an account of thy stewardship. A presbyter whose worth and usefulness, from his vicinity to us, are well known, has been recently taken from us.[9] But a few months since, and this temple witnessed your attendance on the last solemn offices of a venerable Father.[10] The remains of another are now before us. With the exception of one,[11] to whom we still look with reverence, who was the companion of his youth, the associate of his early labors, and the sympathizing friend of his old age, he is the last in this diocese of those venerable men who derived their ordination from the Parent Church, and whose

characters are marked by attachment to evangelical truth, in connexion with primitive order. My brethren, let not their principles descend with them to the grave. Soon our course will be finished; our account will at the great day be demanded; and how awful the responsibility of those to whom Christ hath intrusted the charge of "the sheep for whom he shed his blood, of the congregation which is his spouse and body."

People whom I see before me! you have an account to render—an account of the use which you have made of your talents, your time, your privileges; of the means of grace and salvation. Animating is the reflection, that to the servant who faithfully employs the talents intrusted to him, there is a *resurrection of life*. But let us remember—blessed Jesus—let us remember, and by a living faith lay hold on thee as our refuge—thou hast declared, there is the *resurrection of damnation*.

[9] The Rev. Elias Cooper, Rector of St. John's Church, Yonkers.
[10] The Right Rev. Bishop Provoost.
[11] The Rev. Dr. Bowden.

WILLIAM R. WHITTINGHAM
(1829)

DEFENSE OF THE WORSHIP, DOCTRINE, AND DISCIPLINE OF THE CHURCH.

This I confess unto thee, that after the way which they call heresy, so worship I the God of my fathers, believing all things which are written in the law and in the prophets. [Acts xxiv. 14.]

Unquestionably, the proper office of a minister of the blessed Gospel is to proclaim salvation to a world lying in wickedness and condemnation; to offer the blessings of redemption to fallen man; to present the atoning blood of Jesus as the only means of reconciliation between sinful mortals and their just and holy Maker. He is never at home in his employment, but when delivering this message of love and mercy. In one shape or other—in a grand view of all its features as a whole, or in a minuter examination of its several parts—it must constitute the theme of his public ministrations and his private intercourse. In the temple of God and from house to house, in season and out of season, he must do the work of Him that sent him by publishing the glad tidings of the Gospel of peace.

But in the scheme of man's redemption, as in the operations of His providence in the natural and moral world, God chooses to work by means. He operates upon His creatures by the intervention of second causes. The very existence of a Ministry commissioned with the promulgation of the truths of revelation is a proof of this; since these separated ambassadors of God are one part of the machinery which He chooses to employ to effect His gracious ends.

Now these means, subordinate, it is true, to the ends which they are meant to bring about, have nevertheless a claim upon our attention. It is plain that if in their use anything is left to ourselves, they not only deserve attention, but command it. If there is a choice among them, or between the use and the neglect of them, we are bound (interest as well as duty exacts it) to choose for ourselves, and to endeavor to choose aright. If by adopting them we may render due obedience to God, and by their rejection incur the guilt of disobedience and the danger of condemnation, it behooves us well to examine what they are, and ascertain how far they are in our reach or in our possession. The means of grace are left to us, to choose them or reject them—to use or abuse them. This is one part of our probation. God in His wisdom has so ordained it, that it may appear whether we will receive His gracious provisions for our welfare, or, like Naaman the Syrian leper, prefer "Abana and Pharpar, rivers of Damascus, before all the waters of Israel."

Considerations such as these, my brethren, induced me, on the present occasion, instead of choosing some portion of the grand scheme of redemption, or some minor doctrine of Christian revelation, to call your attention to modes of worship and questions of church government and discipline. The poet may sing, in numbers more harmonious than true,

> For modes of faith let grace-
> less bigots fight,
> He can't be wrong whose life
> is in the right;

but if God has been pleased to prescribe modes of faith and select channels by which to convey His pardoning grace to His rebellious creatures, or give plain directions for our choice, it can not be useless to give our attention to the subject. It sounds well to speak of Christian love and brotherly affection preventing dissensions and doing away with strife; but they may do all this, and yet allow a candid examination of the truth, and a firm adherence to it when discovered. It is a pretty comparison to talk of bands of travelers journeying Zionward by parallel roads; but if the Almighty has marked off a path as safe and direct, it can not be of little importance whether or not we choose to follow it.

Even to those "things convenient" which are left to the direction of our own reason—such as the means of approaching the footstool of the Majesty on high in united worship, "decently and in order"—there is unquestionably a right and a wrong, a better and a worse; and it consists not with our character as reasonable beings, or with the reverence we owe to God, to remain contented in the wrong, or offer Him services which are not the best within our power.

To many of those here assembled, joining for the first time in a mode of worship altogether new, it must have seemed strange, it may have appeared inconvenient, and even improper or absurd. Such impressions it is but natural that I should wish to remove; it is but just that it should be done, if I can. Possessing an opportunity of removing prejudices or correcting misunderstandings as to the views and principles of a portion of Christ's universal Church, it is my duty to embrace it.

I do so, I trust, in the spirit of meekness and Christian humility, and under a sense of responsibility as a messenger of God's truth, to furnish you with what I believe to be reasonable and Scriptural views

of the subjects named; and I hope to speak and be heard with charity and with candor.

First, then, as to the mode of worship of the Protestant Episcopal Church—that which we have joined in this evening. There may be doubts entertained in the minds of many respecting its propriety, because it is a form. For that very reason, and on that account alone, it may have seemed cold to some, uninteresting, unevangelical.

The idea is very prevalent in a large portion of this community that forms must of necessity be formal; to some it may even appear absurd to doubt it. But, in the common acceptation of the words formal and formality to signify something "ceremonious," merely external, having the appearance but not the essence, this is so far from being true, that it would be easy to show that there is much more danger of formality where a single individual expresses as he pleases the supplications and thanksgivings of a congregation, than where all join in petitions and praises with which they are previously well acquainted.

The objection made to our worship, because it is a form, my brethren, will not bear close inspection. It is not more a form than the ordinary services of ministers left to their own guidance. All must have observed that they run into the same style, generally use in their prayers the same set of phrases, and construct them all very much on one unvarying model. They notoriously have to study the art of composing prayers; many use written forms committed to memory; all make use of helps

defense of fixed prayer

of one kind or other. Now, all these are the very essence of a form—that it is studied, composed before using, and unvarying in language, sentiment, and construction. But, admitting the very extreme of probability, that the words of a prayer were never before combined—that its thoughts were never before expressed—it is still, to all intents and purposes, a form to all except the individual who utters it. They must adopt thoughts not their own, and use language selected and arranged for them by another. The only difference, then, between our forms and those to which you have been accustomed is, that ours are previously known to all, have been the production of the combined wisdom of eminently learned and pious men, and have, in part, been handed down even from the Apostles' days; while those of others are the production of a single individual left entirely to his own discretion, and, it may be, arranged at the moment, in haste, and without reflection and close examination.

The use of such precomposed forms as ours, my brethren, is not only unobjectionable and reasonable—it is Scriptural. The children of Israel, when delivered from destruction by the Egyptians, expressed their thanksgiving in a set form. God Himself condescended to compose and prescribe set forms of prayer, for use by the elders of the Jewish cities, when a murder was committed by an unknown hand; for the priests, when they implored His blessing on the congregation, when they took up the ark to commence a march, when they offered the first fruits, and when they set apart the tithes. A great portion of the Psalms are nothing else than written forms of prayer and praise, made for use in the temple-worship by men inspired by the Holy Ghost. It is well known that in our Saviour's time set forms were used in the Jewish synagogues, and we find Him constantly joining in the worship there, without one word of censure, while He freely spoke against all the abuses which the scribes and Pharisees had grafted on God's law. But why should Christ censure forms of prayer in the Jewish synagogues? He has sufficiently declared His divine pleasure (and, one would think, set the question as to the propriety of this way of worship for ever at rest), by expressly prescribing a form, and commanding us all to use it. And, after His example, we find the Apostles and first disciples using a form of prayer, when, on the delivery of St. Peter and St. John from prison, they gave solemn thanks by "lifting up their voice with one accord" (so runs the history in the Book of the Acts), "and saying" a prayer which is there recorded. Since then, that the Church of Christ in all ages has without scruple used this way of worship is too notorious to be denied. It is equally well known that some of the holiest and best of Christians—bright stars in the galaxy of Gospel worthies, and martyrs for the truths of evangelical religion and the principles of the Reformation—have lived in the daily use of forms, and gloried in them, and died with them on their lips.

Let, then, who will condemn our worship because it is a form, he condemns with it all worship that an assembly of men can offer; he condemns the practice of some of the most pious of our race; of the whole primitive Church of Christ; of the Apostles and first disciples; of our blessed Saviour; of the Jewish Church; and of David and Moses, inspired with the Holy Ghost; nay, of God Himself.

But, if there are no just objections to forms in general, some may think there are to the particular kind of which we make use. They may, perhaps, dislike its repetitions, or, because its frequent changes are novel, think them awkward or unpleasant.

The repetitions in our mode of worship are not greater than those which are found to be unavoidable in all others. The best extempore prayer will contain more than can be pointed out in our service for any single occasion. And as to the use of the same forms on all occasions, it is not strictly the case, since appropriate variations are made to suit the time of day, and the whole service of every day differs from that of every other day throughout the year. And if the language and construction of our prayers were always the same, we adopt them because we think them best. Should the mere love of novelty induce us to alter them for the worse? Will God be pleased with ringing the changes upon words?

The character of our form is certainly not liable to exception. Its language is allowed by all to be the very model of spiritual devotion. Its prayers and praises were the breathings of the ardent piety of martyrs and persecuted saints, who learned in the school of afflic-

tion a higher strain of Christian feeling than these degenerate days can furnish. What can exhibit more deep humility and contrition than our Confession? Where is there more fervent praise and comprehensive expression of gratitude than our Thanksgiving contains, or more earnest and pathetic supplications than are in our Litany?

This mode of worship is judicious and useful, too, on account of its provision for the reading of large portions of Scripture judiciously selected and admirably arranged, and by its tendency to explain and illustrate them as they are introduced. For growing families, especially where youth are to be trained up in Christian knowledge and holiness, this continual presentation of the Word of God renders it invaluable. Of the historical books the most interesting and instructive portions are given in regular order. The prophecies are illustrated by being brought forward together with the histories of their fulfillment. The Gospels are yearly read through in course. The Epistles are not read in their regular succession, but joined to selections from the Gospels in such a manner as to exhibit the admirable harmony of both. The Psalms form a stated part of our worship as expressions of Christian prayer and thanksgiving, for which they are so wonderfully adapted.

One feature of our service is the appropriation of the Sundays of the year, and of a few other chosen days, to the commemoration of particular events in the history of the Saviour and the work of redemption. We attach no adventitious sanctity to those days; we do

Church year

not make a merit of their observance; but their appointment provides for the inculcation of the whole round of Christian doctrine, the several parts of which are brought forward in the separate services for the various days. Let what will occupy the pulpit, our worshipers are sure of the Gospel from the desk, and the whole Gospel, and the plain Gospel.

The changes in posture in the Episcopal service, however awkward they may seem to one witnessing them for the first time, have much to be said in their favor. They keep alive the interest; they prevent the fatigue of a long, monotonous stretch of attention without rest or break; and, especially, they are excellently adapted to the nature of the several acts of worship. Kneeling is the posture which the universal consent of mankind has appropriated to supplication, which is of all others most expressive of humility, and which is in many parts of the Scriptures explicitly recognized as proper for prayer. Standing is equally well adapted to the acts of praise, and we know that it was the posture always observed by the Christians of the apostolic age.

Hitherto I have contented myself with noticing objections to our mode of worship. I will state only one, and that one of the least, arguments in its favor. It is certainly a popular worship. There is no dictation in it. All is not left in the power of a single individual, to be the sole organ of the people. They have as much part in our forms as their minister. They choose for themselves, they take their portion in the public duties. There is no au-

worship form in left to clergy

thority in Scripture for the restriction of the public acts of worship to the Ministry alone: they are the sole ambassadors from God to man; but we read nothing of their being made sole agents on the part of men.

Accordingly, the Episcopal Church, while for order and decency's sake it commits the leading of devotion exclusively to the ordained Ministry, enables all to bear a part, gives the people an equal interest, and expressly assigns a portion of the duty to their performance.

I have done, brethren, with our mode of worship. I have said so much on that branch of my subject as to leave less time than I intended, or could wish, for notice of the peculiarities of the Episcopal Church in government and discipline. We differ from our brethren of the denominations respecting the nature and orders of the Ministry of Christ.

The Episcopal Church maintains that Christ established a regular Ministry, to continue in His Church to the end of the world. It also believes that the Ministry was to be perpetuated by a regular succession, each generation receiving its authority from that before it, and the whole commencing with the Saviour, the great Head of the Church. Here the Congregationalists and Independents differ from us, but the Presbyterians and Methodists still keep us company. But we go still further. We believe that our Saviour appointed three orders or classes in the Ministry, and gave the power of imparting again the authority received from Him to the highest order only—

3 orders of ministry

that order being called first Apostles, and afterward, when it began to be thought disrespectful to call uninspired men by a title so dignified, Bishops or Overseers. Of course, as we agree with the Presbyterians in thinking that there can be no Church without a Ministry, and no Ministry without a regular succession derived from Christ, we are consistent, and believe that as the ministerial powers can only be derived through the highest order of the Ministry, or that of Bishops, there can be no succession without that order—consequently, no Ministry—consequently, no true Church of Christ. It would be folly, my brethren, to attempt to set forth fully the grounds of these principles in part of a single discourse; but be they what they may, we bring them forward, not as mere dictation of human teachers, but for candid examination—professing to derive them from Scripture, to support them by Scripture, and to ask only for their comparison with Scripture.

From that infallible source we learn that, while Christ was on earth, He, the Head and source of the Ministry, appointed twelve of an inferior order under Him, and seventy, again inferior to them, all sent to preach His Gospel and minister Baptism in His name—thus constituting, with Himself, three orders at that same time, possessed of ministerial powers. From the Scriptures we learn again that when Christ, having accomplished His mission upon earth, ascended to His heavenly glory, and left His Church below with the promise "to be with it alway, even unto the end of the world"—that then He conferred new powers on His Apostles, investing them with the same commission that He had previously possessed alone. "As my Father sent me," said He, "even so send I you." His Father had sent Him with power not only to be an ambassador to man, but also to perpetuate the embassy, by appointing others; so now, for the first time, He sent His Apostles, not only to minister, to which they had been already chosen, but to impart the ministerial character to others, and to delegate again the power which they had received from Him. Thus, when the departure of the Saviour made vacant what had been the highest of the three orders of Ministry in His Church while He was on earth, the second order, the twelve Apostles, were promoted to be first; and from the Book of Acts we learn that with them and under them were the seventy, now, from the lowest, made the second order, and others chosen in their room as deacons, all of whom preached and baptized—thus making again three orders of men possessed of ministerial powers. From the Scriptures we still further learn that the Apostles, by virtue of their authority derived from Christ, chose successors, to whom they gave power to ordain, to try, and to govern the lower orders of the Ministry; and that under these—for instance, under Timothy in Ephesus, and Titus in Crete—there were elders and deacons subordinate to their rule, yet possessing and exercising the ministerial powers and functions. Yet again, from the same unerring fountain of truth we learn that Christ's Church is a Body, a house, a temple—that is, a visible and organized society, with its proper officers, deriving their powers from its Founder and Head, and from Him alone, and in such way only as He has chosen to appoint. These things, my brethren, and much more to the same effect than I have time to state, we learn from the Scriptures alone, and look to them alone for proof of them. How, then, can we be charged with setting human authority before the laws of Christ? Is it not rather submission to His laws, and anxiety to preserve His religion as He left it, that lead us to lay stress upon matters which some would fain represent as unimportant? If the facts be as I have stated them (and I ask for nothing so earnestly as for diligent examination whether they are not so), are we not in that case clearly justifiable in our pretensions and claims? It is true, we confirm our proofs from Scripture by the united and universal testimony of the whole Christian Church, which for fifteen hundred years retained, without an exception, the Ministry established by Christ, and left by His Apostles, and which now, in nine tenths of the Christian world, possesses that same Ministry. We confirm our proof by this testimony, I say; for we appeal to it only as evidence that our understanding of the Scripture agrees with that of the Apostles, and of their successors, and of all Christians for fifteen centuries. We quote the early Christian writers merely as witnesses, not as judges, or authorities in themselves. We ask them, "How did the inspired Apostles leave the Church constituted? How did you find it?"—and as witnesses to these

facts, their veracity and authority no learned man will attempt to deny, and no ignorant man can shake.

Thus much for those views of the Ministry from which the Episcopal Church derives its name. We adopt them, because we believe them to be the plain teaching of the Word of God. We support them, because they have been maintained in the universal Church of Christ from the days of the Redeemer until now, with the exception of a small portion of Europe and in this country, and there only within the last three hundred years.

But, lastly, there are some points of doctrine and discipline of the Episcopal Church which are grievously misunderstood. I can do scarcely more than name them, and deny the charges that have been erroneously founded on them.

We are thought to favor the errors of the Church of Rome. It is not true. That corrupted branch of the Christian family has had no more determined or dangerous opponent than the Protestant Episcopal Church of England, and has none more ready now to combat her dangerous errors than the Episcopal Church of this country. There is no Protestant denomination that Rome so dreads, because she well knows our ability to maintain our consistent principles, and the validity of our pretensions to the character of a true Church of Christ.

Our opinions as to the sacrament of Baptism have been grossly misunderstood. Because we will not degrade it from its rank as a positive ordinance of Christ, and the appointed seal of covenant between God and man, we are represented as considering it sufficient in itself to insure salvation! We abominate the notion. Christ's all-sufficient merits, appropriated by faith, are the only ground of acceptance with God. But then, while we receive with reverence and awe the Saviour's declaration concerning the want of justifying faith—"he that believeth not shall be damned"—we place equal reliance on His promise, "he that believeth and is baptized shall be saved." Baptism is the covenant ordinance which gives the claim to the privileges that Christ died to purchase for a fallen race; but faith, working of God's Spirit in a willing heart, alone can make those privileges effectual to salvation.

A mere question of words has given occasion to charge us with serious perversion of the "truth as it is in Jesus." Because we speak of Baptism as the means of regeneration, and call baptized persons regenerate, we have been thought to hold that a change of heart accompanied the mere outward ordinance, and thus to subvert that fundamental doctrine of the Gospel that, "if any man be in Christ Jesus, he is a new creature"; "old things are passed away, and all things are become new."

Our whole Book of Common Prayer disproves the charge; it everywhere recognizes the doctrine of the renewal of the heart into the image of God; its petitions are founded on the assumption of that truth. The fact is that, when we speak of regeneration in Baptism, we do not mean by that word what most denominations use it to express—the change of heart. We

adhere closely to the use of the word in Scripture, while others have given it a new meaning, which it has not there. A change of state, an admission to a new condition and relations, is the proper meaning of the term regeneration; and in the only two places where it is found in the Bible it can not have any other; since in one it is applied to the events of the day of judgment, and in the other is expressly distinguished from "the renewing of the Holy Ghost," and made the consequence of "washing," that is, Baptism. The change of heart, then, brethren, we do most explicitly recognize as indispensable to salvation, and we do not consider it as effected in baptism. The regeneration which we speak of in that ordinance is simply a change of state, from being out of covenant, without title to the promises, to the condition of heirs of the promises, by the gift of grace connected with God through Christ.

One more explanation, and I will ask your patience no longer.

It is commonly supposed that the terms of communion in our Church are loose; that she sets wide the doors of heaven to the gay, and insincere, and dissolute, and makes the narrow way to eternal life so broad that but few of the encumbrances of a worldly spirit or a carnal mind need be laid aside to enter it. But what is to be the standard by which we shall decide in a question of this nature? By the conduct of her communicants? Alas! can any portion of the household of faith pretend that all its children are what they profess to be, and what they ought to be, in Christian holiness, and purity, and spotlessness of life? No, brethren; it is what is required of those who make public profession of their faith in Christ, what they are taught to aim at, that is the proper test of the principles of a church. And where are those requisitions more strict, where is the aim set higher, than in the exhortations which are solemnly addressed to all our members, and with still more earnestness and almost awful force of language to the communicants in our formularies? But, it is objected, we do not use discipline; we do not officially admonish, threaten, suspend, or expel unworthy communicants! In cases of flagrant crime our ministers are bound to refuse the participation of the Sacrament to the offender. But in the minor offenses, the shades of indiscretion, and casual sin, and levity or folly, that make up so great a proportion of the scandal to the Christian name, it is granted we do not apply the lash of discipline. Why? Because such conduct is approved? because it is thought consistent with the Christian character? No; but because we deem man incompetent and unauthorized in such cases to interfere between God and His sinful creatures; we leave judgment to Him to whom judgment belongeth, who hath said, "Vengeance is mine, I will repay." We warn the offender of his danger; we set before him the responsibility under which he lies; and then, if he persist in his course of sinful folly, we leave his case to the Almighty, whose ordinances he abuses. The watchman has discharged his trust; "the soul that sinneth," on his own head shall be his blood!

Such, Christian brethren, is the plea which it is my privilege and my duty to make for a mode of worship and a system of church government and discipline which are far too little known and too lightly appreciated in this community. If anything which I have been led to say in the statement of that plea has seemed harsh or unpleasant, it was unintentionally so, and from Christian charity I ask forgiveness. If anything asserted has seemed strange or dubious, examine, candidly and thoroughly examine it for yourselves; go especially to the living fountain of truth—God's Word—and apply to the Source of all knowledge and illumination in humble prayer, and you shall know the doctrine whether it be of God. In this one thing—though on other points, it may be (we think they are) material points, one side must be in error—yet in this one thing we all agree, that Christ Jesus, even Christ crucified, the propitiation for our sins, is the Rock, and the Way, and the Life; neither is there salvation in any other, for "there is none other name under heaven given among men whereby we must be saved."

No excommunication —
accusation

CHAPTER SIX

ROMANTIC REACTION (1844–1880)

In midcentury three important social phenomena challenged the orderly world view of rational orthodox Episcopalians: the growth of the Roman Catholic church, the American Civil War, and the development of factory capitalism. The Roman Catholic church, swollen by Irish immigration, outgrew the Episcopal church; Episcopalians could no longer claim to be the exclusive stewards of the apostolic succession. After the Civil War, few Episcopalians could continue to claim, as had John Henry Hobart, that they reserved judgment on the merits of representative government; who could remain aloof in the midst of such a struggle? The growth of factories took men from cooperative family enterprises and created both a confusion about and unexpected opportunities for women. What did the church have to say to a generation of women who had studied under female church school teachers and who now wanted to enter male professions?

The American publication of the *Tracts for the Times* precipitated a church-wide debate on these issues. The *Tracts* were the product of a small group at Oriel College, Oxford, who decried the increasing secularity of English society. The specific issue to which they responded—Parliament's reform of the Church of Ireland— had little relevance for Americans, but the general issues with which they wrestled were vitally important. Oxford theologians stressed the apostolic succession and attacked the necessity of adult renewal (they believed that a proper understanding of baptismal regeneration made a separate adult renewal unnecessary) at a time in which Episcopalians were in doubt about both. What should high church Episcopalians do with the covenant–apostolic orders argument now that Roman Catholics were so numerous? How could evangelicals continue to press for adult renewal when many American were willing to dismiss doctrine as of secondary importance?

Rational orthodox high church and evangelical Episcopalians sought precise answers to theological questions. A new breed of romantic Episcopalians at midcentury were unable or unwilling to answer in kind. They found comfort in theological pluralism and were as attracted to the artistic aspects of faith as to the doctrinal. William Augustus Muhlenberg (1797–1877) was representative of this romantic turn in the church. He had studied with Bishop White, but was attracted to projects—Episcopal sisterhoods, vested choirs, sung services—that White would scarcely have recognized. For Muhlenberg subscribing to Anglican doctrine was only a small portion of what it meant to be an Episcopalian. For him the church was a vibrant and growing institution with a vital role in the nation. In 1853 he and others drafted a memorial to the House of Bishops suggesting that the church be an inclusive, rather than exclusive body. The penultimate paragraph of the memorial made a daring proposal to the bishops:

> This leads your petitioners to declare the ultimate design of their memorial; which is to submit the practicability, under your auspices, of some ecclesiastical system, broader and more comprehensive than that which you now administer, surrounding and including the Protestant Episcopal Church as it now is, leaving that Church untouched, identical with that Church in all its great principles, yet providing for as much freedom in opinion, discipline and worship, as is compatible with the essential faith and order of the Gospel. To define and act upon such a system, it is believed, must sooner or later be the work of an American Catholic Episcopate.[1]

Muhlenberg offered the memorial at a time when strife was increasing between evangelical and high church Episcopalians. At

[1]*Memorial Papers: the Memorial with Circular Questions of the Episcopal Commission; Report of the Commission; Contributions of the Commissioners; and Communications from Episcopal and Non-Episcopal Divines* (Philadelphia: E. H. Butler & Co., 1857), p. 30.

the General Convention of 1844, evangelicals, angered by the Oxford attack on adult renewal, had proposed condemnation of the movement; high church Episcopalians, finding in the Oxford advocacy of apostolic succession a badly needed support for the covenant–apostolic orders apology, had blocked the effort. The Muhlenberg memorial did not address the Oxford movement directly, but it did offer an ingenious solution to the disagreement over the covenant theology. The more comprehensive ecclesiastical system of which Muhlenberg spoke would give apostolic succession to other evangelical Protestants, thereby removing the high church objection to their inclusion in the covenant. On another level, however, the memorial was simply an appeal for greater pluralism in the church. The Episcopal church could no longer be defined by a narrow set of principles.

Those who were dissatisfied with this new pluralism left the church. (A stream of clergy and laity, including Bishop Levi Ives of North Carolina, joined the Roman Catholic church in the 1840s and 1850s. In 1873 Bishop George Cummins of Kentucky and a group of dissatisfied evangelicals left the Episcopal church to form the Reformed Episcopal church.) Those who remained behind remade their church in important new ways, often creating new institutions to respond to the changed character of American life. Individual priests and bishops gave their sanction to the revival of the female diaconate (the revival began in Lutheran Germany and spread to Lutherans, Episcopalians, and Methodists throughout the world) and the reintroduction of female monasticism. Western missionaries, such as James Lloyd Breck (1818–76), experimented with a monastic school and evangelism center (Nashotah House Seminary) and advocated the establishment of American cathedrals (Bishop White's *Case* had called for the elimination of any distinction for parishes over which bishops presided). William Muhlenberg's ritual innovations at the Church of the Holy Communion in New York were imitated elsewhere.

Anne Ayres (1816–96) came to New York from England at the age of twenty. In 1845 William Muhlenberg, who was her rector, admitted her to monastic orders. She was the first post-Reformation nun in the Anglican tradition. The following selection is from Ayres's *The Life and Work of William Augustus Muhlenberg* (New York: Harper & Brothers, 1880), pp. 175–92. In presenting her idealized portrait of Muhlenberg, Ayres was relatively uninterested in doctrine. She stressed instead the role of the church in creating character. She also included the story of her own decision to enter monastic orders.

ANNE AYRES

(1880)

THE LIFE AND WORK OF
WILLIAM AUGUSTUS MUHLENBERG

CHAPTER XIII: 1844–1846

"Forgetting the things that are behind," was a favorite saying of Dr. Muhlenberg's, and indicative of a marked tendency of his life to press on towards the development of a new thought, as soon as that which he had in hand was fully demonstrated. At this time, an ideal parish occupied his field of vision, through the purpose of his sister, Mrs. Mary A. Rogers, in pursuance of the wishes of her deceased husband, to build a free church in the city of New York. She naturally expected her brother should be the pastor of this church, and there were circumstances which seconded his inclination in that direction.

If the projected college edifice [St. Paul's College, Flushing, New York, a secondary school for boys of which Dr. Muhlenberg was then rector] had been completed, it is possible he might not have felt himself equally at liberty to surrender his present charge, but notwithstanding much earnest and persistent effort to that end, the stone walls of the basement story remained as they were left in 1836, while the buildings in use at the Point, from their insufficiency of private rooms for the students of the higher College classes, had become increasingly inconvenient.

Without a suitable permanent edifice he could not satisfactorily go on, and began to be impressed with the conviction that he had possibly done enough for education in presenting, what he believed to be, the pattern of a true Christian seminary of learning. He was not mistaken in this conviction, for at the time of which we speak, schools modelled, so far as might be, after St. Paul's, had sprung up in all directions. Every diocese became ambitious to have one, and bishops and doctors of the church

had resorted to College Point, and sat at his feet, as learners of his methods.[1]

The contemplated church presented a new and delightful subject for his creative talent, and he hailed his sister's proposition as an opening, in the ordering of providence, for exemplifying his long-cherished theory of the Church of Christ as a Brotherhood, and also for setting forth a more reverent and expressive ritual of worship than as yet prevailed.

The "Church of the Holy Communion" he christened his conception, ere yet the details of the structure were matured. "Why not call your church, 'St. Sacrament,' at once?" said his friend Dr. Seabury, on hearing the name. "Because that is not at all my idea," replied Dr. Muhlenberg; "but communion or fellowship in Christ, of which the sacrament is the divinely appointed bond;" and in his address at the laying of the cornerstone, on July 24th, 1844, he yet more fully explained himself, thus:

Let this sanctuary be called the *Church of the Holy Communion*. Nor let it be only a name. Let it be the ruling idea in forming and maintaining the church, and in all its ministrations. Here let there be a sanctuary

consecrated especially to fellowship in Christ, and to the great ordinance of His love. This will rebuke all the distinctions of pride and wealth. . . . As Christians dare not bring such distinctions to the table of the Lord, there, at least, remembering their fellowship in Christ and their common level in redemption, the high and the low, the rich and the poor, gathered together around the sacred board; so let the same brotherhood prevail, let there be no places for the differences of worldly rank in the Church of the Holy Communion.[2]

The church was to be supported by the offertory, as in primitive times, everyone laying by, according as God has prospered him, against the first-day of the week; and it was not to be placed in the hands of a vestry.[3]

Mrs. Rogers retained proprietorship in the beginning, after which it was conveyed to a body of trustees, of which Dr. Muhlenberg became one. Hence, the Church of the Holy Communion was not represented in Convention. Dr. Muhlenberg always deplored the incongruity of elements, composing those bodies in the church; maintaining that a true Council of

[1]Among the institutions which thus had birth, the Rev. Dr. Libertus Van Bokkelen, names the following: The Raleigh Episcopal Institute, N.C.; the High School, Alexandria, Va.; Rev. Dr. Bowman's Lancaster School, Pa.; Bishop McIlvaine's schools, Gambier, Ohio; Jubilee College, Illinois; St. James College, Hagerstown, Md.; and the schools of Bishops Kemper and Otey, in their respective dioceses.

[2]See *Evangelical Catholic Papers, Second Series,* page 79.
[3]Most Episcopal congregations in the mid-nineteenth century were supported by pew rents. Vestrymen, many of whom served for life, were chosen from among those who rented pews—Ed.

the Church should consist solely of communicating members, and further, that the delegates, representing a parish, should be elected by the communicants of that parish, all voting alike. Speaking of the peace and love which he hoped would always prevail in the new church, he adds: "From one source of contention at least, that of ecclesiastical politics, a church will be free, which will maintain its outward union with the Body at large, only through the union of the Pastor and the people with their Bishop, and so preserve its unity by adhering to the 'fellowship of the Apostles.'"

The architecture of the church, a pure specimen of English Gothic, people called "Upjohn's best." Mr Upjohn was the architect, but both the style of the building, and its minutest details came under the close direction of Dr. Muhlenberg's taste and reverential spirit. He brought to this creation symbolism essentially the same as that which he had so long employed in St. Paul's College, but more artistic and costly. They who were associated with him in those days, remember to have heard little or nothing of this or that ecclesiological authority and custom, as influencing aesthetic points. The question was the signification and beauty of the proposed symbol.

The interior, as he left it, was full of pure evangelic Catholic meaning. The ever-open Bible standing under the simple chancel-cross; below it, on the altar cloth, the unchanging command of our Divine Lord—"This do, in remembrance of me"; high above these, with its primitive forms and sym-

bols, the great east window, making a background of rich soft coloring for the whole. In the centre of the beautiful wheel window of the south transept, a circle enclosing a cross, with the intersected legend—"All and in all;" and in the six sections radiating from this centre, emblems of the offices of our Lord Jesus Christ as our Prophet, Priest, and King, and of the order and ministry of the church;—and the pure white marble font with its carved wreath of water-lilies encircling the words— "He that believeth and is baptized shall be saved."

The building was sufficiently completed for use in May, 1846, and was consecrated by Bishop Ives on the third Sunday in Advent of that year; the diocese, unhappily, through the suspension of Bishop Onderdonk, being virtually without a head. In this emergency Dr. Muhlenberg had anticipated that his old friend, Dr. Milnor, would preside at so much of a consecration service, as, under the circumstances, they expected, but this venerable man died very suddenly, before the church was finished, and when the time came, advantage was taken of a sojourn of Bishop Ives in the city to obtain his services for the occasion.

During the two years occupied by the projection and building of the church, Dr. Muhlenberg gave himself with unremitting fidelity to his charge in St. Paul's College, revolving at the same time many plans for the continuance of the Institution when it should pass out of his hands. Eventually the Rev. Mr. J. G. Barton, the Senior Professor of Greek and Latin, of whom honorable mention had been made in connection with the College commencement of 1839, became his successor. But, owing to various causes, the work did not long survive the withdrawal of its founder. Within three or four years St. Paul's College ceased to exist, and the buildings and land were sold to a private purchaser. This last, however, not without an endeavor, fruitless through the pressure of his city work, to preserve the place to the church as a country orphanage.

The education period of Dr. Muhlenberg's history was so eminent in results that his scholars may be justified from their standpoint, in claiming as they do, that his best work was comprised within these eighteen years, though in reality those labors were but the foundation of yet greater works, which one after another grew with his life into one symmetrical whole of usefulness and beauty. But it is true, that "beyond all the ties of family he belonged to his boys." They were his children and know better than any other could do the lovableness of his character, "so grand in its simplicity, so full of tenderness, while replete with power, so childlike in its true humility," and so totally unselfish, that his actions were neither tarnished nor trammelled by any aspiration after earthly honor or gain.

One of his oldest spiritual sons throws light on the interior life of the school and its master in the following extracts from a recent letter:

. . . . Dr. Muhlenberg had no eccentricities of mind or manner, no oddities of any kind, nothing in short differing from most men that I have ever met, except the deep reality and entire unselfishness that pervaded the whole tone of the Christian man. . . . All that I can now recall of special incidents at the Institute, resulted directly from some principle in practical life taught by him to the boys. For example: One day he called them together and read to them from the newspapers, a statement of destitution and distress among some German emigrants recently landed in New York. He then asked them whether they would like to give something in relief. One said, "I'll give two dollars," another, "I'll give one," another three, all were ready to give something, and thus a large sum was, at once, subscribed. But the boys, by a standing rule of the Institute, were not allowed spending money, except to a very limited extent, and there was not money enough, in the pockets of all of them put together, to pay more than a small portion of the sum they wanted to give. The Doctor then said to them that he had no doubt their parents would be gratified to pay the several sums named, if made an item of charge in their school bills, but what he, at present, wanted to know was what they would give themselves, without calling upon their parents, *i.e.*, he wanted them to give *their own* alms. And so, he asked them, "Are you willing to give these poor creatures your dinner?" There was a general response of assent, but it was not vociferous like the other. It was subdued, yet earnest and sincere. Then the matter for decision was, How shall it be done? And it was decided thus, to select two of the most expensive weekday dinners—for Sunday was always a feast—to make their own meal on plain bread and molasses for those two days, and to give, through Dr. Muhlenberg, the difference in cost to the needy emigrants. This difference, in a large family amounted to a goodly sum, which was thus the result of the self-denial of the boys and others. This incident illustrated the principle taught by the Doctor, that self-denial for the purpose of giving is held to be a part of acceptable giving at all times. There is no such thing as giving of that which costs us nothing.

Again almost all the lessons for recitation were prepared in two rooms, called the "Large Study," and the "Little Study." In the former there was always an instructor to preserve order, and to have a general oversight. In the "Little Study," used by the older and more merito-rious boys, there was not the presence of an instructor, the boys were expected to refrain from conversation, and to attend faithfully to their studies; and were at liberty to leave the room at their discretion. This plan of trusting to the honor of the boys worked admirably well. It was a great matter to be promoted from the big to the little study. . . . A similar practice was observed in regard to quiet in the dormitories, and keeping within the bounds of the Institute grounds.

Occasionally, when a boy became so frequently troublesome as to be on the point of being dismissed from the school, one of the others, who was of exemplary habits, or sometimes one of the instructors, in order to avoid the boy's dismission, became security for the delinquent for a time, say for one, two, or three weeks. The meaning of *security* was fully explained, and the recipient of the kindness was made to understand, that any future misconduct of the kind complained of, would be charged to the security. . . . This gave an unusual, and powerful stimulant to the boy who had done ill, to do well in future. It was necessary to conduct the whole matter, very discreetly, and in most cases, the result was very favorable. It fostered sentiments of kindness and love on both sides, touched the secret of family love, gave the thoughts of one mediating for another, and thus suggested, and helped to keep in mind, the infinitely higher love, and greater mediation of which we all are recipients. . . .[4]

Another pupil, writing to his former schoolmates on a special occasion, indulges in the following tender retrospect:

Doctor Muhlenberg was never the schoolmaster to *us*. I remember as though it were yesterday, the first time I was placed under his care. It was the autumn of 1829. I was almost an orphan, and although quite young had already passed three years at boarding school, when I was sent to Flushing. The first evening we were summoned to family prayers. This little circumstance, with the fervor of him who led the devotions, were things so new to me that they made a lasting impression. I remember distinctly the room, and all the circumstances, and I think every pupil who ever came to Flushing must have known intuitively, at the very first contact, as I did then, that he was forming a tie, which differed from that of master and pupil. Young as we were, I am quite sure

we realized that it was not for earthly gain, nor earthly honor, that our Principal had withdrawn himself from the world, and from society, where he was so fitted to shine. A loftier aim was evident, even to our youthful apprehensions,—and we saw that he esteemed it little profit to us, if we conquered the subtleties of language or mathematics, and thought not of a higher victory. You all know how warm and often tender a friendship, seemed to spring up towards him in the breast of all who came to him; how it seemed untouched by the boyish resentment which usually follows correction and punishment; and how, even with the incorrigible, the parting was always in sorrow, perhaps in tears, but never in anger or unkindness. We remember, and can never forget, that voice of gentle remonstrance, which so affectionately pleaded with us to beware of evil, and turn to Christ, in the day of our youth.

At the beginning of the Institute, Dr. Muhlenberg had most fervently prayed that among the sons who he should bring up might be some who would become ministers of the Gospel. This was the one earthly reward he asked, and it was signally granted. As early as the year 1834, he saw this fruit on which he had set his heart, beginning to ripen under his hand, and in his private diary thus pours out

[4]Rev. Dr. J.W. Diller to the writer, Aug. 10th, 1879, in reply to a request for some incidents of the Institute days.

his happiness: "The prospects are animating—Oh, the joy of being a coworker with God—of being the means of raising to his glory a temple on earth where many souls may be born to life everlasting—I have enough success to believe that God is with me, and to be an earnest that he will enable me to do what I long to do for the honor of His Name."

He estimated the number of pupils during his rectorship as approximately nine hundred, about fifty of whom, counting some of his college students who accompanied him to New York to complete their studies, entered the ministry of the church.[5] Bishop Bedell of Ohio, may be named from the fact of his having been one of the earliest pupils of the Flushing Institute. He entered on the first day of the occupancy of the building and before work was actually begun. The following extract from a tribute of the bishop's to his "dear old Master," in a Convention-address, is to the purpose here: "During these years Dr. Muhlenberg laid the impress of his character upon some eight hundred boys. Those who survive are now men, most of them are in position where they touch the very springs of society, and direct the forces that are moving this age. One has played his part well in diplomacy, and still is wielding political influence.[6] Another stands to-

day among the chiefs in our commercial metropolis, and lately welcomed the president into that great company which controls the finances of our land.[7] Another, the sweet boy-singer leader of the school choir, is now heard through his hymnal in hundreds of our churches and leads the devotion of thousands of souls as he learned to do when we were boys together at Flushing.[8] Another stands prominently among critics of the English tongue.[9] Others lead at the bar or in medical life. Many are clergymen. Three are bishops—of Northern New Jersey, Pittsburg, and Ohio."[10] Bishop Bedell further says—"I chanced to go into a butcher's stall in a market in New York a year or two ago, and casually dropped Dr. Muhlenberg's name while speaking to my companion. The butcher laid down his knife and asked, 'Do you know him?' I replied. And then he said, 'I once went to school to him for a year. How I would love to see him! Do you think I might call on him.' I met the doctor that day and told him the incident. The next morning scarcely had the butcher opened his stall, when his old master—nearly eighty years of age—stood beside him, and the hard hand of toil was clasped within the loving grasp of one to whom every scholar was a dear child never forgotten. . . . Blessed the boys that had such a teacher and fragrant is his memory to every one that ever sat as a learner at his feet."

[5] The Rev. Dr. Jacob W. Diller and Bishop Kerfoot of Pittsburg were among the first-fruits of the school. Bishop K., for some years, as chaplain of the College, rendered valuable assistance in spiritual work among the boys.
[6] John Jay, Ex-Minister to Austria; later, Chairman of Civil Service Reform Committee, investigating New York Custom House.

[7] Samuel D. Babcock, President of Chamber of Commerce, New York.
[8] John Ireland Tucker, D.D., of Troy.
[9] Richard Grant White.
[10] The late Bishop Odenheimer, Bishop Kerfoot, and Bishop Bedell.

The part of his life given by Dr. Muhlenberg to the Institute and College was necessarily a period of much retirement and comparative obscurity. Beyond the repute of his work, and the publicity incident to the conduct of its immediate affairs, he came, personally, little in contact with the outer world, and was not much known even to his brother clergymen in the city of New York. During the last years of these labors, zeal for the honor of his church forced him for a little while into some prominence, but in a matter so wholly apart from his own history that it is not necessary here to revive its painful details.

In the summer of 1845, he gave the initiatory impulse to a Church Sisterhood, but unconsciously and indirectly, in the first instance, both on his own part and on that of the subject of his influence; and through the rest of his life, he would revert to the particulars which follow as a remarkable Providence.[11] He was "on the crest of the advancing wave" in the matter of sisterhoods, as in other points of church progress. There was then no organization of the kind in the Episcopal Church, either in America or in England. The Lutheran deaconesses were beginning to be spoken of as doing a good work in the little village of Kaiserswerth, on the Rhine, and the picture of a community of Christian women, consecrated to the service of charity, had entered into his dreams of the church he was about to establish, but he had not given his mind to any plans on the subject, nor

[11]Miss Ayers refers to herself here in the third person.—Ed.

taken a step towards the embodiment of his idea, when it was somewhat signally precipitated.

It was on a Sunday, in the little chapel of St. Paul's College, College Point, where Dr. Muhlenberg's sister and niece and some lady friends were spending part of the summer vacation. The rector preached a sermon on "Jephtha's vow," with an application glancing at the blessedness of giving one's self undividedly to God's service. The suggestion was covert and guarded. Reading over the manuscript later, there seemed little in it to produce a very marked effect, yet the arrow from the bow thus drawn "at a venture," was guided by a Higher Power, straight to the heart of at least one of his hearers. The latter at that time was too little acquainted with the preacher to speak freely of the deep impression received. All that was ventured in meeting him casually after the service, was a brief expression of the interest felt in the discourse and the conviction that there *was* something better and happier than the ways of our every-day Christianity. "Yes," Dr. Muhlenberg rejoined; "No man that warreth entangleth himself in the affairs of this life that he may please him who hath chosen him to be a soldier," and after this single utterance passed out of the room. But the text thus spoken, "was a nail in a sure place," which thenceforth, through a lifetime, was never to loose its hold; and from this germ, was developed later, the Sisterhood of the Holy Communion, so called, from the parish under whose first pastor it originated. The formal organization of the community took place later. This first Sister was consecrated one winter evening in the church, at the dispersion of the congregation after daily service. Besides the pastor in his surplice within the chancel, and the Sister in her accustomed dress kneeling at the rail, the only other present was the good old sexton, waiting to put out the lights. The whole was as simple as it was solemn.

Those were days of great excitement in the Episcopal Church. The secession of Mr. Newman and others of the Oxford School to Rome was then recent, and all parties were filled with alarm at whatever they thought tending in that direction. The very name "Sister" would have been obnoxious. But it was not so much prudence, as a sense of the sacredness of the engagement, which ruled in the privacy of the above occasion. Observation and talk would kill what there was of divine life in this germ. All true growth is hidden and silent. So a reserve on the subject seem mutually, almost tacitly, understood.

While arranging for the occasion, it transpired that the pastor had made a partial engagement to be present at the consecration of a church out of town; but learning the Sister's wish, he immediately set this aside. On her demurring at any change of plan on her account, Dr. Muhlenberg at once replied, "What is the consecration of a church to the consecration of a life!"—a trifling incident, yet illustrative of his habitual, instant sympathy in any spiritual endeavor. How great a power for good that quick Christly sympathy has been to hundreds and to thousands will be best appreciated by those who

were ever favored to be the recipients of it. Coming within its influence, was as if one passed from under a cold, gray November sky, with its leaden landscape and prospective drudgery of winter toil, into the inspiriting warmth and color of a fine June morning. The powers of heart, mind, and soul would spring to Christian work, as though treading on air, or rather as borne along by the felt support of those words which were so often his parting charge to his disciples: "Be strong in the Lord, and in the power of his might." So did he dignify, enoble, idealize, whatever of Christian service he came in contact with.

Thus was obtained the womanly element essential to the domestic administration of the various charities, already, to Dr. Muhlenberg's mental vision, clustering around the Church of the Holy Communion. He saw the future Sisterhood. But in its first member he received more than a beginning of the community he desired to organize; for counting it the noblest of privileges to work under such a leader, she threw her life heartily and unreservedly into all his plans and aims, with unceasing thanks to God for the opportunities of usefulness so largely opening up to her through his wise and holy guidance. Assuredly, as one had expressed it, "Dr. Muhlenberg met the supreme test of true goodness and true greatness; for to none was he so good and so great, so pure, so tender, and so loving, as to those who knew him best and were most with him."[12]

[12]Bishop Littlejohn of Long Island.

Naturally, as time went on, the relation thus formed grew to be essentially a paternal and filial one, the difference of age itself inducing this. The church-sister became the church-daughter, and the constant companion of his labors throughout the rest of his consecrated life.

The spiritual element was always indispensible to Dr. Muhlenberg in any thing like friendship. To a young man, a stranger, who, in a very remarkable manner, once ardently importuned his affections, but whose way of life lay in quite a different direction, he said with his habitual frankness: "I never cared much for any one not helpful to me in my work for the Lord;" and in a letter to one whom he had educated, and who was, at the time, ably assisting him in the induction of the work at College Point, he wrote: ". . . Therefore it is, my dear son, that you must be more to me than a business man in the College. There is no communion of heart in dollars and cents, in, etc., etc., etc., . . . You must be my partner in the service of Jesus Christ. You must unite with me in leading the young to the kingdom of Heaven— our souls must work together."

CHAPTER SEVEN

THE LIBERAL CHURCH
(1880–1920)

In 1881 William Reed Huntington (1838–1909), chairman of the liturgical committee that was preparing a revision of the Book of Common Prayer for the General Convention of 1883, offered a rationale for revision. His first and most carefully argued reason was "the changed conditions of national life." Huntington went on to explain:

Shrewd and far-seeing as were William White and his coad jutors in their forecast of nineteenth century needs made from the standpoint of the Peace of Versailles, they would have been more than human had they succeeded in anticipating all the civil and ecclesiastical consequences destined to flow from the memorial event. Certainly it ought not to be held strange that this "new America" of ours, with its enormously multiplied territory, its conglomeration of races, its novel forms of association, its multiplicity of industries not dreamed of a generation ago, should have demands to make in respect to a better adaption of ancient formularies to present wants, such as thoughtful people count both reasonable and cogent. That a prayer-Book revised primarily for the use of a half-proscribed Church planted here and there along a sparsely inhabited sea-coast, should serve as amply as it does the purposes of a population now swollen from four million to fifty, and covering the whole breadth of the continent, is marvel enough; to assert for the book entire

[handwritten margin note: Country has changed needs — new BCP]

adequacy to meet these altered circumstances is a mistake.
"New times, new favors and new joys," so a familiar hymn
affirms, "do a new song require."[1]

For Huntington and many other Episcopalians neither the rational
orthodoxy of the early part of the century nor the romantic vision
at midcentury were adequate for a new and vibrant industrial
America. The church needed a new flexibility and a new appeal
to the industrial worker, the foreign immigrant, and to the modern
businessman. Huntington believed that the Episcopal Church
could respond to these needs better than other denominations.
Combining strands of both the high church covenant–apostolic
succession argument and the more egalitarian evangelicalism, he
envisioned an American church with episcopal orders and a commitment to American democracy that he did not find in the Roman
Catholic church of the Day. Huntington's *Church-Idea* (1870) was
his attempt to describe such a comprehensive church.

Alexander Crummell (1819–98), a missionary, an author, and
priest, was one of the most prominent black Episcopal clergymen
of the nineteenth century. Returning to the United States in 1873
after twenty years in Liberia, he became a spokesman for blacks
in the church. In 1883 he played an important role in defeating
the "Sewanee proposal," a suggested canon that would have
created a separate nongeographical jurisdiction for blacks, thereby
removing them from any participation in the dioceses in which
they lived. Crummell's sermon titled "The Discipline of Human
Powers" was preached in the "manly religion" vein—an attempt
by clergymen who feared that a romanticized church lacked appeal
to men to stress the masculine nature of Christianity. Crummell,
aware of the constant effort needed by black Americans in order
to gain equality, handled the genre well and also touched upon the
dangers of modern skepticism in his sermon.

While the dreams of such as Huntington and Crummell were
not fully realized, the Episcopal church did make considerable
strides during these years toward becoming a more compassionate
and inclusive church. Among the accomplishments to which Episcopalians could look as evidence of this change were: (1) At the
General Conventions of 1886 and 1892, the Episcopal church be-

[1]William Reed Huntington, "Revision of the American Common Prayer," *American Church Review* 33 (April 1881), pp. 15–16.

came the first American denomination to go on record as favoring improved conditions for the industrial workers. (2) The 1916 Christian Nurture series, the church's first graded Sunday school curriculum, emphasized missions and social action. (3) In 1918 Henry B. Delany (1858–1928) of North Carolina and Edward T. Demby (1869–1957) of Arkansas became the first black Episcopal (suffragan) bishops to serve in the continental United States. (4) The General Convention of 1919 amended the church's constitution to make the presiding bishop an elective rather than a seniority position. At approximately the same time many individual congregations abandoned perpetual vestries in favor of a rotating leadership, and a "Nation-Wide Campaign" (a coordinated national canvass in 1919) helped individual pledging replace the vestiges of the pew rent system. (5) Professor Vida Scudder (1861–1954) and other Episcopalians interested in more humane national policies supported the Christian Socialist Fellowship that drew nearly one million votes in 1912. Economist Richard T. Ely (1854–1943) challenged prevailing economic theories that appealed to natural law to give businesses a free hand in dealing with employees. (6) Female Episcopalians formed national organizations in order to gain a stronger voice in the church: the Woman's Auxiliary to the Board of Missions (1871), the triennial of the Women of the Church (1874), and the United Thank Offering (1889). (7) Episcopalians expanded their ministry to blacks (Bishop Payne Divinity School in Petersburg, Virginia began to prepare black clergy in 1878), orientals (Deaconess Drant's True Sunshine Mission to Chinese-Americans in San Francisco opened in 1905), hispanics, and other ethnic groups. (8) The Reverend Thomas Gallaudet (1822–1902) led the way in opening the church to the deaf.

The selection from Huntington's *The Church-Idea; An Essay Toward Unity* is from the fifth edition (Boston: Houghton Mifflin, 1928, pp. 1–33). Crummell's sermon is from *The Greatness of Christ and Other Sermons* (New York: Thomas Whittaker, 1882, pp. 285–311).

William R. Huntington
(1870, 1899)

THE CHURCH-IDEA

I

THE GOSPEL OF THE KINGDOM

Dissatisfaction is the one word that best expresses the state of mind in which Christendom finds itself to-day. There is a wide-spread misgiving that we are on the eve of momentous changes. Unrest is everywhere. The party of the Curia and the party of the Reformation, the party of orthodoxy and the party of liberalism, are all alike agitated by the consciousness that a spirit of change is in the air.

No wonder that many imagine themselves listening to the rumbling of the chariot-wheels of the Son of Man. He Himself predicted that "perplexity" should be one of the signs of his coming, and it is certain that the threads of the social order have seldom been more intricately entangled than they now are.

A calmer and perhaps truer inference is that we are about entering upon a new reach of Church history, and that the dissatisfaction and perplexity are only transient. There is always a tumult of waves at the meeting of the waters; but when the streams have mingled, the flow is smooth and still again. The plash and gurgle that we hear may mean something like this.

At all events the time is opportune for a discussion of the Church-Idea; for it is with this, hidden under a hundred disguises, that the world's thoughts are busy. Men have become possessed with an unwonted longing for unity, and yet they are aware that they do not grapple successfully with the practical problem. Somehow they are grown persuaded that union is God's work, and separation devil's work; but the persuasion only breeds the greater discontent. That is what lies at the root of our unquietness. There is a felt want and a felt inability to meet the want; and where these two things coexist there must be heat of friction. Catholicity is what we are reaching after. But how is Catholicity to be defined? And when we have got our definition, what are we to do with it? The speculative and the practical sides of the question are about equally difficult to meet. The humanitarian scheme would make the Church conterminous with the race; the ultramontane would bound it by the Papal decrees.

Clearly, we have come upon a time for the study of first principles, a time to go down and look after the foundations upon which our customary beliefs are built.

The more searching the analysis, the more lasting will the synthesis be sure to be.

The present papers presuppose in the reader a certain amount of Christian faith, enough, at least, to give him a general interest in the subject under review. They do not, however, take for granted any definite conclusions as to the nature or intent of the Christian Church. We will begin, therefore, at the beginning, with the Church-Idea itself.

And first of all this very expression must be justified. What is the Church-Idea?

Briefly it is this, that the Son of God came down from heaven to be the Saviour not only of men, but of man; to bring "good tidings of great joy" not only to every separate soul, but also to all souls collectively. He died, not only to save the scattered sheep, but to gather them that they might be *scattered* sheep no longer. If we would receive the Gospel in its fulness, we must recognize it as a message endowed with a twofold significance, sent with a twofold purpose, freighted with a twofold blessing.

Not that there are two Gospels—God forbid! St. Paul would have his Galatians hold accursed even the angel who shall dare to preach to them a second Gospel. But this single Gospel has a twofold outlook; in the one direction it fronts upon the individual, in the other it fronts upon society.[1]

Every man that breathes has his own personal need of pardon at God's hands. The Gospel meets him with its promise of forgiveness. Again, the great family of men, as a family, asks to be reconciled and set in order. The Gospel meets this want with its announcement of a Kingdom organized upon the principle of holiness.

"The Gospel" ought to be regarded as the entire blessing resulting to the world from the birth, life, death, resurrection, and ascension of our Lord Jesus Christ. In this aggregate of blessing, the interests both of the one and of the many have a place. It is an injury to the balance of truth when either aspect is dwelt upon to the exclusion of the other. Many a weary estrangement in religion owes its origin to this mistake. If, in a rough way, we define the error of Romanism to be an overestimate of the value of organized Christianity, we ought also to admit that the error of Protestantism has lain in an underestimate of the same. The one theology tends to sacrifice the in- *RC* dividual to the Church; the other tends to sacrifice the Church to the *Prot* individual.

But we shall come to "the Roman Question" by and by. At present we are concerned with the abstract Church-Idea, and in determining whether it has, or has not, any intimate relation with the Gospel of Christ.

A glance at the very first instance in which the word "Gospel" occurs in the New Testament will give us light upon this point. The Evangelist St. Matthew tells us, in one of his earlier chapters, that as soon as our Lord's ministry was fairly begun, He "went about all

[1] The Schoolmen wisely recognized this distinction in their theory of "The Seven Sacraments." Two of the seven, namely, Matrimony and Orders, were held to confer grace on society, as the other five conferred it on the individual. It cannot be denied that a profound truth is latent here.

Galilee teaching in their synagogues, and preaching the Gospel of the Kingdom."[2] Now we know what "Gospel" means, and we know what "Kingdom" means. Gospel is good news. A kingdom is one of the familiar forms of organized society. When, therefore, we are told that Jesus preached "the Gospel of the Kingdom," the natural and straightforward inference from the statement would seem to be that He announced to the people the coming of a new and better social order. It will be remembered that this had been the key-note also of the Baptist's cry in the desert. He had bidden men repent and be ready, because there was a kingdom close at hand. When the King came, his first utterance was but the amplification of what his harbinger had said. He also preached "the Gospel of the Kingdom."

But we are not left wholly to our own devices in searching out the meaning of this phrase. We have even better evidence than that of the ordinary laws of language. The discourses spoken in those Galilean synagogues and elsewhere on mountain, lake, and plain, are largely preserved to us. In sermon and parable we have the outline of the new Kingdom sketched, and so sketched as to persuade us that it is meant to be a thing very tangible and real. The impression given is that of a new society about to be established here on earth, a regenerate social order, that shall dwell within the older order, while yet wholly independent of it, the one community bearing to the other

[2]Matt. iv. 23.

the relation that the embryo butterfly sustains to the larva it inhabits. There is to be brought in among the kingdoms of this world a Divine polity fruitful of change and sure of triumph; a polity that shall fulfil the promise of the Magnificat, putting down the mighty from their seats, exalting them of low degree; filling the hungry with good things, and sending the rich empty away.

But how does all this square with the ordinary definitions of "the Gospel"? To the question, What is the Gospel? the usual answer would be something like this: "The Gospel is the blessed promise of pardon through the blood of Christ. It is the assurance that for me the Saviour died." A true answer, doubtless; but is it the whole truth? Can it be the whole truth? Is this the Gospel that was preached by Jesus Christ in his own person?

Manifestly if the benefits of Christ's death were preached by Him while He was yet treading the soil of Palestine, and before He suffered, they must have been preached prophetically. But do we find this to have been the case? Do we discover in his recorded discourses very plentiful allusions to the Preacher's coming sacrifice of Himself? We certainly do find mysterious hints of what is to be wrought upon the Cross. Calvary looms heavily as we approach the close of the Gospel story. But do we find in the reported sayings of our Lord anything like the same prominence given to the distinctive doctrine of his sacrificial death that we find in the writings of the Apostles? Waiving for the moment those intimations and foreshadowings of a truth more fully to be revealed, do we discover among the words of Jesus any such plain, direct statement as this, for example, "The blood of Jesus Christ, His Son, cleanseth us from all sin"? No one, whatever his theological bias, will assert that we do. And yet "the Gospel" was preached even while

The Word had flesh, and wrought
With human hands the creed of
creeds. *before* †

The Gospel was preached then, for we are expressly told that it was, and it was Jesus Christ Himself who preached it. He, if any one, must have known what the Gospel meant. And how did He preach the Gospel? The Evangelists tell us. Their record makes it plain, that, from the beginning of his preaching and teaching, Jesus presented his Gospel in the twofold aspect that has here been claimed for it. He taught the duty of personal allegiance to Himself. "Follow me," He said. That was the side of the Gospel that fronted on the individual. Again, He spoke repeatedly to his disciples of "the things pertaining to the Kingdom of God." That was the side of the Gospel that fronted upon society.

It is to be observed that neither one of these two bearings was clearly discerned until after the Saviour's death. It was only when Pentecost had completed the cycle of the redemptive work that the "salvation which, at the first, began to be spoken by the Lord" could be either taught or received in its completeness.[3] The death and res-

[3]See Bernard's *Progress of Doctrine in the New Testament.* Chap. vii.

urrection of the Gospel-bringer threw a flood of light upon what He had said about his kingly claims. Men began to see why so large a measure of personal loyalty was demanded of them, when they were shown how He who asked it had died to take away their sin. And they began to understand what was meant by the Gospel of a Kingdom, when they saw rising everywhere about them the walls and turrets of the new-founded City of God.

It will be seen that the writer's view identifies "the Kingdom" with the institution known in history as the Christian Church.

Against such an identification of the Kingdom with the Church, two arguments may be brought. The two are independent of each other, and, to a certain extent, in conflict; but since each has found distinguished, as well as numerous upholders, it will be worth our while to examine them with carefulness.

The first of these two negative arguments may be compactly stated thus: Christ's Kingdom means his spiritual supremacy in the hearts of his several followers. It is not, as its Founder never intended it to be, a visible organization. The second is this: Christ's Kingdom means that coming down of the heavenly Jerusalem to earth, which we are to look for when the present order of the world passes away.

Of these arguments, the first supposes that the Kingdom has been already started in the world, but is invisible; the second holds that the Kingdom will be visible when it comes, but that it has not yet come. There is truth in both *early Church as Visible kingdom*

views. There is Scripture in support of both. Their error lies in their one-sidedness. The larger doctrine that is to include both must set forth a Kingdom at once visible and invisible, present and future.

Let us first look at the argument for invisibility. It is undeniable that the phrase "Kingdom of Heaven," or "Kingdom of God," admits of a subjective as well as an objective interpretation. Christ Himself says, "The Kingdom of God is within you,"[4] and this word of his has been the main reliance of the "invisible" hypothesis. But, when we think of it, every kingdom is, in one sense, "within" men. The essence of a kingdom does not lie in thrones, and crowns, and sceptres, and palaces, but in the king's consciousness of rightful authority, and in the people's consciousness of an obligation to obey. The true kingdom is "within" the subjects' hearts. And yet for all this, kingdoms, as we know them, are very real and visible things. Granting that Christ meant his Kingdom to be inward, does it follow that He did not mean it to be outward also? In such a discussion, the burden of proof rests upon those who deny the outwardness or visibility, not upon those who affirm it.

The Apostles are commonly believed to have known the mind of Christ as well, at least, as most modern theologians, and they certainly could not, after Pentecost, be called unspiritual men; yet these Apostles went forth from their forty days of intercourse with

the risen Lord, and built up all over the world a society as visible and tangible as it well could be. This society had its terms of membership, its officers, its laws, its sacramental observances, its rites and usages. Long before the books of the New Testament had been gathered into a volume, the existence of this society was as real and evident to the eyes of men as that of the Roman Empire itself. There was nothing shadowy or uncertain about it. It was actual. It had a name. That name was The Church. This point will be more fully brought out later on; just now it is merely noted as a formidable fact in the way of those who would disprove Christ's intention of founding a visible Kingdom.

The parables of our Lord hold a very interesting relation to this question. They are almost all of them concerned with the nature of the Kingdom of Heaven; and it is a significant fact that while some of them are most readily interpreted of that Kingdom which is "within," and some of that which is "without," there are yet others that admit with equal ease of either interpretation.

Every student of the parables must have noticed this. Indeed, it is but another illustration of that law of duality which, as we have seen, runs through the whole system of revelation. The very fact that these symbolic sayings are illustrative of the Gospel causes them to partake of the Gospel's twofold character. Take, for example, the Parable of the Mustard Seed. We may understand it of God's truth sown in the heart of the believer and growing up into what

[4]Some critics prefer the marginal reading "among you," in Luke xvii. 21.

we call ripe character, a tree beautiful in foliage and vocal with the song of birds. Or we may understand it of the seed of the new social order sown in the world, and springing up into a tree whose branches reach out over all lands, and whose top touches the sky. Either interpretation is beautiful, and probably both were intended.

The old philosophers were fond of calling man a microcosm, or little world in himself. So the Christian may be a little Kingdom of Heaven in himself. But as the microcosm does not exclude the macrocosm, the little world and the great world being admirably adjusted to each other, so neither does this double aspect of the parables at all impair their meaning.

The variety of limestone known as calc-spar crystallizes in the rhombohedral form. It is a peculiarity of this mineral that if you shatter a crystal of it by a blow of the hammer, each little fragment will be found to be a perfect rhombohedron in miniature. All that was true geometrically of the planes and axes and angles of the large crystal is also true of the planes and axes and angles of the tiny one. The same scientific formula that described the unbroken mineral answers equally well for any fractured part. The only difference is in respect of magnitude. Let us interpret this parable of stone. It shows us that a law of spiritual proportion may be applicable to the individual man, and yet not for this reason inapplicable to the "colossal man," society. It indicates also what is the right answer to those who would oppose the spirituality of the Kingdom to its visibility, namely this: the Kingdom was meant to be both spiritual and visible, internal and external; a Kingdom within the soul, and yet a Kingdom into which both soul and body have the power to come.

There remains the argument of futurity, as it may be called. Did Christ, in all that He said about the Kingdom of Heaven, intend to be understood as speaking of that perfected social state which is to ensue upon his coming again? In a word, did He mean the heavenly state itself, that which we look forward to when we pray, "Thy Kingdom come"?

Again let us resort to the parables. Two of the most familiar of them can settle this point in a moment. The Kingdom of Heaven, Jesus tells us, is like a net cast into the sea, that gathers of every kind, good and bad. And yet of the heavenly city of the future, that perfectly pure and holy city, we are told that there cannot enter into *it* anything that defileth, worketh abomination, or maketh a lie. In another place the Kingdom of Heaven is likened to a field of wheat in which an enemy sows tares. The wheat and tares grow together until the harvest. And when is the harvest? The harvest is "the end of the world." Clearly, then, the Kingdom of Heaven, as Christ uses the words, must be something that begins long before the world ends; otherwise how can it possibly be like a field in which wheat and tares grow together *until* the harvest?

The right way out of the difficulty seems to be this. When our Lord spoke of the Kingdom of Heaven, He had in mind a Kingdom

He meant to establish at once here on earth, but a Kingdom, nevertheless, which should find its fullest and ripest development in the world to come. He was to lay the foundations in time, of a building whose battlements and spires were to mount up into eternity. If this was indeed his purpose, then it is certainly an unwise spirituality that allows itself to speak slightingly of organized Christianity as the "*mere* visible Church." Thus contemptuously to set aside the Church-Idea as being no part of the true Gospel of Christ, but only an accidental, perhaps dangerous appendage, is virtually to make ourselves wiser than our Lord Himself. Let us beware of endeavoring to be more spiritual than He whose gift the Spirit is.

We are sometimes warned of the great peril of putting the Church before Christ, or in the place of Christ. If by putting the Church before Christ be meant the worshipping of forms and ceremonies, instead of the worshipping of Almighty God, the caution is not amiss. But if it be meant that the Gospel of the Kingdom really interferes with or obscures the Gospel of the Cross, then the warning, however well meant, is a mistaken one. The New Testament couples together the two thoughts, "Christ" and "the Church." To this agrees St. Paul. He confesses that the mystery is great; "but," he adds, "I speak concerning Christ and the Church." To this agrees St. John: "The Spirit and the Bride say, Come." The Spirit is the Spirit of Christ; the Bride is the Church. In those high and mystic nuptials of which the Apostle speaks, the invisible and visible are wedded. What are we, that we should strive to have it otherwise? "Those whom God hath joined together, let no man put asunder."

Thus far we have been busy with determining the single point whether our Lord Jesus Christ did or did not mean that there should be built up in the world, after his departure, a visible and organized society bearing his name. Our next step will be to mark the manner in which the creative thought took shape and body in the hands of those who received it directly from the Founder.

We shall then review successively the three principal misapprehensions to which, in the progress of human history, the original thought has been subject, namely,—

(*a*) Romanism, or the Exaggeration of the Divine Idea;

(*b*) Puritanism, or the Diminution of the Divine Idea;

(*c*) Liberalism, or the Distortion of the Divine Idea.

Lastly, we shall confront the difficult problem how in this strange new America of ours, good Christian people who sympathize fully with neither Romanism, Puritanism, nor Liberalism, but who desire to give each one of these its just due, may best be loyal to the true Church-Idea.

Let no one say that the inquiry is an idle one. Leastwise let no Christian man or woman say so.

For an unbeliever to boast, "The Church is nothing to me," is natural enough. But a believer has no right to use this flippant tone. In him indifference is blameworthy. He is as much bound to feel solicitude for the well-being of the Church, as the good citizen is bound to care for the prosperity of the State. For a Christian to declare that his whole religion consists in watering and weeding his own spiritual garden-plot, and that he has no time to look beyond the hedge, is blank selfishness. We call the man who acknowledges no obligation to the community in which he lives a churl. The Church is the commonwealth of souls, and every Christian owes it fealty and service.

In following out the plan thus sketched, it will be the writer's aim to use perfectly explicit language so as to avoid being misunderstood. If at any time this plainness of speech should seem to the reader too plain, let him be assured that there is no intention of unkindness or discourtesy. The single purpose of these papers is to promote reconciliation and peace, a purpose which any least tinge of bitterness would thwart. But unity is to be sought through the truth; and if we would reach the truth every man must say out honestly just what he thinks. When, therefore, in the course of our inquiry, different systems of religion are freely criticised it will be understood that this is due to no inability or unwillingness to appreciate what is good in them, but is only the fruit of an honest desire to get at the truth.

Any other method would be at once feeble and unsatisfactory. To say nothing directly, and to leave everything to inference, may be an inoffensive, as it certainly is a safe way of expressing thought. But what the most charitable of men has called "sound speech that can-

not be condemned," is speech of another sort. It can only mean such utterance as is straightforward, intelligible, and to the point.

II

THE THOUGHT AND ITS CLOTHING

Life, of whatever sort it is, looks for a lodgment in organization. Perhaps the remark ought to be limited to life as we know it upon this planet. What the vital conditions may be elsewhere, we cannot tell. Here, certainly, life is forever taking on shapes that are at once its clothing and its expression.

Vegetable life finds its organization in roots and stalks, leaves and branches, plants and trees. Animal life breathes itself into flesh and bones, and seeks a dwelling in the bodies of all moving creatures, in birds, beasts, and men. There is yet a higher kind of life than either the vegetable or the animal. We call it spiritual life, the life that differences man from the brute.

Now where and how does this spiritual life find organization? In a partial and meagre way the question is answered whenever spirit and flesh are welded together in one living man. But this embodiment is of necessity incomplete. It is the incarnation of *a* spirit, rather than of spirit. We must look for an ampler tabernacle than the human frame, and we find it in that large and complicated body, society. This is the law that binds men together in communities, girding the earth with a chain armor of families, each link nearly or distantly connected with every other link.

The individual is conscious of incompleteness, and seeks instinctively, by joining himself to others of his kind, to realize that "fulness" which really can be gathered up in no one person save the Word made flesh. This, then, is the rationale of the Gospel of the Kingdom. This is the marrow of the Church-Idea. Because there has always been spiritual life in the world, *therefore* there has always been society. Because it is possible for the spirit of man to live either with God or apart from Him, *therefore* there has always been an inner or elect society,—the Church. Because Jesus Christ brought into the world a vast access of spiritual life, *therefore* the new society of the elect in which this life has found embodiment is called, in distinction from the national election it displaced, the Catholic or Universal Church.

Now it is one thing to admit the truth of abstract statements like these, and quite another to discern their true bearing on the history of the past, and the needs of the present. We have undertaken to study the divine idea of the Church, but the attempt is hopeless without the aid of some sort of illustration.

Moreover, we want an illustration that shall carry with it the weight of authority. A man is at liberty to pick and choose illustrations when he is setting forth his own thoughts; but when he undertakes to interpret a revealed thought of God, we demand that he employ similitudes stamped with the sanction of the Revealer.

Our Lord provided for this necessity very fully when He promulgated his Gospel of the Kingdom. He knew well that men would never catch his idea unless He put it into pictures, and wrote his own *Fecit* on the canvas. Both He and his Apostles after Him took pains, therefore, to employ very striking comparisons as a means of expounding the nature of the new society. Some of these comparisons illustrate one aspect of the divine idea, others another aspect.

Thus the Church is likened in the New Testament to a field of wheat, to a fisher's net, to a vineyard, to a kingdom, to a ship, to a sheepfold, to a family, to a bride, to a tree springing from a seed, to the human body. Of all these various similitudes, the last is richest in suggestion. Nothing in Nature is so marvellously wrought as the house that man inhabits, and it is no wonder we find it the best symbol of that Divine society whose Head is Christ, and whose many members are destined to constitute at last "the perfect man."

Besides, this illustration of the body falls in admirably with our present purpose, which is to ascertain in what way the Divine thought as it came from the mind of Christ took on, at the hands of his immediate successors, the clothing of actual fact. The Apostle with whose activity in missionary labor we are best acquainted, was the same whose eye seems to have caught most readily the resemblance between the body and the Church. We are likely to find, therefore, that the analogy is as rich in practical suggestions as it is useful in the interpretation of ideal truth. Let us see.

The first and most obvious attribute of a body is Visibility. Undoubtedly there are bodies that we cannot see,—microscopic bodies, for example, and ethereal bodies too subtle for our vision; but when we speak of such bodies as invisible, we really only mean that we have not the eyes to see them. Letting alone such fine-spun distinctions as this, the remark is perfectly true that the most obvious attribute of a body is visibility. It is, indeed, this very visibility that, in the common judgment of men, distinguishes body from spirit. Spirit is something that cannot be seen; body is something that can be seen. When the disciples after the resurrection were frightened because they thought they had seen a spirit, Jesus, while He reassured them, gently reproved their error of judgment. "Why are ye troubled? Behold my hands and my feet that it is I myself. Handle me and see, for a spirit hath not flesh and bones as ye see me have."[5] Here sight is made, by the highest authority, the criterion of the body's reality. "Handle me and *see*." It is a true body, because it is a visible one.

If, then, the Church is a body, in any real and satisfactory sense, the Church must be a society that is visible, open to the eye. And what is a visible society? It is any union of men that confesses itself a union by having terms of admission and symbols of membership. The societies called "secret" are just as visible as any others, so far as the evidence of their existence goes. The nearest approach to an invisible society, if the very coupling of the two words does not involve a contradiction, is in the case of men banding together for the attainment of some object, and agreeing solemnly that their relation to each other shall not be indicated by any outward sign or token whatsoever. But we have a distinct name for such a union as this. We call it a conspiracy, or mingling of breaths. Yet even a breath upon a cold day takes form and shape such as the eye can see. So hard is it to disconnect the idea of visibility from the idea of a society.

Why, then, do we hear so much in these days about "the Church Invisible"? There certainly is no warrant for the phrase in Holy Scripture. Nowhere in the Word of God, from the first page of it to the last, is there any mention of a Church Invisible, save of that which is only invisible because it is in heaven, not on earth. We must remember that there is a difference between "things not seen" and things that cannot be seen. The heavenly Church is among the things not seen as yet, but this is not because it is a Church Invisible by nature. It can be seen, and will be seen, even as in vision it has been seen. Here is the picture of it. "After this I *beheld,* and lo, a great multitude, which no man could number, of all nations, and kindreds, and people, and tongues, stood before the throne, and before the Lamb, clothed with white robes and palms in their hands; and cried with a loud voice, saying, Salvation to our God which sitteth upon the throne, and unto the Lamb."[6] This is indeed a Church to us invisible,

[5]Luke xxiv. 39.

[6]Rev. vii. 9.

and it is the only "Church Invisible" of which the Scriptures speak.

In the previous paper the argument against the theory of invisibility was rested upon the words of Christ Himself, and the question of his intention was made the central point. A glance at the actual practice of the men who were commissioned by Christ to carry out his plan, will show whether the inference there drawn from the language of the King finds warrant in the acts of his lieutenants.

Let us see what was St. Paul's notion of edifying or building up that Body of Christ of which he said so much.

The Apostle goes into a certain city of Asia Minor, or Macedonia, or the Greek Peninsula, and he preaches there the Gospel of Jesus Christ. The soil is an outworn and unpromising one, but into it he bravely casts the seed. What follows? Some of the inhabitants of that city repent and believe. What follows next? The Apostle satisfies himself of the genuineness of their repentance of faith, and he then receives those persons and their households into the circle of the Kingdom, the Fold of the Church, the Body of Christ. How does he do this? He does it by that sacrament of Holy Baptism which the Lord Himself ordained as the door of entrance to the new society. They become regenerate, or new-born into the family of God.

The Apostle goes away. His missionary errand carries him to some far-off city of the Mediterranean. Presently he learns, either by some chance comer or by a special messenger, that all is not going on well in that city where he planted the Kingdom, and left it to be cared for at the hands of others. There has been a falling away from the faith, or dissensions have sprung up, or gross sins have crept in and defiled the flock, so that purity of life, as well as of faith, is put in peril. What does the Apostle now? He takes his pen, or he bids some fellow-missionary take the pen for him, and he writes a letter of counsel to those far-off Christians, telling them how sadly grieved he is to learn that anything has gone wrong, and pointing out in what way all may be set right again. But how does he address this letter? How should we expect him to address it, according to the "invisible Church" theory? Should we not look to find him drawing a sharp line of distinction at the very outset between those in the Church who had come up to his expectations, and those who had not? Should we not expect him to state explicitly that he regards those who have been in fault as no Christians at all? Ought he not to tell these last that their baptism was a nullity, that events have proved the sacrament to have been in their case an empty form, and bid them reflect that their membership of the mere "visible Church" avails them nothing?

This is what we might very naturally expect. But do we, in point of fact, find the Apostle taking this line? We know that the Christians of Corinth were, at one time, fallen into much such a state as has been pictured. St. Paul wrote to them. What was his address? "Paul, called to be an Apostle of Jesus Christ, through the will of God, and Sosthenes our brother, unto the

Church of God which is at Corinth, to them that are sanctified in Christ Jesus, called to be saints, . . . grace be unto you and peace."[7] The whole spirit of the letter is in harmony with this beginning. The Corinthian Christians, one and all, are dealt with throughout as those who had been sanctified, set apart to be holy, made members of the Body of Christ. The appeal to those of them who have gone astray, is made to rest upon this very fact that they do belong, in virtue of their baptism, to the sacred Body of the Lord, and that they ought to be deeply penitent for having defiled that Body.

"As many of you as have been baptized into Christ have put on Christ;" this is the promise that underlies all his reasoning, the solemn reminder that gives weight to his every rebuke. Even when he is expostulating with the offenders themselves, his argument is that they are defiling the temple of God, "which temple," he significantly adds, "ye are." Does this look as if St. Paul had always in mind two Churches, an outer and an inner, a visible and an invisible, a husk and a kernel? Does it not rather look as if he regarded the whole body of the baptized as being the one Church of Christ on earth, a Church not without its unworthy and sickly members, even as the Lord had said should be, but still one Church, to be addressed as brethren, to be taught, to be guided, to be built up, to be ministered unto, to be led on in holy living, and, at last, to be judged, not by him, Paul, but by that One who

is ordained to judge both them and him.

The mention just now made of the temple suggests a second point in the analogy between the Church and the living human body. What is it that gives honor to this complicated organism of flesh, and blood, and bones, and nerves, and muscles we call "the body"? It is the solemn fact that the body is the appointed dwelling-place of a spirit. So long as it can claim this august tenant as its own, the body has dignity; but no sooner is the spirit fled from out it than the body begins to return into the crude and worthless elements of which it is built up. Beauty and power alike forsake it. Only dust remains.

Now what is it that makes the new society whose nature we are exploring worthy of the high and glorious titles given to it in Scripture? Doubtless it is the indwelling in this Body also of a Spirit. And what Spirit? God the Holy Ghost. Here lies the distinction between the Church and any other society whatsoever. The Church has the promise of its Divine Founder that He will be in it always.

And only consider what the presence of a spirit in a body involves. It is a most marvellous thing, this connection between ourselves and the temporary home in which we think and feel. The wit of man can formulate the law that keeps the stars in their courses, but of the law that links body to soul, it tells us almost absolutely nothing. We can philosophize upon that mysterious union, and invent all manner of hard names to describe it, but we get no nearer to understanding it by doing so. All

[7] 1 Cor. i. 1.

that we really know about it is that it exists, and that it answers the purpose of making the body the servant and instrument of the soul. Thus, for example, you wish to express a thought in writing. Your will determines that your hand shall take the pen, dip it in ink, put it on the paper, form the words. But how did the mandate, which was a spiritual thing, find its way to the muscles of your hand? And when it had reached them, how did it compel obedience? You answer, "By the power of volition." Yes, but are you any nearer to understanding *the thing,* because you have the phrase that describes it at your tongue's end? Not one whit.

And if we cannot understand how the spirit impels the body to action, neither do we know any better why it is that an injury done to the body brings grief and anguish to the spirit. By what strange electricity the nerves of feeling are empowered to carry to the soul their nimble messages of warning, and, as it were, bring down the spirit to the suffering part, who can comprehend? We only know that thus it is. The ancients used to say, The soul is all in every part. We moderns have not got beyond the paradox.

It is impossible to appreciate the wealth of St. Paul's illustration unless we take into account this omnipresence of the spirit in the body. Let the reader summon up to his mind the image of a vast society of living men, all animated, actuated, and controlled by one central spirit. Let him imagine that spirit sending out commands to every remotest point of the complex organism, just as a human will telegraphs its orders to hand or foot, to eye or lip. Let him imagine again that spirit receiving intelligence from all these various members, learning of their necessities, knowing when they suffer, sorrowing, as it were, with their sorrow, rejoicing in their joy. "Now the Lord is that Spirit": His body is the Church. His going forth upon the nerves of motion we call "grace." Our coming to Him upon the return nerves of feeling we call "prayer." What a marvellous similitude it is! How can we enough adore the wisdom that has thus made the seen things the mirror of the unseen; our perishable and earthly frame the type of that Body Mystical which is the dwelling-place of Christ!

A third important point in this analogy is that which bears upon the question of the Church's unity. That the Church ought to be visibly, as well as spiritually one, is a direct corollary from the two truths already brought out. It is wonderful that even the usages of common speech do not teach people to see more clearly the connection between life and unity. Thus, for instance, while a man is living, we say that he is one person, but after he is dead, we speak of his "remains." Why this change of number from the singular to the plural? It is because a body, taken by itself, suggests manifoldness of parts; and when the tenant whose presence brought all things into unity has fled, the characteristic which was before subordinate, becomes conspicuous. Similarly we make "dissolution" a synonym of death; and what is dissolution but a sundering into parts of that which before was

lack of unity & death

lack of unity in Church

whole? Are those who maintain that the competition of sects makes the life of the Church, aware that what they advocate is really nothing less than the dissolution of the Body of Christ? Indeed, is it not something worse than dissolution? The demoniac who had Legion for his guest would probably have chosen death as a relief; and yet the only way by which sectarianism can escape the charge of crucifying the Lord afresh, is by taking refuge in the idea of a Body multitudinously possessed. An alternative more awful it would be hard to name.

We are assured that there must be "diversities of operation," and hence sects. By all means let us admit the first proposition; by no means let us consent to the inference. Diversity is perfectly consistent with oneness; sectarianism not at all. Nature is running over with variety, but it is a variety in unity, a diversity that is absolutely obedient to law.

That the modern interpretation of the phrase just quoted would have been wholly alien to the mind of its author is evident from the peremptory way in which we find him dealing with the sectarian principle in his own times. He does not seem to have regarded the Cephas party and the Apollos party as harmless "diversities of operation," in which the Corinthian Church might safely be indulged. On the contrary he did not hesitate to say that such divisions savored more of worldliness than of godliness. No, this theory that the eye of the Almighty discerns in sectarian Christianity a harmony hidden from man's weaker vision is but a poor make-shift at best. The definition of unity that it implies is such a definition as would not be admitted for a moment in connection with any of those forms of community-life most familiar to us. Who, for instance, would dream of organizing a commonwealth, an university, an army, or a navy, upon this principle that outward and visible unity need not be considered as particularly important? And if, the higher we rise in the development of social life, the more we feel the need of a perfect order, why should we imagine that in the structure of the ideal community, the Church, this point may be safely disregarded?

But these are questions that properly belong to a later stage of our inquiry. At present they are only noted in their connection with the argument from analogy. If the Church be a living body, unity belongs to it of right.

One more resemblance. In every human body that lives and breathes there goes forward a process of ceaseless change. The vital energies are constantly engaged in discarding old material, and assimilating new. The atoms of carbon, hydrogen, oxygen, and nitrogen, that have done their work, go on their way to build up other bodies, and fresh atoms come in to take their place. Physiologists have not decided what precise period of time is required for an entire change of fleshly clothing; but that such a change does take place many times over in the course of an ordinary life they are agreed. The identity of a man's body is, therefore, something quite different from that of a marble statue,[8] for it is an identity that must, somehow, be consistent with perpetual change. Now and then there come crises in the history of a body. We call them diseases. They may leave the man in a better condition than they found him, or they may leave him in a worse. They may alter his outward appearance for the remainder of his life, or, again, they may alter it only temporarily. In either case, and in any case, a man's body, so long as he inhabits it, remains his body still.

The bearing of these facts upon the phenomena of Church life is important. We talk about Reformations of the Church, and argue whether they are desirable or not. Reformations? Why, the whole life of the Church ought to be a continual Reformation, a constant taking out of the way that which is effete, and re-forming the tissue with new material. Those who fancy that in order to demonstrate the identity of the Church they must import into the nineteenth century the cultus of the thirteenth are under a delusion. As well refuse to own your friend because his countenance at forty is not what it was at twenty-five, as turn suspicious of the Church of your fathers because it does not look to you precisely as it looked to them. Provided the historical continuity of the Church be kept, and the original deposit of faith preserved intact, it matters not how many reformations are ex-

[8]Much confusion of thought with regard to the Christian doctrine of the Resurrection of the Body would be avoided if this distinction between the two sorts of identity—identity of material and identity of growth—were always kept in mind.

perienced. An unintermitting reformation would be the best of all.

Thus we gather from this analogy of the Body no less than four notes, or characteristics of the perfect Church:—

1st. Visibility.

2d. The indwelling Spirit of the Lord.

3d. Unity.

4th. Capability of perpetual renewal.

But how has it fared with this Divine idea in the actual history of the world? This is a question upon which we have yet to enter. We must approach it prepared for some measure of disappointment, and even of mortification.

Every one is familiar with the distinction between an idea and its realization. A man conceives some grand and noble thought, and he attempts to give expression to it, but he invariably fails. What we call works of art are but the forms or shapes into which men have cast their various thoughts and imaginings. The one word written upon them all is Imperfection.

No matter what the work is, be it a picture, a poem, a statue, a building, a machine, an oratorio,— the maker of it will be the first to acknowledge, if he be an artist indeed, that that which seems so perfect in the eyes of others, does, in his own, fall short of what he can imagine. Between a high idea and man's embodiment of it there is always a great gulf fixed.

It is told of the famous Danish sculptor, that in later life he was once found in his studio laboring under deep dejection. He gave it as the cause of his melancholy that he had just completed a work that satisfied him. "My powers must be on the decline," he added, "when I find that I am contented with anything that I accomplish." This must always be the confession of honest human endeavor. Our best achievements lag behind our visions of what might be.

The history of the Church of Christ is but the record of a long and painful effort to clothe in actual fact the divine idea of a heavenly kingdom upon earth. But in this, as in all else with which man has to do, the result has been lamentably imperfect.

Is it objected that such an admission is inconsistent with what has been said about the divine origin of the Church-Idea? Not at all. The divine thought, it is true, must be perfect for the very reason that it is divine. But the working out of the thought has been left, to a great degree, in the hands of men. Part of the purpose was that in this building of the Temple we should be "laborers together with God." God's share in the work has indeed been perfect; ours very far from perfect. This is why it was said that we should find cause for mortification; for is anything more mortifying, when we have the picture of what might be, and of what was meant to be, before our eyes, than to observe in what a sad and terrible way human wilfulness, and human pride, and human enmity, have marred and disfigured in the fulfilment the fair beauty of the promise?

And yet, along with our mortification, we shall feel gratitude and joy, if we discover that, after all, the lines of the original painting are still traceable upon the stained and torn canvas, and that underneath the incrustations of long ages there lies the pure and perfect outline of the Mystical Body of the Lord.

ALEXANDER CRUMMELL
(1882)

THE GREATNESS OF CHRIST
AND OTHER SERMONS

THE DISCIPLINE OF HUMAN POWERS
The Twenty-first Sunday after Trinity

Endure hardness as a good soldier of Jesus Christ.
[2 Tim. II:3]

There are two senses in which we can take this exhortation of St. Paul. We may understand the word hardness in the sense of suffering and tribulation; or we may regard it as referring to trial—that general trial which is equivalent to the discipline of life in its various stages, out of which comes such vigorous strength as fits men for the changes and chances of life. The Apostle seems to refer to this latter signification rather than to the former—not indeed to the exclusion of the idea of suffering. For it was then a time when the whole Christian Church had much to endure, when distress and tribulation were the universal condition of the faithful servants of God.

This address, however, to Timothy, who was then little more than a youth, would seem to be equivalent to counsel somewhat of this sort: "Resist the seductions of ease. As a Christian man and minister, put away the inducements to mere gratification. Choose rough usage in the Christian life. Task your powers with severity. Take rigidity as the rule of life, and make discipline your habit." "Endure hardness as a good soldier of Jesus Christ." This exhortation is addressed to no particular section of our being. It is evidently general in its meaning, befitting every segment of our constitution, applicable to the whole apparatus of our nature. Hence the discipline of life is not merely a corrective of the body, giving license to the intellectual powers or to the spiritual faculties; but it is to subject the *whole* man to rule. And so St. Paul, in his Epistle to the Thessalonians, says, "And the very God of peace sanctify you wholly; and I pray God your whole spirit, and soul, and body be preserved blameless unto the coming of our Lord Jesus Christ." Now as St. Paul indicates hardness as an instrument to the sanctification of his son Timothy, it is evident that it must reach every part of his being, and that the whole man be brought under the discipline which the text implies and teaches. In this sense, and with this wide meaning, I propose to address you upon the text before us.

1. First of all, then, reversing the order of the text, as it is written, I wish to exhort to endurance with regard to the body. It is one of the greatest of our personal and moral needs. In the original state of man this necessity did not exist. There was *then* such a correspondence, such a genial concord between the animal and the spiritual of man's being, that all his constitutional tendencies were harmonious, and beautiful, and free. But man's departure from original righteousness has caused that internal disruption in his being, whereby, to use St. Paul's language, "the flesh lusteth against the spirit, and the spirit lusteth against the flesh." It is this antagonism, this aim of the fleshly desires to get the ascendency over man, which creates the duty and necessity of bodily discipline. In speaking of the flesh, it is not meant that there is any guilt in matter, any sin in our bodies. The word is a figurative expression, which signifies our carnal tendencies, of which the body is the master instrument. But the two are so thoroughly identified, that a single word serves to give a most distinct and unmistakable impression. Everybody understands by the

flesh the whole apparatus, internal and external, of gross and carnal desires.

Now we maintain that the flesh, as thus defined, and the body especially, as its agent, is to be brought under rule and into subjection to the habits of endurance.

At all times, under all circumstances, this is a duty. But the urgency of it comes especially in our day and in our country. It may be doubted if there ever was a time, since the days of degenerate and luxurious Rome, when ease, indulgence, and keen worldly self-enjoyment were such universal objects of desire. It is not of indulgence in gross sin, or of the prevalence of abominations that I am speaking. What I have reference to is the tendency to softness, the anxiousness we see on every side to avoid hardness and severity of duty. In every sphere of life one sees a shrinking from hardy toil, a reluctance to meet the strain and tug of tasking, physical endeavor. Then, next to this negative aspect of the case, one cannot fail to observe the ambition for all the agencies and appliances which minister to ease and delightful relaxation.

Remember, then, that our bodies are the agents and the instruments of work in this world. Man's "staff of accomplishment" in material efforts is his body and its members. If it is strong and vigorous, so much the more effective can it be in the work of life. If it is impaired and feeble, by just so much does it meet with hindrance and encounter opposition. We are not responsible for the constitution with which, in infancy, we came into this world. If that is strong, well; if weak, that is our misfortune; but even in that event, we are responsible for the powers we have, feeble though they be, and our duty is to use them to the best advantage, and to train them to the highest tone and vigor for the service of life. And surely nothing can be more evident than that men and women who are sluggards, people who indulge in soft, luxurious, and heating beds, people who shun the cares and burdens of life, the youths who want their fathers to do everything for them, whose highest ambition is to skim along the surface of existence with hands of baby softness, begloved and bescented, so delicate and gentlemanly that they can neither handle a hoe, nor wield an axe; or the girls, so refined and elegant that they lack the muscle to scrub a floor, wash their clothes, or cook, with their own dainty fingers, a meal of victuals—creatures of such a frame and with such habits, where can they get the physical energy which is needed for the work of life, in the Family, the Church, and the Nation? The enervating habits of life cannot yield to any of us strength and bodily vigor. If you banish the cares of life and strive for ease, if you work little and play much, if you indulge in revelry, if you avoid active and healthful toil, then it is very certain that the body will grow weaker and weaker, and lassitude and feebleness will ensue, as the certain and direct result. With the physical weakness which is the result of indolence comes the mental dullness, which is its legitimate fruit. It is your strong, robust men who *live*. Mind, I say they live, not stay. They live, both mentally and physically. A paralysed man may *stay* here in the world ninety years, and *be* nothing, and *do* nothing. A weak and sickly man, if he have conscience and will, may do much in the world. Such paradoxes are seen. But, as a rule, it is your strong men who perform the greatest achievements. They make the great statesmen, the great thinkers, the great preachers, the great workers of the world. Even if they live but a brief time, they crowd into a lifetime the vast and wonderful works, which tell, not only upon their own generation, but which go down with lasting influence through ages after ages.

The basis of life, then is the strength and endurance which comes from exercise, right living, and proper habits. If men will not, by these means, secure a sound condition of their flesh and blood, they must surely fail, as well in body as in mind. To do the work of life we must have somewhat of a sound bodily constitution. And to attain this grand advantage in the battle of life, begin first of all with the appetites and passions. Keep the body down. Bridle its lawless lusts. Avoid the heating stimulants which send the blood racing through the veins with the heat and speed of lightening, and which sweep away the brains. No bodily endurance can be gained without these precautions, no animal strength secured without these yokes. Put the rein upon yourselves in all these outward aspects of your nature. Husband your powers, and so get strength for maturity, and preserve vigor for old age. Even if you have feeble constitutions you will find these rules of abstinence and regulation powerful tonics for the acquisition of physical endurance. And then, next to this, for the practical habits of life, it is well for us all to avoid luxurious and pleasing habits for the body, and to accustom ourselves to stirring employments, vigorous exercise, and plain living. I do not say that comfort should be shunned; rather, I say, we should seek comfort in life. But if we would have physical endurance we must not nurse ourselves too much, nor yield to indolent tendencies. Strength comes from hardihood. Even invalids find restoration in physical severity and bodily toil. To rise betimes in the morning, to sleep on a hard bed, to eat plain food, to abstain from stimulants, to take robust, and even tiresome exercise, is the regimen often given to enfeebled constitutions, and even to aged men. Even the wealthy seek with eagerness the season when they can leave the haunts of luxury, and rough it, like tramps, in the woods. It is the part of wisdom, of reason, and religion, so to use our bodies that we may get out of them, for as long as possible, all the effective strength and activity that nature warrants, that providence assures, that duty calls for, and that the glory of God requires.

2. But not only do we need the subjection of the body to severe discipline; the like duty pertains to the mind. *It* too, as well as the animal nature, needs the tonic of endurance; calls for the stringency of rule and government; requires the training and the tasking which are essential to sanctity. It is not merely that the fools' eyes wander

to the end of the earth; sad as it is that there are fools who give license to the eyes of the mind, and allow them to roam incontinently to every quarter of the globe. The evil of the matter is that people who are not fools, people of sense and understanding, set up a claim to independence in the domain of intellect, and declare that they are a law to themselves in all the habits of thought and intelligence. The idea that mind itself, mental activity, the range of thought in the spheres of acquaintance, that books, both the instruments and the agents of the thinking faculty, that these are, in any way, matters of responsibility, has never entered the thoughts of thousands. And as the fruit of such gross heresy, one sees everywhere in society, freedom to the very verge of license in the conversation of men and women; the handling, on the one hand, of the most delicate subjects with ignorant rudeness, or the flippant disposal of the most mysterious and awful themes, as though they were holiday pleasantries. So, too, in reading, one sees, on all sides, the same self-release from the sense of duty and responsibility. In the family, children are allowed to read what they please. The parents who would shriek, or go into convulsions if their girls should, by mistake, swallow Prussic acid, are utterly unconcerned when they see them reading, with eagerness, books which inflame the youthful imagination, and which serve to fasten the most damning principles upon the soiled surface of their souls. Youth, and young men, too, who hate the reading which tasks the mind, which demands attention, which sends the soul peremptorily to sound the inward oracles of reason or of faith, run with eagerness after the trashy literature of the day, which give unthinking pleasure, and which is alien to every idea of truth and virtue.

Worse than all, not few are the numbers who secretly dabbled in the dirty waters of impure literature, and corrupt the very fibres of their inward nature by the reading which comes from the devil, and which bears the imprint of damnation.

Now it seems the most evident of all things that we are responsible for our thoughts and for our habits of thinking. Our minds, in their several faculties, just the same as our bodies and limbs, are our instruments. As our own instruments, they are under our control and direction. The thoughts of the soul are the generators of all action. As the thoughts of a man, so is his life. "As a man thinketh, so is he." If the master tendency of the mind is toward evil, then the "thoughts of the wicked are abomination." If they tend, in a man, to the excellent, then the "thoughts of the righteous are right."

It is a matter, then, of the greatest concern, for men to secure rectitude in the intellectual provinces of their being; for everything depends upon right thinking. If they seek ease in this section of their being, if they would fain avoid care and burdensome duty, if they choose to have only the things pleasant and delightful, if they would fain avoid what brings trial, toil, and perseverance, then most surely all tone and vigor will pass away from their mental faculties; they will become dwarfed and imbecile in the next grandest element of their being.

Hence, as an effort toward the mental endurance which I maintain is an obligation, it is our duty, first of all, to aim after the regulation of the intellect. By this I mean that we should bring our minds under such rules and laws of discipline as that we may have our minds and all their faculties under our control. You say, perchance, that this is the business which belongs to scholars; business people cannot attend to intellectual discipline. But I beg to say that if you cannot have your wits at your command, if you do not train yourselves to interior rules of order, then you cannot do the work of life. In this, my brethren, resides all the success of life. Your successful and effective people, whether farmers, or laborers, or merchants, or mechanics, or sailors, as well as scholars, are men who have their powers at command. Says the Apostle St. James, "Behold we put bits in the horses' mouths, that they may obey us, and we turn about their whole body. Behold also the ships, which though they be so great, and are driven of fierce winds, yet are they turned about with a very small helm withersoever the governor listeth." In precisely like manner every man should endeavor to put his personal self in the centre of all his powers and faculties, and regulate and dispose of them as he wills.

One great difficulty with most men is that they are possessed by their powers. Thus some men are mastered by prodigious memories;

but they have no judgment, and ply no reasoning faculty. Then there are others who are carried away by a vivid and inflamed imagination. Another class are hard and iron thinkers, but there is no illumination of fancy, no treasure-house of golden memories.

The vice of disproportion and excess is always a great hindrance to self-command. When men are controlled by any one or several master faculties, then they come into a species of slavery to themselves, and lose the freedom of their wills just as much as when they are mastered by some special vice. The true remedy is to so train and regulate ourselves by proper habits, that we can use our mental capacities when we want them, and as we will. And this, in a degree, is in the power of all men; for as an actual fact we see this steady, constant mind in men of all classes. We see sailors, soldiers, shoemakers, and carpenters, men in all callings, in perfect self-possession, who know their own powers, know how and when to use them, and who turn themselves, with full command, any way they wish with self-assurance and telling effect.

Besides the subjection of the intellect to rule and control, our next aim to the attainment of its strength is the use of the mental powers for the glory of Christ. It is with the intellect as with the bodily powers—by tasks you bring out its force and energy, by toil it gets hardihood and endurance. So, too, the intellect. Give it the nobler duties, and it, too, by every effort, gains to itself unusual and extraordinary might. And nothing in the range of the sciences, nothing in the circle of philosophy and letters, gives scope for the exercise of man's noblest powers as the religion of Christ. Hence it is that Lord Bacon declares that "theology is the prince of all the sciences": transcendent, that is in bringing out the forces of our mental manhood, and unequalled in the reflex influence which they give back to the soul as the fruit and reward of diligent spiritual study.

Now the special requirement, in this regard, is first a *negative* one, and that is that we guard intelligently the entrance of any intellectual poison into our minds. Do not tamper with scepticism. There is a wisdom that, in our day affects to hold that all greatness calls for the intellect to deny God, the word of God, and the grand attributes of God. This wisdom, so-called, but which after all is nothing but folly, would tells us that religion is a weak and fond thing only fitted for women and children. But then remember that the weak and simple ones who adored Christ, reverenced His holy name, and who held Him precious to their souls, are, with millions of others, such historical and learned persons as Hannah More, Sarah Coleridge, Catherine Hershel, Mrs. Browning, and Florence Nightingale. And the *other* weak ones who have worshipped the Christ were Augustine, and Jerome, and Gregory; and in modern times Newton, Barrow, and Pascal, Cudsworth and Butler, Edwards and Faraday, and Coleridge and Bushnell. A fine lot of simpletons, of both sexes, who gave way to superstition, and evidenced the shallowest brains! And if you will listen to the wise people

of our day you will get the notion that to be intellectually great you must tramble upon the faith of these grand persons, and take to your hearts the aid and unbelief of infidels and atheists.

Do not tamper with scepticism. It takes away sense, morality, and strength of mental being, and can only serve to bring weakness and imbecility to the intellectual powers.

Add to this the other grand accessory of power in the domain of intellect; that is, to lay hold of the great truths and noble ideals of the Christian Faith. Nothing will sooner and more directly give you strength than the grappling with lofty truth and majestic principles. Go to the fountain head. Reach up to the primary, fundamental ideals of the Christian system. Take these ideas, turn them over, look into them, study them, and try to master them. The effort will indeed try and puzzle your best brains; but you will surely come out of the trial strong and robust men. Old Jacob, weak, tricky man as he was, when he met the mysterious man at the ford of Jabbok, grappled with him, mighty as he was and prevailed. He came out of the tussle, it is true, with a disabled thigh; but he got power from it, and was ever after called Israel, "for as a prince he had power with God and prevailed." So, too, your intellects shall gain majestic strength by familiarity with the noble truths of the religion of Jesus. Seize, then, upon the vital principles of the Christian Faith, in all the ways and modes it can be brought home to you. Make companions of the great Christian thinkers. Stick to the great Christian books. Above all, familiarize yourselves with the deep reasonings and the exhaustive discussions of St. Paul; and, in the private regions of the mind, store up texts and paragraphs and chapters of the revealed Word, until by such a regimen your weak nature attains tone, strength, and masculine power. "Endure hardness, as a good soldier of Jesus Christ."

3. We have been considering the duty and the need of discipline and hardihood in the two distinct sections of our being, that is, the body and the mind. One other higher domain of our nature calls for notice, and that is the soul or spiritual being of man. It is difficult to make, in express terms, a distinction between the mind and the spirit. A very clever work appeared not long ago, in England, which maintained the doctrine of "The Tri-part Nature of man;" that is, that man is a being with three different elements in his nature, viz., body, mind, and then a third essence called spirit. There are two or three passages in the New Testament which, on the surface, seem to warrant this opinion. One already referred to is 1 Thes., v, 23, and another is Heb., iv, 12. But I apprehend that the true doctrine both of mental science and of the Bible is that man's immaterial nature is a unit, and that soul and spirit in Scripture only refer to two distinct departments of the inward nature; one which we commonly speak of as intellect, and the other more especially the image of God, the soul or spirit.

This soul or spirit, is, as all the other sections of our being, im-paired by the Fall, and needs the discipline which trains to divine rectitude. The soul, as well as the body, and just as the intellect, must need endure hardness. It cannot thrive by indulgence. It cannot reach to sanctity by being pampered. On the other hand it must be brought under the subjection of rule, laid under the burden of tasks, pass the ordeal of endurance. Hence we read the commands of our blessed Lord to the duties of humility and meekness, to lowly-mindedness and peace, to fasting and prayer, to forbearance and submission. Read the Sermon on the Mount, and observe how our Lord inculcates the precepts and the practices which serve to chasten the spirit into patience, endurance, and calm submission to man; yea, to the evil, as well as to God. Read the inspired Epistles, and see how St. John, St. Peter, and St. Paul, in the spirit of their master, enjoined the habits which bring the soul into austerity and strict obedience. Turn to the beautiful pictures and grand panorama of the book of Revelation, and see how conspicuously there, tribulation is brought before us in the conflicts and the triumphs of the saints; is set before us, as the heritage of the blessed, in all their inner spiritual experience, as well in outward circumstances. Indeed, brethren, to use the words of another, "All regulation is limitation, and regulation is only another name for reassured existence." All our life, even our spiritual life, is only a series of limitation, to the end, as St. Paul puts it, "Casting down imagination, and every high thing that exalteth itself against the knowledge of God, and bringing into captivity every thought to the obedience of Christ."

The duty and the need of endurance unto hardness, in the three different portions or division of your one grand nature, have thus been brought to your notice. Two or three suggestion which may serve to fasten the train of thought that has been presented, and lead to some deep insight into the realities of life, in conclusion may be added.

1st. Remember that life is no toy, no jest, no dance, not a thing of mere revelry. Everywhere life— that is, in rational spiritual beings—is a grand, downright, and active service. We begin with God Himself; and of Him, that august and awful Being Who fills all things, Who presides over all creatures, and decides all destinies, of Him we have that most singular and mysterious utterance of His blessed Son our Saviour—"My Father worketh hitherto, and I work." It is but a glimpse, indeed, into the secrets of awful Deity, but it is sufficient to show us the ever-weaving active spring of that infinite mind which stretches out invisible to every quarter of illimitable space, and touches all things and all beings, and by that touch imparts that "active principle" which moves the universe. Yes! God is the greatest worker in the universe; carrying on multitudinous operations, in matter and in spirit, through Jesus Christ the eternal Son, by the agency of the Holy Spirit—here on earth and amid the hierarchies of highest heavens. And all these works are deep, noble, majestic, awful, as is God Him-self. Nothing of levity is, in any way, associated with them. God's work, everywhere, even in nature, to say nought of the spirit world, is sacred, earnest, absolute, beautiful and glorious though it be.

2d. With this may be joined the other reflection that the final end of all God's work, whether that work is by Himself, or through the energies of His creations, the final end is God's own glory. The work of the universe terminates in that special point, and was designed to culminate in that grand consummation. And so indeed it will. Even the wrath of men shall praise Him. But what a corrective is this grand truth, to the selfish regards which lead men to set up their own personal good as the main object of existence!

O, happiness, our being's end
     and aim,

the exclamation of a great poet, is the creed of the Epicurean and the Bacchanal. Not so! Happiness is *not* the terminal point of our being. The end of our existence is a something out of and beyond ourselves. It is a grand fact which reaches over to another and a higher nature than our own. It is a reality in which is involved a struggle and fight to rise beyond self to a somewhat infinite and ineffable, beyond the skies. In this resides the obligation of work and high endeavor. There is an infinite goal to reach, a high mark for the soul to attain unto. And herein is no place for levity or foolish pastime. We were baptized to be soldiers. The call of soldiers is to endurance and hardness in the camp and on the battle-field. And with this idea, as the central point of the morning's teaching, I can do nothing better for you and for myself than to repeat the trumpet-call of the day's Epistle—"Finally, my brethren, be strong in the Lord, and in the power of His might. Put on the whole armor of God, that ye may be able to stand against the wiles of the devil. For we wrestle not against flesh and blood, but against principalities, against powers, against the rules of the darkness of this world, against spiritual wickedness in high places. Wherefore take unto you the whole armor of God, that ye may be able to withstand in the evil day, and having done all, to stand. Stand, therefore, having your loins girt about with truth, and having on the breastplate of righteousness; and your feet shod with the preparation of the gospel of peace; above all, taking the shield of faith, wherewith ye shall be able to quench all the fiery darts of the wicked. And take the helmet of salvation, and the sword of the Spirit, which is the word of God."

CHAPTER EIGHT

PUTTING THE BRAKES ON LIBERALISM—
Reaction and Reorganization (1920–1945)

In 1920 Warren G. Harding followed Woodrow Wilson into the White House. Americans, sobered by large waves of immigration and exhausted by the costs of waging the First World War, began to question Wilson's dream of a world safe for democracy and to edge toward a more isolationist stance. In Wilson's second term Congress had already rejected participation in the League of Nations. Under Harding it soon added legislation severely limiting foreign immigration.

The 1920s were a volatile decade, a time of contrasts. Within the American churches innovative liberals and a growing conservative countermovement that took its name from a series of pamphlets on the fundamentals of the faith that had been distributed earlier in the century clashed over the content of faith. Conservative Presbyterians withdrew to form the Orthodox Presbyterian church. Disciples of Christ and the Churches of Christ divided over theological liberalism. Liberal Baptist pastor Harry Emerson Fosdick (1878–1969) openly criticized Fundamentalists, and conservative Presbyterian biblical scholar J. Gresham Machen (1881–1937) questioned whether liberals were Christians at all.

A growing tension was evident within the Episcopal church as well. A small number of black Episcopalians, dissatisfied with the spread of segregation policies in the church, withdrew in 1921 to form the African Orthodox church. In 1923 a special session of the House of Bishops issued a pastoral letter reaffirming the Virgin

Birth to counter complaints that the autobiography of Bishop William Lawrence (1850–1941) had repudiated the doctrine. The following year Bishop William M. Brown (1855–1937) of Arkansas was found guilty of heresy for his vocal advocacy of communism. In 1928 350,337 signatures on a petition helped convince the bishops and deputies at General Convention that it would not be wise to discard the Thirty-nine Articles of Religion from a new edition of the prayer book.

Yet, despite these conflicts, the Episcopal church was in a better position to weather the fundamentalist-liberal controversy than many other denominations. The American concern with East European and Oriental immigrants and the consequent cutoff of open immigration had triggered a new national preoccupation with English roots that turned the Episcopal church's connection with England from a liability into an asset. The church, though a voice for temperance in the early nineteenth century, was not as a denomination identified with the imposition and failure of prohibition. Moreover, Episcopalians in the previous century had already wrestled with and reached some accommodation about greater religious pluralism. In the 1920s they could believe that their church had a grasp of the American scene that allowed them to deal with modern intellectual freedom better than most other denominations.

With the Depression large scale debate on theological liberalism halted. Parish budgets fell drastically with some congregations closing or merging with stronger parishes. Domestic and foreign mission work slowed.

Despite the hardships of the depression, however, a revival of scholarship was taking place on seminary campuses. Some within these communities, taking advantage of the theological latitude that their church offered, became deeply interested in continental theology of crisis (Karl Barth, Emil Brunner, etc.). They laid the groundwork for an outpouring of neoorthodox theology after World War II. Others became attracted to the liturgical movement that was stirring in certain quarters in Europe, a movement that would in time lead to the liturgical revival of the 1960s and 1970s.

Selections from two authors follow. William Lawrence's *Fifty Years* (Boston: Houghton Mifflin Company, 1923, pp. 66–77) was the book that some feared had questioned the validity of the Virgin Birth. Dean William Palmer Ladd (1870–1941) of Berkeley Divinity

School was a participant in the seminary liturgical movement. He wrote a series of essays on liturgy for *Witness* magazine. These were then published under the title *Prayer Book Interleaves* (New York: Oxford University Press, 1942, pp. 93–94, 162–167). His humorous essay on crucifers and his notes on the modern liturgical movement are reprinted.

WILLIAM LAWRENCE

(1923)

FIFTY YEARS

Without these Creeds many people feel that the foundations of the Church would be endangered.

Are we so sure of this? Do we not make a mistake in thinking that the Creeds are our chief instruments in binding us together in unity? Surely thinking alike has no such unifying power as common prayer, common associations of worship, and a common loyalty to the great traditions of a common faith, and a supreme loyalty to the Personal Christ. The great mass of people in the recital of the Creed do not understand the articles in detail. What meaning does the average worshipper attach to the article, "of one substance with the Father," or "He descended into Hell"? Far deeper and more spiritual bonds than the Creeds hold the Church together and inspire the people to go forward. It was

generations after the Apostolic days that the Creeds, those great monuments built up gradually to express the Faith, took their place in public worship. The Creeds were the living and exact expression of the doctrine of those days; and the echo comes down to us through the ages of doctors, soldiers, saints, martyrs, and the whole people repeating and believing every sentence that they spoke, and with the original intent of their framers.

At the close of the American Revolution, when this Church separated from the Church of England, our fathers stated in our Book of Common Prayer that "this Church is very far from intending to depart from the Church of England in any essential point of doctrine, discipline, or worship"; and yet, in adopting her Prayer Book, this Church dropped one of the three

Creeds of the Mother Church, the Athanasian Creed. The Athanasian Creed still stands in the Prayer Book of the Church of England, and clergy and people are required by law to recite it on the great Feast Days. But one would have difficulty in deciding as to whether the Mother Church, with three historic Creeds, or this Church, with only two, is the more loyal to the Faith. Giving up a creed does not necessarily involve a loss of the faith for which the creed stands. It may even involve such a deepening of the faith that the form of expression seems too inadequate to satisfy the faithful.

I have said that the antiquity of the Creeds, the Apostles' and the Nicene, their forms of expression adapted to their day, their emphasis of fundamentals, invite varied and very free interpretation. The articles of these Creeds, too, are not of equal importance. To this I think all churchmen agree. To illustrate, the phrase, "He ascended into heaven, and sitteth on the right hand of God," was interpreted literally many centuries ago. To the people of fifty years ago, to myself as a boy, heaven was local, up there, and Jesus was taken up there bodily; it was to me what the man in the street would call "a real thing."

"I believe in the Resurrection of the body" used to mean, of course, the resurrection of the flesh, the same material body that was buried in the earth. As late as 1884, when in Westminster Abbey, I myself heard Bishop Wordsworth of Lincoln, one of the most learned Biblical scholars of his day, object to the cremation of the dead on the ground that it would weaken faith in the resurrection of the body. These words now have a deeper meaning, more spiritual than before, that He who humbled Himself and became obedient to death upon the Cross, who gave to us in His life the revelation of the Father, overcame the power of all spiritual enemies, overcame death, and entered again the life of the spirit victorious, his personality holding its integrity through to the end and in eternity.

Upon my return from England that summer, I found a group of people, some of them physicians, who had been given the impression by some prominent religious leaders that, because of its supposed overthrow of the doctrine of the Resurrection, cremation was a pagan form and forbidden by the Church. Fearing that this misunderstanding, based on such an unspiritual interpretation, would create an additional cleavage between science and religion, and determining to throw my influence against such a cleavage, and in behalf of a more spiritual conception, I immediately joined a cremation organization, of which I have been ever since a Vice-President. I have no particular interest in the cremation or the burial of my body; but know that my action had a helpful influence in creating a right understanding.

I was brought up to believe that "Jesus Christ, His only Son our Lord, was conceived by the Holy Ghost, born of the Virgin Mary"; and in my earlier ministry assumed, as has been assumed throughout a large part of the Christian era and in Christian theology, that this fact was an essential element in the Incarnation.

It is now well recognized that scholars are divided upon the question of the Virgin Birth, as to whether the stronger evidence leads to the confirmation of this as a fact, or whether it is a tradition which must be reëxamined. These scholars are not mere critics and sceptics, but are upon either side men of equal reverence, faith, and belief in the Incarnation.

With the conservatism of my nature, I have always acceded to the tradition, but with a mind open to further light. Some thirty years ago, however, I was convinced that there is no essential connection between the belief in the Virgin Birth and a belief in the Incarnation. In giving expression to that conviction, which was founded on the careful study of a few American scholars, I was charged by friends dear to me with heresy. It is now a source of satisfaction to read in Bishop Gore's later works wherein he is defending the doctrine of the Virgin Birth, that he has come to the same conclusion.

There are, as we well know, clergymen, a number of them, who find it difficult if not impossible to accept the doctrine of the Virgin Birth, whose belief in the Incarnation is sincere and firm; indeed, whose belief has been made the firmer by their release from this doctrine. Their reasons are to them convincing; and inasmuch as the two Creeds stand for the essentials of the Faith, and as belief in the Virgin Birth is not to them an essential, I am clear that with an honest heart they may join in the recital of the Creeds.

I well know that this position may bring sorrow to those whose faith in the Incarnation, whose habits of thought and worship have been interwoven with the doctrine of the Virgin Birth. But their interpretation of the Creeds and their comfort in them are in no way affected by the different interpretations of others.

Since my first canonical examinations, as Bishop I have never asked my candidates their position on that point; for knowing the division of judgment among scholars and saintly men on the subject, I have not wanted to commit them to a decision before they have enough maturity of thought to make one. I believe that the results of this conduct have justified themselves. Those candidates have as a whole been loyal to the Faith of the Church, and especially to the truth of the Incarnation of our Lord.

Indeed, experience has convinced me that the vital test of a young man as he enters a high calling is not as to what particular doctrine he believes to-day, but what is the essential trend of his thought, what his attitude toward the ever-revealing truth; not in what he does, or thinks, but what, in the long run, he is, what spirit, character, or temper controls him. Hence, in examining young men for Holy Orders I delegate[d] to the Examining Chaplains the testing as to their knowledge and intellectual abilities, but I want to be sure as to what they are, their attitude of mind, their capacity of vital faith, their humility and their courage in facing in Christ's name the world and its revelations of error and truth.

I remember that as a young candidate my theological convictions were largely those of my last teachers. From these convictions I moved the very next day toward, I hope, a fuller knowledge of the truth as it is in Christ. Every day since then the emphasis and proportion of my beliefs have changed. By inheritance and temper I am a conservative. Taken off my guard, I should like to have things stay as they are. It is so comfortable to have habits of thought and life, principles and beliefs, that never alter. I should so enjoy life if I were always orthodox. What a relief it would be never to worry, think, or struggle! And then a shaft of fresh truth, gleaming with heaven's brilliance, strikes across my path, and I leap toward it tingling with the spirit of adventure.

Some one wrote a while ago that the American youth are looking deep for the foundations of faith, they are fundamentalists. True in a sense; a strong structure must have strong foundations. But I like another figure better. I believe that the American youth, inheriting religious faith, mental powers, and alert bodies, are best won when faith is made an adventure, and when that adventure leads on through questions, struggles, sacrifice toward the truth. Surely that was the spirit of the young man of Nazareth, Judea, and Jerusalem. On and on He went, ever gathering, ever revealing Truth. "Ye shall know the Truth, and the Truth shall make you free." "The Spirit of Truth will guide you into all truth." Mark the challenge which brought Him to the Cross. "Ye seek to kill me as a man that hath told you the Truth." In Christ's service complete confidence in the truth has been my great source of exhilaration in these fifty years.

Moreover, I have found it impossible to stand still in thought and beliefs for two consecutive weeks. The movement of thought and action, religious, social, political, scientific, philosophic, has been such in fifty years that one cannot live and not move. One cannot hold fast to the dock by the cable at the stern as the ship sails out. With sails full and helm true, but with the charted stars and continents, with unerring compass, she leaps into the open sea.

WILLIAM PALMER LADD
(1942)

PRAYER BOOK INTERLEAVES

Some Reflections on How the Book of Common Prayer Might
Be Made More Influential in our English-speaking World

49. A WORD ABOUT CRUCIFERS

If our Prayer Book services, as I have argued, have dramatic character, they should be rendered artistically. But this the clergy do not seem to realize. For example, I get many letters from different parts of the country saying how badly the clergy read, but I have never known one of the clergy themselves to admit that his reading could be improved. The same applies to the conduct of services. The clergy do not work at the art of public worship as an actor works at his art, or an architect at his.

These thoughts have come to me recently as I have been watching the antics of one of those crucifers of the familiar type who parade up the church alley with gauntleted hands, cross pressed against chin and nose, eyes peering into space, body stiffly leaping forward in a sort of goosestep at each beat of the music. I am hopeless of trying to open the eyes of the clergy to the absurdity and vulgarity of this performance, and to the discredit which it must bring on the Church in the eyes of people of

good taste and reverent feeling. What can be done?

It occurs to me that, since the evil cannot be suppressed, the best plan would be to work toward making the crucifer's parade into a really artistic production, something like a sacred dance, for which there is, of course, considerable historic precedent. For example, instead of pressing the cross *against* the chin, the crucifer might be encouraged by the rector to balance it *on* the chin, varying the performance by balancing it on the *nose* on saints' days. Then, on very special Church festivals, he might be trained to twirl the cross and toss it into the air as drum-majors do with their batons. Such a ceremony would have the additional advantage of attracting young people to the church, a matter which is of special concern to the clergy in these indifferent times. Further interest might be secured by having the gauntlets colored green, violet, or red to correspond with the Church seasons. This would involve some extra expense, but the rectors of our larger congregations would be sure to know sentimental and well-to-do ladies who would be glad to pay and do their bit in this way for the Church.

It further occurs to me that it is dull for our crucifers to proceed straight ahead at a uniform pace. Between the verses of the hymn they could leap zig-zag from side to side, and for this maneuver the organist could prepare special compositions which would allow variety in movement and speed. In fact, between every two or three verses of the processional hymn it might be effective if the crucifer should not go ahead in any direction; he could pause and *whirl,* an exercise which the Moslem dervishes have found to contribute greatly to religious emotion. The difficulty of training crucifers in this novel form of movement would not be insuperable: doubtless expert oriental advisers could be secured from the W.P.A. lists of the unemployed.

Needless to say I do not pose as a specialist in the dance, least of all in the religious dance. I am only making suggestions which can be worked out by wiser minds. Some of them may seem rather extreme. But the American people like extremes. And if we went far enough in the direction I have indicated, there would doubtless be a reaction. Then we might once more have crucifers who would lead our choir processions with simplicity and dignity, and without gauntlets.

THE HISTORY OF THE LITURGICAL MOVEMENT

The celebration of our own 150th [American] Prayer Book anniver-sary would seem a fitting time at which to survey the growth of the liturgical movement in the Roman Catholic Church, for there is no doubt that this is one of the most interesting religious developments of our time. It has not gone very far in this country, nor has it made any great progress in any country among the rank and file of the clergy and laity. To a great extent it is a movement which belongs to scholars and theologians. It is thus a continuation of the important contribution made by members of the Roman Church since the Reformation to the understanding of its historic liturgy.

This contribution has been largely the work of the monastic orders. In the XVII and XVIII centuries the center of liturgiology was the great Benedictine Congregation of St. Maur, with its mother house in Paris, which edited the well-known Benedictine editions of the Fathers. Mabillon (+1707), a member of this Congregation, first published the famous *Ordines Romani,* which record the ceremonial of the Mass from the first *Ordo* of about 700. Edmund Martène (+1739), a member of the Congregation, produced the *De Antiquis Ecclesiae Ritibus,* a work of lasting value, partly because it gives an account of liturgical documents since lost. Among the French Oratorians of this time were Pierre LeBrun (+1729), perhaps the greatest of all liturgical scholars, and Eusèbe Renaudot (+1720) who, with LeBrun, investigated the Oriental liturgies and demonstrated the place of the invocation in the Eucharist, somewhat as the English and Scottish Nonjurors did in the same period. In the XIX century one of the best known liturgiologists was Dom Prosper Guéranger (+1875), who desired to revive the Maurist Congregation, which had been suppressed at the time of the French Revolution, but was forbidden to do so by the pope. He then founded the monastery at Solesmes which became the center for the revival of the Gregorian chant. Among other well-known Roman Catholic liturgical scholars in France in the XIX century have been Delisle, Cagin, Andrieu, Duchesne, and Cabrol; in Germany, Ebner, Dreves, and Casel; in Belgium, Callewaert and Morin; in England, Edmund Bishop.

The modern liturgical movement may be said to date from the period following the Great War, and its development from the first has been largely under the leadership of the Benedictine monks of Maria Laach, near the Rhine in Germany, which traces its inspiration back through Beuron in Bavaria to Solesmes. The influence of this monastery has been very great, not only in the field of scholarship but in the spiritual life of the German Roman Catholic Church. Competent observers have said that that church could hardly have withstood the Nazi persecution as it has done had it not been for the leadership of Maria Laach. The movement is strong in Belgium, where in its inception it had the patronage of Cardinal Mercier. It is well established in Rome; some, in fact, look on the *Moto Proprio* of Pius X on church music, issued in 1910, as a landmark in the history of the movement. On this continent it is favored by the present Archbishop of Quebec, and at Collegeville, Minnesota, a Benedictine monastery is furthering the movement by issuing much popular liturgical literature, including a valuable magazine, *Orate Fratres.*

The essence of the movement is a return to primitive standards of worship. This means a decided repudiation of the degenerate eucharistic doctrine and ceremonial which prevailed in the late Middle Ages and which continued in an exaggerated form in the Roman Church of the Counter-Reformation period. It means a protest against the rigid liturgical uniformity so successfully advocated by Dom Guéranger at the time of Pius IX, the result of which was the suppression of ancient local usages such as those of the Lyons diocese—"a lamentable result of ignorance and bad will," to quote the words of the distinguished Roman scholar Dom Morin. It means the repudiation of what a Roman bishop has recently called "that falsely sentimental and superstitious piety which constitutes a grave spiritual malady in our own times."

The Mass in spite of its many defects has preserved some of the best features of the ancient liturgies. Thus "Back to the mass!" which is one of the watch-words of the movement, means a restoration of congregational worship; for the Mass is not a service to be said by the priest *for* the people (the medieval idea), but is the prayer of the whole congregation—"*we* pray and beseech thee, *we* offer, let *us* give thanks," etc. It means a return to the emphasis on offering rather than the medieval emphasis on presence and adoration. Cardinal Faulhaber has revived the primitive offertory procession in which the people bring their bread, wine, and other food to the altar, a timely move in face of the Nazi opposition to all the charitable enterprises of the church. There is a return to the old custom, still found in the Roman basilicas, of the priest standing behind the altar facing the people as he celebrates mass. Churches have been built with an altar in the center, around which the people gather, that they may see and understand what goes on at the altar and join intimately with the priest in the successive parts of the liturgy. In many churches there is a "dialogue mass" in which the people take their part in the Latin responses. Every attempt is made to surmount the difficulty of worshipping in an unknown tongue. Sometimes a second priest repeats whole sections in the vernacular for the benefit of the congregation. People's missals, with Latin on one side and the language of the country on the other, have been issued in enormous quantities. All this tends to emphasize the fact that in the Mass the laity exercise their priesthood. And there is a reformulation of the whole doctrine of the sacrifice of the Mass.

How far these ideas have penetrated even the English Roman Catholic body may be judged by two quotations taken at random from recent numbers of the *Dublin Review*. One contributor speaks of "the ignorant superstition not merely that the Latin Church is the Catholic Church, but that there is something essentially superior about the Latin rite and those who have the privilege of using it." (What a shock to our fellow churchmen who have been for so many years trying to persuade us of the essential superiority of the Latin rite!) Another refers to "the popular illusion that the mass is simply a means of procuring the sacramental presence of our Lord in order that we may receive him in Communion." In the Mass, he says, "the oblational must predominate over the adorational."

It is apparent that the ideals of the Roman liturgical movement are similar to those that animated Cranmer and the other reformers in their preparation of the English Book of Common Prayer. They too were liturgical scholars. The honorable tradition of liturgical scholarship begun by Cranmer and continued by the Caroline divines and the Non-jurors still survives. We may well be proud of the contributions made to liturgical study and indeed to the liturgical movement by our own Church in modern times. Important publications of original documents have issued from the Henry Bradshaw Society and the Alcuin Club. The names of Frere, Brightman, Wilson, Feltoe, W.C. Bishop, Wickham Legg, Percy Dearmer, to mention only a few, are well known. And the publication of Dr. Easton's *Apostolic Tradition of Hippolytus,* Parsons and Jones' *American Prayer Book,* and Dr. Cirlot's *Early Eucharist* is a good omen of the revival of liturgical study among ourselves.

But the Oxford Movement bequeathed to us an evil heritage. Instead of building on the fine liturgical tradition of the Non-jurors, which had been so successfully popularized by John Wesley, its leaders turned with longing eyes toward Rome. To a serious degree they were mere copyists and sentimentalists. We can today make a sober estimate of their achievement in the architectural field. We see them roving about England, desecrating its cathedrals and parish churches, spending vast sums on "restoration" and replacing the old by their childish make-believe Gothic. Such ideas carried into the liturgical field produced the "ritualists" who tore down Anglican tradition and copied all the wrong things. They replaced the parish communion by high and low mass. They imposed vulgar ceremonial on long-suffering congregations just because it had been pronounced "correct" by the papal Congregation of Rites. They pursued the same ultramontane ideal of uniformity which Dom Guéranger had inflicted on the continental church. They ignored the fact that their beloved Roman ceremonial came out of the period which Father Gregory Dix has described as one of "unexampled liturgical decay," and they spread the cultus of many forms and ceremonies which are anathema to learned and orthodox leaders of the Roman liturgical movement today.

At the present time there is a considerable liturgical movement in the Church of England, led by Father Hebert of the Society of the Sacred Mission, author of *Liturgy and Society*. Its weakness is that it is the outgrowth of "ritualism." Its leaders have been so long travelling on the pro-Roman road that they find it difficult to turn about. They undervalue Anglican tradition, and they are so devoted to their "Western use" that they find it hard to face realities. An illustration is furnished by Father Hebert in his really valuable book entitled *Parish Communion*. He makes an eloquent plea for a Sunday morning communion at which the whole parish shall communicate—by which he means all who come fasting! "Some of the Anglo-Catholic clergy are," he admits, "more rigid than the Roman Church, but we must uphold fasting communion as a rule." Those who have to eat before the parish communion are to get a dispensation from the parish priest! It is hard to suppose that many of the intelligent laity will accept this advice, or that many of the clergy will desire thus to sit in grave judgment on the dietary habits of docile parishioners.

Nothing is more important than that the liturgical movement should take the right direction in this country at the present time. It ought not to be left to the guidance of those clergy who dare do nothing without Roman sanction. Evangelically-minded churchmen are faced with a great opportunity. By carrying the Prayer Book reform inaugurated at the Reformation a step further forward, and by adapting our inherited forms of worship to the modern situation, they can prepare the Church to meet the needs of a generation it has done so much to mislead and to alienate.

CHAPTER NINE

REVIVAL AND GROWTH
(1945–1965)

When the soldiers returned home from the Second World War and rushed to establish families and to enjoy a renewed American prosperity, the "mainline" American Protestant churches entered into a period of unprecedented prosperity. Following the rising middle class to the new suburbs the Methodist, Presbyterian, Episcopal, Congregational, Lutheran, Disciples, Brethren, Reformed, and Baptist churches grew rapidly in both numbers and social importance.

While the closing and consolidating of marginal rural and inner-city congregations that had begun in the Episcopal church in the depression continued, the large new suburban congregations rapidly increased average congregational size. In 1918 the average congregation held 129 communicants; by 1963 that number had more than doubled to 292.

Theologically, neoorthodox theology—the post–World War II Americanized version of the continental theology of crisis—held out the hope of both retaining the intellectual insights of the liberal theology of the 1880–1920 period and asserting the traditional truths of the Christian faith. The Episcopal church's Seabury series (the first comprehensive Sunday school material since 1915) and a church teaching series for adults both reflected the insights of neoorthodox theology.

Organizationally, the Episcopal church mirrored the hierarchical American culture of the postwar years. Men exercised all major decision-making positions. A woman had been seated at the General Convention of 1946, but the following Convention reversed the situation, excluding any women from participation. The decision would be reaffirmed throughout the 1950s. In most cases parishes and dioceses followed the same pattern; only men could sit in diocesan convention or on vestries. Women were limited to participation in a series of parallel organizations. Women's auxiliaries, often meeting in the same location and at the same time as the official bodies from which they were excluded, functioned at parish, diocesan, and national levels. Children also had a slot on the hierarchy. Because of the large numbers of children in the baby boom generation, children were often excluded from part or all of the major service of worship. They gathered at children's chapel services and at a variety of functions designed for their age group.

On an institutional level Episcopalians were removing some of the bars that separated blacks and whites. John T. Walker (b. 1927), later bishop of Washington, entered Virginia Seminary as the first black student in the fall of 1951. Payne Divinity School in Petersburg, Virginia, a major training institution for black clergy since its founding in 1878, merged with Virginia in 1953. After a mass faculty resignation protesting segregation, the trustees of the School of Theology at the University of the South allowed the first black student to enter in that same year. Dioceses abandoned indirect representation schemes that had limited the number of black clergy and congregations seated at diocesan conventions. Yet these changes had not yet reached a parish level. Black and white Episcopalians had little contact on a local level.

The following selection is taken from the *Christianity and Modern Man* series. In 1947 A.T. Mollegen (1906–84) and Clifford Stanley (b. 1902) of the Virginia Seminary faculty responded to a request from a group of interested lay persons in the Washington, D.C. area by beginning a weekly series of lectures on the Christian faith, with the help of a number of others it would continue until 1965. Like James Pike (1913–69), a church-teaching series author who as dean of St. John the Divine Cathedral in New York hosted a weekly religious television show in the 1950s, Mollegen and Stanley found that American Christians, troubled by the events of the Korean and Second World wars and by sweeping changes in American values, were hungry for the intellectual presentation of the Christian faith that the Episcopal church could offer.

It was an optimistic and exciting period for the Episcopal

church. Volumes of the *Episcopal Church and Its Work* in the church teaching series carried an appendix showing that the denomination had consistently grown in proportion to the U.S. population from a 1 in 415.851 ratio in 1830 to a 1 in 86 ratio in 1960. The Episcopal shield and flag (adopted by the 1940 General Convention) appeared frequently in the new suburbs, and the establishment of a major seminary in Texas (The Episcopal Theological Seminary of the Southwest in 1951), the first new Episcopal seminary in the twentieth century, signalled that it was not only on the East Coast that the church was growing.

A.T. MOLLEGEN
(1947, 1948)

CHRISTIANITY AND MODERN MAN

First Lecture: Classical Christianity

INTRODUCTION

We are very grateful to Dean Suter and Canon Cleveland for their hospitality and the use of the Library books.

I should like to say a few introductory words about the theme of the course and the theme of its presentation. I am a man under orders in this whole affair. The plan is entirely the plan of representatives of the discussion groups which have been running for a period of years—none of them less than two consecutive years. This course is the result of an experimental Christian university, which ran in the basement of the Francis Lin-coln home all during last year. Visiting lecturers met with them once a week on the basis of the reading and studying which they had pursued during the previous week.

Even the broad outline (the syllabus) of the course is one which was designed by that original group. I contributed very little to that outline except perhaps a bit of wording here and there when their committee met with me. Their intent and purpose in designing this course is not primarily to furnish a series of inspirational talks. As they said several years ago, it is possible in the city of Washington to study anything that one desires, unless it happens to be Christianity. One can study sociology, politics, modern languages, chemistry, physics—ad infinitum, but if one wants a respectable course in Christianity, one has tremendous difficulty in finding any place where such a course is given.

So they designed one; in fact, this is the second one they designed. What they had in mind in this particular design is something like this: One had to begin somewhere, so they said, "Why not begin where Christianity had a unified point of view, that is, with the fifteenth century? Having begun there, let's make a statement of Medieval Catholicism, then of the essential elements of the Reformation. Let's watch this original and Classical Christianity as it was subjected to the criticism of modernity, to the rise of the critical spirit, to the development of the empirical scientific method, to the stresses and strains and criticisms of a completely new type of society—modern democratic, technological capitalism, that is, western civilization in the form it had until recently. Then let's give a portion of the course to the restatement of Christian faith in the light of the criticisms and purgations which have come about as a result of the developments since the fifteenth century—that is, let's state Christianity as it emerges from the acid tests of modernity."

This design emerged as a result of an experience which they had in the discussion groups. They found that the Church was not antiquated to the degree that a good bit of the modern world seems to think it is, that the Church has accepted and applied to its documents, its history, and to its theological outlook the best scientific methods and the most rigorous self-criticism. They found it was quite possible to hold and to believe the old Classical Christianity that they, themselves, wanted to know more about and to share with their friends and others who were interested in this course of lectures.

We shall be attempting to do two things: On the one hand the purpose of the whole course is to provide professing Christians with a statement of the Christian faith without any sacrifice of its essentials, yet which is compatible with the best in the modern spirit and does not require the sacrifice of the integrity of the human mind. On the other hand we shall be presenting this same Christian faith to those who, in all sincerity and honesty, have not found themselves able to come in and be a part of the Christian fellowship in the institutional churches because of intellectual doubts or disagreements. This course welcomes the full and free expression of the minds of those who are professing Christians and those who are not professing Christians. We have come to this point in our development out of a long process down to the bedrock matter of discussion, so that we are relatively immune to insults, criticisms, or cross-fire, and we welcome that, provided that it comes in the spirit of honest seeking for the truth and in terms of the expression of the integrity of someone's mind. So we shall welcome any atheist or sincere agnostic as well as those Church people who are seeking to enhance their

understanding and their practice of   15 October 1948
the Christian faith.

Fifteenth Lecture: Faith, Hope and Charity

This afternoon I want to speak very personally and informally, as a kind of summary of what we have done. I want to begin by speaking on the historical situation at this time.

Many of us have in the last twenty years learned two rather bitter lessons as Americans. First, we have come to feel that the major difference between American history and the history of Europe is that we are younger than the Europeans, and that, since we are part and parcel of Western civilization—both of its economic order and its political order—we have yet to go through in America many of the trials and tribulations which the European nations have already seen. That is, it is neither pessimistic nor is it bold or courageous to guess that within one decade we shall know a return to an economic crisis such as characterized Europe before the war, and such as we knew in the thirties; that this economic crisis will precipitate, in our political order, the same increasing cleavage between the left and the right that appeared in the life of every Western nation in the original economic crisis, and appeared in the life of our country in the New Deal period; that we were saved from the immediate workings out of the last depression, and that cleavage between left and right in the political order, by a New Deal, pump-priming, a social service State—a temporary expedient—and then saved by war expenditures; and that now we are being saved by a war-starved consumers' demand, by tremendous increases of capital resources to meet this consumers' demand, and by a heavy expenditure for the rehabilitation of Europe, and for the upkeep of an Army and Navy such as we have never known before.

All of those factors are temporary, so that we have in America still to look forward to a period of very tortuous and precarious existence, when the breaking of our economic order shall throw increasing tensions upon our political order and shall make us wonder if democracy can be maintained under such divisive pressures.

That is the first bitter lesson. It seems to me that many Americans have learned during the last twenty years that we are part and parcel of Western civilization and shall not for long be delivered from the agony of the nations.

The second bitter lesson is: America is part of one world which is deeply divided and constantly poised on the brink of war. There was a time, I suppose, when there was a modicum of truth in American isolationism—when history substantiated the dream that, because we lived in a Western Hemisphere guarded from the rest of the world by two mighty oceans, and because we were a powerful nation threatened by no nation of comparable power in that hemisphere, we could pursue our own destiny and leave the rest of the world to itself. That is obviously no longer true.

We emerged from World War I with a bit of a "Sir Galahad" complex. Europe had got into a miserable mess, and "Sir Galahad" descended from the heights of peace and security—from the Western Hemisphere—and pulled the chestnuts out of the fire, and saved the world for democracy. And we thought we had made the world safe for democracy forever.

In a self-gratulatory mood, we felt that our responsibility to the rest of the world had been, if anything, overdone, and so we shirked the responsibility of membership in the League of Nations. We pursued an economic policy in regard to the rest of the nations of the world, which was utterly and completely self-centered, and even shortsighted from the standpoint of self-centeredness.

One sign and symbol of American guilt in producing the world situation out of which Nazism emerged and the World War came (and I mention this only as a kind of "litmus paper test" of our guilt in producing that kind of world) is the fact that Hitler came to power in Germany by using an economic depression that was precipitated first by the withdrawal of long-term loans, and then by the withdrawal of short-term loans by America.

We could have kept the Weimar Republic going indefinitely if we had been willing to finance the Government as a social service, Government-spending State which was the only solution to the economic crisis which any nation found for itself in the late twenties and throughout the thirties. This attitude of irresponsibility which America manifested toward the rest of the world, both in terms of its absence from the League of Nations and in terms of its own economic policy toward the community of nations, still manifested itself after the Nazi foe had arisen and shown his true nature.

I was a part of the interventionist forces during the last half of the thirties; and at the moment of Pearl Harbor I could not have honestly said that I believed the United States would have, of its own free will and volition, taken up its responsibility and stood alongside the democracies to defend them from the Nazi foe, and to destroy that foe. I did not know whether America was going into the World War voluntarily or not.

In the light of Biblical history, these war years can be read as the judgment of God. The judgment of God is that a nation which possesses the greatest power in the world, and which uses that power irresponsibly among the nations, helps to create a world situation far more desperate and terrible by reason of its irresponsibility, and is finally dragged into a debacle that it helped to create. Because we would not be there responsibly, the world situation got worse, and then we were dragged by Pearl Harbor into the pit of fire which we had helped create. It is a kind of Divine judgment upon our irresponsibility, is it not?

So also in regard to the first point: it is only the blindness that comes upon a culture that is immersed in the immediate and the sensational which cannot read the picture and realize that our immediate years of inflation and boom are short-lived. The fate of Europe will begin to be our fate in the not too distant future. Sin blinds, and blindness means more sin, which blinds the more. So it is a Divine judgment that we who will not deal with our basic maladies plunge more deeply into those maladies: God punishes sin with more sin.

One of the continuing threads of our previous fourteen lectures has been an attempt to understand how man got himself into this modern predicament, when he had a past that was so steadily a march of progress that people could mistake it for the really significant and important movement of history, and believe in a doctrine of progress by which man was thought to march upward forever and forever. Our lectures attempted to give an interpretation of modern man which saw him turn from God in the late Middle Ages, and set up step by step his own reason and self-confidence as the standard, and the power by which he could achieve a good future for himself. We saw the progressive disintegration of that point of view, which is now lumped under the great label "humanism." (I don't like the label, because it is a libel on the humanism of Plato, Aristotle, and the Stoics, and upon the Christian

humanism of the Renaissance. Perhaps it should be called humanitarianism, or self-sufficiency— humanitarianism at any rate is the essential dogma of that great movement of the human mind which was the Renaissance as it broke free from its Christian environment and its Christian background.)

We saw this begin with certain great philosophers who did not themselves indoctrinate the whole of Western civilization with their own perspective, but whose voices were articulations of a culture's turning away from the Christian world view, from Christian worship, and from the Christian Church in which it had been begotten. In the consciousness of the West, we saw God cease to be a Living Reality who created human existence, who was the Judge with whom men had to reckon, the Redeemer to whom men could turn, the Savior in whom men found life and culture remade by Divine influence—the Holy Spirit. We saw God cease to be that for a culture, and begin to be an idea at the end of a rational series of logical steps, the beginning of which was man's only sure knowledge—that he, man himself, existed. We saw Cartesian philosophy as an articulation of the self-confidence of Medieval man, who made the fatal mistake of identifying himself with natural man, forgetting that he was Catholic man—man made over a period of a thousand years by the action of the Holy Spirit through the Church.

Western culture began its fatal descent with the original act of sin that brought Adam to his terrible predicament: he made himself God—I will sum it up with that one sentence. Christian man, Medieval man, Catholic man, said that he was natural man. And when he said that he was natural man he was on his way to daemonic man as expressed in Nazi culture.

One might say, therefore, that our study of the rise of secularism, by which man lost the fundamental and original Christian religious experience which had brought Western culture into being and sustained it, is summarized by St. Paul when he spoke of the disintegration of Graeco-Roman culture in the first Chapter of Romans. His words become a review of Western secularism:

> They are without excuse; for although they knew God they did not honor him as God or give thanks to him, but they became futile in their thinking and their senseless minds were darkened. Claiming to be wise, they became fools, and exchanged the glory of the immortal God for images resembling mortal man or birds or animals or reptiles.
> Therefore God gave them up in the lusts of their hearts to impurity, to the dishonoring of their bodies among themselves, because they exchanged the truth about God for a lie and worshiped and served the creature rather than the Creator, who is blessed forever! Amen.

One might use that passage as a kind of outline for the pilgrimage of man to destruction as we have been sketching it. "For although they knew God"—in the thirteenth century they did know God—"they did not honor him . . . or give thanks to him." Man said, "I am natural man; I am sure of myself; God must be demonstrated as existing out of my surety of myself" (Descartes—I am using him only as a kind of sign and symbol of the turning from the Holy Spirit). Therefore, setting themselves up as a standard, "claiming to be wise, they became fools, and exchanged the glory of the immortal God for images resembling mortal man."

And we saw the "religion of man" of Auguste Comte, out of which came Marxism and the great titanic attempt of man of his own powers—uncriticized by, untransformed by, indeed unaware of, the Almighty God—to bring a Utopia by obedience to the dialectic of history as it was interpreted by Karl Marx. God was removed from the throne of worship in Western civilization, and man was put upon that throne.

We saw the descent continue in psychology: we used Sigmund Freud as the typical psychologist and depth point of a movement. When man does not stand in the presence of God, he cannot understand himself. And so the image on the throne of worship in Western civilization ceased even to be a man, and man was thought to be explicable only in terms of the vital powers which he had in common with the animals. Sigmund Freud began to dominate Western civilization. Here again it is not that he indoctrinated a culture with his own cult, but that he is an articulation of a much wider expressed understanding of man that is less technical and not confined to psychology. So the image passed from that of mortal man to animals— "birds or animals or reptiles." Man understands himself only in terms of his vital forces.

There has been a kind of negative thread that has run through our lectures, and we saw, at the end of that process, a civilization which had so lost the fundamental religious experience that it was the victim of perhaps the most widespread anxiety that any human culture ever knew on the face of the earth. *Anxiety* became a kind of key word, which described man as an individual standing on the brink of existence and peering into the void—into absolute nothingness. Man had, therefore, to huddle in groups again, and to believe in a particular culture as the only meaning of life, thus starting the whole religious pilgrimage of mankind all over again. Empty, anxious, sophisticated man became pagan: we saw primitive religion arise again.

We saw some men take an old solution to the problem of existence—we saw them become Stoic again.

We saw man taking mystic flight out of this dilemma.

Men have to have a religious answer to the problem of anxiety. And here we reiterate the great work of the Swiss psychologist, Carl Gustav Jung, who taught us much about the inevitable religiosity of mankind and much about the situation of anxiety which lies at the root of all modern existence

and in the heart of every modern man.

In the story of Western civilization, as it parallels St. Paul's analysis, sin comes first—then comes anxiety. The anxiety of modern man is created by the sin of modern man—the sin of Western civilization which has forsaken its Creator.

The positive side of our lectures tried to present the point of view from which we can understand our culture's descent and face our future—the point of view from which man departed and the point of view to which he is beginning to return. I think it is fair to say that there are indications that the finest and best of Western culture is beginning to rediscover Christianity, and enter again into the heritage it once had. And that made us state Christianity again in terms of modern conceptions, reviewing the whole of the scientific method, the whole criteria of the modern critical spirit, and showing that Christianity is in no way antiquated or outmoded—that it is not at all a superstition which modern science made incredible.

We were able to say that a rise of modern secularism was in part due to the sin of the Church—the Medieval Church—and of the classical Protestant movement which came in the sixteenth century. So we have not made a "Church criticism" of the world: we have made a Christian criticism of both the Church and the world, as we developed our understanding of Western culture to the present.

We found a way—at least I have found a way, and I hope many of you go with me—where the great classical creeds of the Church become living again, and relevant to our modern situation. We learned again what faith, hope, and charity could mean to an individual drawn into the great fellowship of the Church, looking upward to God as He descended in Christ and made Atonement for the sins of the world by the Cross, as He transforms the faithful segment of the world with His Holy Spirit and produces a first installment of the kind of humanity which He will inevitably bring about because He is all-powerful.

We found a way to believe the Nicene Creed again. We found a way to enter into this institutional Christianity which sometimes looks, from the outside, stupid and complacent, unaware of the present world distress. We found a way to enter the Church and know the presence of God in the ancient sacraments, because they had become our baptism and our Eucharist. That has been the positive side of our course. It meant a re-statement of Christianity: What we really mean by the Christian doctrine of Creation; what we really mean by the Fall of mankind; what we really mean by Original Sin; what we really mean by God's preparation for the Incarnation by the story of the Jews; what we mean by the Incarnation, by the taking away of the sins of the world, wrought on the Cross; what we mean by the Ascension, and the Church as a fellowship; what we mean by the Communion of the Holy Spirit, and the sacraments— Baptism and Holy Communion; and why we are so sure that God's victory means eternal life for the individual, and the consummation of history and of the universe.

Now it has become possible for the most sophisticated and intellectual products of Western culture to be profoundly and simply Christian. I used a phrase—coined extemporaneously — "super-sophisticated, child-like Christianity." It seems to me that modern man, as he becomes Christian, acquires again some of the child-like simplicity of trust in prayer and the use of the sacraments, some of the child-like trust in the future which is so characteristic both of children and of profound Christians in other ages. And yet he does so by having been a sophisticated critic of his past history and of his whole Western civilization.

If we stand within this Christian world view, and within the living encounter with God (which is being a Christian), we can face the future as many profound Christians have faced the future in times of crisis in the past.

I think we spoke of one of Augustine's prayers on his deathbed, when the barbarians had laid siege to the city of Hippo in which he was dying. It seems to me that profound Christians today can pray that prayer in the face of our future. Augustine prayed, "O lord, save the city." And we shall pray, "O Lord, save Western civilization." When a Christian prays, it is the articulation of his active labor. You cannot be absolutely sure that to labor is to pray. To labor is good, but to labor and not be self-consciously in the presence of God cannot really be called prayer. But you can be sure that to pray is to labor: that is, if one is really open to the life of the moving, dynamic God, one cannot stand in His presence and be in communication with Him without working toward the end that God sets before us. So to pray—to pray profoundly and truly, to know God intimately—is to labor.

So when the Christian prays today, "O Lord, save Western civilization," it means that his life is on the battlefront for the salvation of that civilization—on the battlefront for social justice where the tension between the races is to be found; for social justice where the precarious nature of our economic situation depresses us; for social justice where equality before the law is at stake; for social justice where American responsibility before the bar of the nations of the world is at stake. "O Lord, save Western civilization" means "O Lord, empower and encourage and illumine us to labor for the salvation of Western civilization."

Here must come a word of warning. We cannot worship the Almighty God in order to save Western civilization, because that means that Western civilization is our God, and we are trying to bring the true God in as a *deus ex machina*—a god out of the machine—at the end of the tragic play, to save the real God that we worship and adore: namely, ourselves, our culture, our way of life. But we can let the disintegration of that which we have participated in and loved—of Western civilization—we can let its crisis become a sign of warning, a chastizing blow of the Almighty God which makes us know our present time as the occasion for our turning back to God.

If Western civilization is saved, it will be saved as the by-product of the return of its best elements to the true and Christian worship of God.

But Augustine was a realist, and he knew that his will and his hope and his desires were not always identical with the will and hope and desires of God. So when he had prayed for the salvation of the city of Hippo, he moved to a deeper level of prayer and said, "If that be not Thy will, give us the courage to endure."

I am not prophet enough to know whether Western civilization can be saved or not. All I know is that under God I have to try. But I have also seen—in history—civilizations come and civilizations go. And I have no doubt that our civilization will go some day into the graveyard of civilizations. And this may be the day. So I always have to pray the second prayer with Augustine: "If it be not Thy will, O God, to save civilization, give us the courage to endure." And I think that perhaps profound Christians will be the only people who will have the courage to endure.

The Christians were the only people who had the courage to endure when Roman civilization fell. Because they believed in God and knew Him; because their life was constituted in, and given meaning by, the power of God; because they lived in a fellowship which was the community of the Living Spirit of the Almighty God; for these reasons, the Christian Church survived as a solid, cohesive group. After the disintegration of Roman civilization, Christians courageously set their hands to work rebuilding the civilization and bringing a new culture into existence.

I do not know whether Western civilization can be saved or not, but I do know from history and from the power of God who shall be in His Church that the Christian Church will have the courage to endure, and save out of the catastrophe the goods of Western civilization, and begin again that long and torturous effort to rebuild another culture. Our day may be like the day before Hippo fell to the barbarians: if so, there may be a Christian culture so much better that God will be vindicated by the end of ours.

But on a still deeper level, St. Augustine prayed, "If that be not Thy will, take me to Thy heavenly bosom." I do not think it likely, but the scientists tell us that it is possible that an atomic war might mean the eradication not only of civilization but of mankind. If this becomes true, it will not mean that Christianity is not true. If man destroys himself off the face of the earth, it would only be to vindicate what St. Paul once said to the Christians in Rome (Romans 3): "Let God be true if it makes every man a liar." And so even here the Christian has not lost his last trench. He will fight for the West in the first trench. If he loses that, he will fight for a new and more Christian culture—that is the second trench. But if God chooses to wind up the human experiment, he still has the last trench, which no man can take away from him—the bosom of the Heavenly Father. He is grounded in the eternal heart of God. He knows that no power on earth—the daemonic power of Nazism (I am paraphrasing St. Paul in Romans 8), of Communism, the decadent power of a Western economy as it sinks from maturity into senility, the frenzy of racial prejudice, the impersonal power of modern science used in warfare—nothing can separate us from the love of God in Christ Jesus. And, since nothing can separate us from that, we have a joy which the world cannot take away from us. So we pray as Christians also on that deepest level.

If the city does not stand, and if there is to be no enduring and rebuilding, then take us to the final consummation: that is, to the heavenly home, the eternal abode in the skies. We face the future, then, with great trepidation, with a sense of solemn responsibility, but never with anything approximating ultimate despair, because we have *faith.* Faith is our personal trust in God, our response to God's personal self-revelation, which was made once and for all in Christ and is continuing in His Church. We, therefore, have hope—hope for the immediate future, hope for the day after tomorrow if this immediate future becomes bitter and is destroyed, and an ultimate hope which no power in this world can take from us. Because by faith our life is lived in response to God's movement toward us in Christ, and because our life is founded on the hope which cannot be taken away from us, we are the only people in the world that can *love* and sustain the world without answering vindictiveness with vindictiveness. For in St. Paul, charity is an attitude toward man—not toward

God: *Faith* toward God, *Hope* toward the future—immediate, remote, and ultimate—and *Love* toward our fellow men. We are the only ones who cannot be ultimately and finally frightened, who are safe from the hysteria that will try to save itself by the destruction of the other.

Faith, Hope, and *Charity*: Faith in God through Christ; Hope for the future; and Love of our fellow men. These theological virtues are the helmet and shield and sword with which any man can truly and adequately face the future.

8 February 1948

CHAPTER TEN

GROWING PAINS
(1965–1980)

By 1965 the suburban revival of the church began to stall. Part of the reason for the decline was demographic. The baby boom was over; the rapid population rise of the suburbs that had fed the rapid gains of 1945–65 had slowed. There were, however, other important factors at work. As many suburban congregations paid off their mortgages and completed their building programs, they found ethical and theological differences about which they had postponed discussion. The train of national events—the Civil Rights Act of 1964, the war in Vietnam, and the Women's Rights movement—exacerbated this situation. What did the church have to say about desegregation? What was to be the role of women in the church? What did the church have to say to young men facing the draft?

There were as well important issues for discussion arising from within the church. In 1953 the House of Bishops had authorized "special use on a particular occasion" of alternate forms of worship prepared by the Liturgical Commission. The liturgical movement had been gaining steam since the depression. What was to be done about the prayer book? Dennis Bennett (b. 1917), a priest who had a charismatic experience while serving as rector of St. Mark's, Van Nuys, California, became an effective spokesman for the charismatic renewal movement, a rediscovery of the role of the Holy Spirit in the Christian life that often was accompanied by such experiences as speaking in tongues. How would the church at large react to such phenomena?

In the period from 1965 to 1980 Episcopalians vocally discussed all these issues. They reshaped their denomination in many ways. Even a partial catalogue of changes is staggering: (1) The role of women. In 1964 female deputies were admitted to General Convention and deaconesses were granted permission to marry. In 1970 all distinctions that remained between male and female deacons were eliminated. (Prior to 1970 deaconesses had been covered by different canons from male deacons. They had had different educational requirements and different pension benefits.) The General Convention of 1976 opened the priesthood and (theoretically) the episcopate to females. (2) Family life. In 1973 a new marriage canon was adopted that greatly eased the possibility of remarriage in the church for divorced persons. Following a 1968 discussion of baptism at Lambeth, the General Convention reexamined and then dropped the requirement that a person be confirmed in order to receive communion. Young children were able to receive the eucharist in the Episcopal church for the first time. (3) Liturgy. In 1967, 1970, and 1973 trial use liturgies were approved. In 1979 a new prayer book was adopted. Three years later a new edition of the hymnal would follow. (4) Parish life. In 1967 the General Convention adopted a report on clergy deployment that led to a new method of calling clergy. In most cases in the past parish vestries had either undertaken the search for a new rector or relied upon small committees. Under the new deployment system parish search committees used congregational surveys, drew up parish profiles, and examined computerized statements prepared by clergy. The new system was more democratic, for it gave more people a part in the search process; but in many cases it greatly increased the time necessary either for a parish to choose a rector or for a rector to find a parish. (5) Theological education. The period was a difficult time for theological seminaries. Three—Philadelphia Divinity School, Bexley Hall, and Berkeley—were forced to merge with other institutions in order to remain open. Seminary administrations were forced to walk a difficult line between providing experiential and socially responsible curricula desired by activists within the church and not alienating some of the more conservative church members who had traditionally contributed to seminaries. Students asked for and received more flexible programs of study and greater voices in seminary policy. General Convention countered by requiring an-

nual statements from seminaries on the character and prepared-
ness of students and by instituting a new set of national general
ordination examinations (GOEs).

These were difficult years. Between 1966 and 1978 the number
of baptized persons fell from 3,647,297 to 3,057,612. In the latter
year a group of dissatisfied conservatives left the church to form
the Anglican Church in North America, a breakaway group that
would itself splinter into a series of bodies.

Episcopalians were torn between the knowledge that changes
were needed in order for the church to preach the gospel to a
changing world and a fear that the very effort to change was alienating existing parishioners. They were no longer able to reconcile
the two elements—engagement with modern critical thought and
attachment to classic Christianity—that neoorthodoxy had promised to hold together. Two documents follow that illustrate this
tension.

The first is the 1967 report to General Convention of the Committee to Study the Proper Place of Women in the Ministry of the
Church. Committee secretary Elizabeth Bussing (b. 1901), an active laywoman who served as an editor for the *Episcopalian* and
as the chair of the diocese of California's commission on prayer,
was the primary author of the report, which urged careful consideration of ordination for women. The second document is taken
from the special session of the House of Bishops of 1974. In the
Convention of 1973 the House of Bishops had voted for women's
ordination; the proposal was blocked, however, in the House of
Deputies. On July 29, 1974 three bishops—DeWitt, Corrigan, and
Welles—convinced that the time for careful consideration had
passed, irregularly ordained eleven women to the priesthood. The
minutes of the House of Bishop reveal some of the confusion and
pathos of the time; how could the bishops balance the needs of
those who felt that change could wait no longer with those who
felt that too much had changed already?

The texts are taken from the *Journals of the General Convention of the Protestant Episcopal Church* (printed for the Convention) of 1967 (pages 35.4–35.12) and 1976 (pages B312–B357).

PROGRESS REPORT TO THE HOUSE OF BISHOPS
from
THE COMMITTEE TO STUDY THE PROPER PLACE OF WOMEN IN THE MINISTRY OF THE CHURCH

October, 1966

The creation of the Committee to Study the Proper Place of Women in the Ministry of the Church was authorized by the House of Bishops in September, 1965, and its members were subsequently appointed by the Presiding Bishop. The Committee consists of

The Bishop of Rochester [George W. Barrett], *Chairman*

Mrs. Irvin Bussing of California, *Secretary*

The Bishop of New Hampshire [Charles F. Hall]

The Bishop of Oklahoma [W.R. Chilton Powell]

Mrs. Charles M. Hawes III of the Virgin Islands

Rev. Dr. Alden D. Kelley of Bexley Hall

Mrs. Theodore O. Wedel of New York.

Of the women serving on the Committee, one has been an executive in public relations and advertising, another has been engaged in professional Church work for many years, both in this Church and on an ecumenical level, and the third has recently received a Bachelor of Divinity degree.

The Committee presents this preliminary Report, indicating the direction of its thinking and making some initial recommendations to the House of Bishops.

SCOPE AND URGENCY

The Committee presents this preliminary Report, indicating the place of women in the Church's Ministry demands the facing of the question of whether or not women should be considered eligible for ordination to any and all Orders of that Ministry. No one would deny that women are part of the lay ministry of the Church, and the Committee does not think that another examination of the status of Deaconesses alone would do justice to the matter.

The Committee is convinced that a number of factors give the question a new urgency, require a fresh and unprejudiced look at the whole issue, and warn against uncritical acceptance of beliefs, attitudes, and assumptions that have been inherited from the past and strongly persist at the present time. Three such factors seem especially important:

a. *The growing place of women in professional, business, and public life,* in medicine, in teaching, in politics and government, in the Armed Forces, even in high executive positions within this Church.

b. *The development of new forms of ministry* that permit greater flexibility and call for many more specialized skills than is the case when the ministry is limited largely to one priest in charge of one parish, a generalist rather than a specialist. As one member of the Committee put it, "We need to stop talking or thinking of the ministry as though it were a single unitary vocation. Rather, we need to think of the many functions of ministry which are needed today—the sacramental ministry, preaching, theological and Biblical research, teaching, pastoral work and counseling, social service, etc. In an age of specialization and of a tremendous explosion of knowledge we must face the fact that no one person can possibly be adequate in all these areas. ... We need to encourage specialization according to a person's gifts and interests and organize our corporate life to use specialists." This fact requires consideration of how women may be used in a changing and increasingly specialized ministry.

c. *The growing importance of the issue in ecumenical relationships.* The question is being discussed in many parts of the Anglican Communion. ... The initiation of a study of the experiences of ordained women was urged by the World Conference on Church and Society, meeting at Geneva in the Summer of 1966. In this country, the Consultation on Church Union has reached the point of considering the drafting of a plan of union, involving this Church and a number of others that now admit women to the ordained ministry, and the question of the ordination of women in such a united Church obviously must be faced as the negotiations proceed.

Nor does it seem that the question of the ordination of women in the Orthodox and Roman Churches can be regarded as finally and forever decided in the negative, particularly in view of other changes that have occurred, especially in the Roman Church.

There is a sentence in one of the official documents of Vatican II that reads, "Since in our times women have an ever more active share in the whole life of society, it is very important that they participate more widely also in the various fields of the Church's apostolate." (*The Documents of Vatican II,* Walter M. Abbott, S.J., General Editor. Guild Press, New York, 1966. page 500.) The Archbishop of Durban, South Africa, Dr. Dennis Hurley, recently predicted that "there are going to be some fantastic developments" in the role of women in the Church. (See *Christian Century,* September 15, 1966.) And in an interview with the Secretary of this Committee, given on October 11, 1966, the Rev. Dr. Hans Küng, Professor in the University of Tübingen (Germany) stated, "There are two factors to consider regarding the ordination of women to the Sacred Ministry of the Church. The first is that there are no dogmatic or bib-

lical reasons against it. The second
is that there are psychological and
sociological factors to be considered. The solution to the problem
depends on the sociological conditions of the time and place. It is
entirely a matter of cultural circumstances."

BURDEN OF PROOF

The Committee has become increasingly convinced that the burden of proof is on the negative in
this matter.

For, to oppose the ordination of
women is either to hold that the
whole trend of modern culture is
wrong in its attitude toward the
place of women in society, or to
maintain that the unique character
of the ordained ministry makes
that ministry a special case and
justifies the exclusion of women
from it.

REASONS GIVEN AGAINST THE ORDINATION OF WOMEN

Mental and Emotional

The alleged mental and emotional
characteristics of women are said
to make them unsuitable to serve
as clergymen. Such arguments are
never very clear, consistent, or
precise. Sometimes, the weakness
of women is stressed, despite the
fact that women are healthier and
live longer than men. Or, it is
claimed that women think emo-
tionally rather than rationally and
that they over-personalize problems or decisions.

The same sort of arguments
could be used to show that women
are unfit for almost any business,
professional, or public responsibility. They were used against the admission of women to higher education, to the practice of medicine
and law, and against women['s]
suffrage. They are still being used
against the admission of women to
the House of Deputies of the General Convention.

None of these negative arguments has been borne out in any
other walk of life. Women have
proved to be capable, often bril-
liant, lawyers, statesmen, scientists, and teachers. They have
enriched the practice of medicine,
and politics have neither been redeemed nor debased by their participation.

As experience has demon-
strated, only experience can show
the extent to which women might
fulfill a useful role in the ordained
ministry, as well as ways in which
their role might be different from
the role of men. Here, as in other
callings, women would need to be
better than men in order to compete with them.

Emil Brunner states, "It is absolutely impossible to put down in
black and white, as a universal
rule, which spheres of activity 'belong' to women and which do not.
This can only become clear
through experience; and for this
experience, first of all the field
must be thrown open."

Because the field has not been
thrown open, any judgment based
on the Church's experience with
professional women workers is limited and inadequate. With the highest respect for the contributions
these women are now making, the
Committee is convinced that an
absolute bar at the level of ordina-

tion has a deterring effect upon the number of women of high quality who enter professional Church work or undertake theological study, and that this same bar places theologically trained women in a highly uncomfortable and anomalous position.

Marriage versus Ministry

There is alleged the impossibility or impracticality of combining the vocation of a clergyman with domestic responsibilities, with marriage, as well as the bearing and care of children. Would it be possible for a wife and mother of a family to bring to the priesthood the required degree of commitment, concentration, and availability?

First, it must be said that many women choose careers and never marry, others combine marriage and careers. The Church recognizes that the latter is an entirely legitimate vocation, both in the secular world and in the Church itself.

Secondly, the question of married women is partly answered by the fact that married men are permitted to serve as bishops, priests, and deacons in the Anglican Communion. Such permission implies an acknowledgment of the strong claims that the wife and family of a married clergyman rightfully have upon his time, his money, and the conduct of his vocation. All would grant that a clergyman has a duty, as well as a right, to take into account his wife's health, or his children's education, in considering a call, in negotiating about his salary, in determining his standard of living and the amount of money he will give away.

While other, and perhaps more serious, problems might exist for a woman who wished to combine ordination with marriage, the Commission is by no means convinced that such a combination would not prove practical in many instances. Even such demanding professions as teaching and medicine are finding ways of using skilled and trained married women with children, both on a part-time and a full-time basis. Many intelligent women find that they are better wives and mothers by combining an outside calling with the care of a family. Many also can look forward to years of full-time professional work after their children are grown.

The Commission would ask whether the leadership of the Church does not possess resourcefulness and imagination similar to that displayed by other institutions in using married women, if not often as ministers in charge of parishes, yet as assistants, or for the specialized types of ministry that are sure to develop much more rapidly in the future. It is thought unlikely that any great number of women would seek ordination, considering the very real difficulties involved. But difficulty is not impossibility, and at the least there need be no fear that women will "take over" the Church.

Theological Arguments

Then there are certain theological objections which seem to the Committee to present a strange mixture of tradition and superstition.

Biblical

Some of the objections rest on a rather literal approach to the Bible and fail to take into account the degree to which the Bible is conditioned by the circumstances of its time. It is not necessary to dwell upon the Creation Story, in which woman is created after man and taken from him, nor be influenced by the fact that women were excluded from the covenant-relation of God with Israel, any more than one would support polygamy or slavery because both have clear sanction in the Old Testament. Nor is one moved by the familiar argument that our Lord chose only men to be his apostles. Any sound doctrine of the Incarnation must take full account of the extent to which Jesus lived and thought within the circumstances and environment of his own time. To deny such facts is to deny the full humanity of Jesus and to subscribe to a grotesque Docetism. Our Lord did choose women as close associates, even if he did choose men as the transitional leaders of the new Israel. The Committee also believes that St. Paul, as well as the authors of *Ephesians* and the Pastoral Epistles, were sharing in the passing assumptions of their own time, as well as advising wise strategy for the First Century Church, in recommending that women keep silent at services, cover their heads, and be subordinate to their husbands; just as St. Paul thought it wise to send a run-away slave back to his master. Much more permanent and basic are St. Paul's words, "There is neither Jew nor Greek . . . slave nor free . . . male nor female; for you all are one in Christ Jesus."

Image of God

Then, there is a cluster of theological objections based on the assumption that the female is a less true or complete image of God than the male; and that, therefore, woman is less capable, or is quite incapable, of representing God to man and man to God in the priesthood, and of receiving the indelible grace of Holy Orders.

This line of reasoning has a number of curious sources. In the Bible, God is thought and spoken of as "he," for the most part, as would be entirely natural in a culture first militant and warlike, always patriarchal, and with a developing monotheism. Even so, God can be compared with a mother who comforts her child.

Jesus Christ was born a man. Obviously, God's unique child would need to be born either a man or woman; and, again, in a patriarchal culture, only a man could fulfill the role of Messiah, Lord, or Son of God. When one calls God personal, one can mean no more than that human personality is the best clue we have to the nature of God. Perhaps male personality is a better clue than female personality in a masculine-dominated society, but who would presume to project such sexual differentiation upon the very nature of God? The first of the Anglican Articles of Religion states that God is "without body, parts, or passions." To call God "he," implies no more than to call the entire human race "man" or "mankind."

The view that the female is a less true or complete image of God than the male is sometimes still supported by a tradition coming from Aristotle and St. Thomas Aquinas, which holds that woman is an incomplete human being, "a defective and/or misbegotten male." This tradition was based upon the pre-scientific biology which held that woman was an entirely passive partner in reproduction. On this subject, the Rev. Dr. Leonard Hodgson has commented, "We should be unwise to base our theological conclusions on notions of a pre-scientific biology which has never heard of genes or chromosomes."

Emotional and Psychological Pressures

The Commission is also aware that all the intellectual arguments against the ordination of women are connected with and reflect strong emotional and psychological pressures. These pressures *may* point to profound truth about men and women and their relationship to each other. Or, they *may* reflect magical notions of priesthood and Sacraments that linger on in the most sophisticated minds. Or, they *may* reflect the fact that our deepest emotional experiences in the life of the Church, experiences often associated with the birth and baptism of children, maturity and Confirmation, worship and Sacraments, the pastoral ministry in times of crisis, joy and sorrow, are all closely associated with an episcopate and a priesthood that is exclusively male. Or, they *may* illustrate the sad fact that histori- cal and psychological circumstances frequently make the Church the last refuge of the fearful and the timid in a changing world and that, the more rapidly the world changes, the stronger become the pressures to keep the Church safe and unchanged. Or, they *may* represent a threat to the present ordained ministers, to their wives, to lay men or lay women. The Commission is disturbed by the scorn, the indifference, the humorless levity, that is occasioned by the question of seating women in the House of Deputies, let alone their admission to ordination.

Finally, one cannot place much weight upon the common opinion that women themselves do not wish to be ordained. Who knows? Most women obviously do not, just as most men do not wish to become clergymen. But some women do. Kathleen Bliss has written, "This is not a woman's question, it is a Church question." The Church's answer must be determined, not primarily by what is good for woman, but what is good for the Church.

RECOMMENDATIONS

Upon the basis, then, of its work up to now, the Commission makes the following proposals:

• That the Lambeth Conference of 1968 be asked to study the question of the ministry of women again in a fresh and thorough manner.

The fact that Lambeth has dealt with the question before is hardly decisive. In 1920, the Lambeth Conference condemned contraception; in 1930, it gave it rather grudging approval; but, in 1958, it implied that family-planning was a marital decision.

• That this Committee be continued, or that a similar one be appointed by the Presiding Bishop, to carry forward the study of the proper place of women in the ministry of the Church, keeping abreast of new developments and the wealth of new material appearing on the subject, and reporting any significant trends to this House, to the Presiding Bishop, and, through him, to those responsible for preparing for the Lambeth Conference.

• That the Committee be asked to communicate with other groups in the Anglican Communion making similar studies.

• That the Joint Commission on Ecumenical Relations be asked to explore the implications of the issue in its negotiations and conversations with other Christian Churches, Protestant, Orthodox, and Roman, and that the studies of the Committee be made available to them for such purpose.

• That the Committee be asked to collaborate with the Division of Christian Ministries of the Executive Council, with the Committee now studying theological education under the chairmanship of the President of Harvard University, with the Joint Commission on Education for Holy Orders, and with the Joint Commission on Women Church Workers, and that this last Commission be commended and encouraged in its efforts to improve the training, canonical and professional status, and compensation of the lay women now engaged in professional Church work or who shall be so engaged in the future.

SPECIAL MEETING OF THE HOUSE OF BISHOPS 1975

FOURTH DAY

Portland, Maine
Monday, September 22, 1975

REPORT OF THE
COUNCIL OF ADVICE

[Presiding Bishop John Allin convened his Council of Advice, following the Philadelphia ordinations of 11 women. The Council, composed of the presidents of provinces, delivered its report to the fourth day of the 1975 special session of the House of Bishops. Bishop Frederick B. Wolf of Maine presented the first portion of the report ("Where We Have Been"); Bishop William Creighton of Washington, the second portion ("Where We Are Now"); and Bishop C. Kilmer Myers, the third ("Some

Perspectives"). In addition to receiving the report of the Council of Advice, members of the House of Bishops also heard from Bishop of Ohio John H. Burt and the Bishops' Committee on Theology. After consideration of these reports and considerable debate the bishops voted to censure four of their number for participation in irregular ordinations.—Ed.]

WHERE WE HAVE BEEN

On or about July 19th, 1974, the Presiding Bishop read the announcement in the *New York Times* of the proposed service in Philadelphia on July 29th. He immediately made efforts by telephone and telegram to dissuade the bishops from proceeding with this proposal.

The bishops held the service on July 29th. Immediately thereafter the Presiding Bishop had a conference call with the Advisory Committee to the House of Bishops. It was their unanimous decision to call a Special Meeting of the House, which the Presiding Bishop called for August 14–15, 1974, in Chicago. At this Special Meeting of the House in Chicago every effort was made to deal with the question of order in the Church and to avoid any suggestion of judicial procedure so as in no way to jeopardize the rights of those who might subsequently be charged with a canonical offense.

Having no judicial functions, the House of Bishops confined itself to a faith and order resolution as follows:

The House of Bishops in no way seeks to minimize the genuine anguish that so many in the Church feel at the refusal to date of the Church to grant authority for women to be considered as candidates for ordination to the priesthood and episcopate. Each of us in his own way shares in that anguish. Neither do we question the sincerity of the motives of the four Bishops and eleven deacons who acted as they did in Philadelphia. Yet in God's work, ends and means must be consistent with one another. Furthermore, the wrong means to reach a desired end may expose the Church to serious consequences unforeseen and undesired by anyone.

Whereas, Our Lord has called us to walk the way of the Cross through the questions and issues before us, resulting from the service in Philadelphia on July 29, 1974; and

Whereas, The Gospel compels us to be as concerned with equality, freedom, justice and reconciliation, and above all, love, as with the order of our common life and the exercise of legitimate authority; therefore, be it

Resolved, That the House of Bishops, having heard from Bishops Corrigan, DeWitt, Welles and Ramos the reasons for their action, express our understanding of their feelings and concern, but express our disagreement with their decision and action.

We believe they are wrong; we decry their acting in violation of the collegiality of the House of Bishops, as well as the legislative process of the whole Church, and be it further

Resolved, We express our conviction that the necessary conditions for valid ordination to the priesthood in the Episcopal Church were not fulfilled on the occasion in question; since we are convinced that a Bishop's authority to ordain can be effectively exercised only in and for a community which has authorized him to act for them, and as a member of the episcopal college; and since there was a failure to act in fulfillment of constitutional and canonical requirements for ordination; and be it further

Resolved, That we believe it is urgent that the General Convention reconsider at the Minneapolis meeting the question of the ordination of women to priesthood, and be it further

Resolved, That this House call upon all concerned to wait upon and abide by whatever action the General Convention decides upon in this regard."

Subsequently (in late August) charges were filed against the bishops who participated in the Philadelphia service. This action required the Presiding Bishop to appoint a minimum of three bishops to determine whether or not the accusations if accepted as true did constitute a canonical offense. The Presiding Bishop did appoint a committee consisting of

The Rt. Rev. Christoph Keller, Chairman

The Rt. Rev. John T. Walker

The Rt. Rev. Hal R. Gross.

These bishops met in the office of the Diocese of Washington and considered the charges as presented and found that the facts as charged did constitute a canonical offense. They then proceeded to select and appoint a canonically required Board of Inquiry.

On the 12th of December, 1974, the Board met for the first time and chose the Rev. Charles Newbery as chairman. After a series of meetings their report was submitted to the Presiding Bishop as required by canon. The substance of the report was that, although there had been violations of constitution and canons, they refused jurisdiction because of its belief that the canonical and constitutional violations were inextricably bound with doctrinal issues involving Title IV, Canon 4, Section 2, "for holding and teaching publicly or privately and advisedly any doctrine contrary to that held by this Church."

As a consequence of this finding the Board did not bring a presentment.

In March of 1975, pursuant to canon, this report was made to the Presiding Bishop, who forwarded it to the Secretary of the House of Bishops to be filed in the archives. This report was shared with the members of the House and the press.

As a result of the strong reaction throughout the Church, reflecting both frustration and misunderstanding of the canonical responsibilities of the Presiding Bishop and the House of Bishops, the Presiding Bishop conferred with the Acting Chancellor, the Hon. Hugh R. Jones, and subsequently requested the Advisory Committee to the House to meet with him, which they did on June 25, 1975.

After consideration of the many alternatives which had been suggested to the Presiding Bishop there was recognition that no further canonical procedures existed. The Advisory Committee requested the Board to determine whether or not it would be willing to re-examine its findings more specifically in line with the requirements of the canon. A majority of the Board expressed their refusal to reconsider.

WHERE WE ARE NOW

We must understand that this terminates legal procedures under the canons. Those procedures which were instituted have now been terminated in conformity with our constitution and canons. To many people this is frustrating but we must accept our frustration and recognize that it comes through and out of our own system. No doubt many are tempted, out of this frustration, to force the structure or to stretch its provisions. We must recognize that, while condemning violations of our constitution and canons and the integrity of the household of faith, we of all people must live within them. We are called upon to recognize that the House of Bishops is not a judicial body, nor is the Presiding Bishop a judicial officer. We must accept the fact that the judicial process has run its course in relation to the charges filed in August, 1974, that put the process in motion.

Proposed resolution of discussion in small groups:

Whereas, The House of Bishops at previous meetings has affirmed and then strongly re-affirmed its support of the Ordination of Women, and

Whereas, Its members both individually and corporately are committed to an orderly process under the Constitution and Canons of this Church, be it

Resolved, That this House deeply regrets the actions of several of its members because of the damaging and divisive and disrupting effect of their actions upon the life of the Church, and be it further

Resolved, That this House hereby censure them and record this censure in the records of this House.

SOME PERSPECTIVES

The Anglican Communion has in its history endured and survived many serious and divisive conflicts. The issues, for example, raised by the Reformation and their accommodation to Catholic faith and order represent the internal, often violent, struggles of a communion attempting to find its way.

Once again our Church is divided over an issue which some call theological and others a matter of justice—that of the ordination of women to the priesthood and episcopate. Sincere men and women on both sides of this issue are distressed—even desperate—as, in the past, were the many who found their way into the Roman Communion or the Reformed Episcopal Church.

The main body of the Church, however, remained intact, although often shaken, during such trials. It remained so by its acceptance of the inevitability of some ambiguity, its recognition of pluralism within the Church and of a hierarchy of theological truths.

In the past certain controversies were dealt with pragmatically by allowing dioceses individually to deal with them. Such certainly was true of the churchmanship issue in which diocese developed their own life-styles often so varied that a stranger wandering through them might conclude that there were several rather than one Episcopal Church. But this pluralism was and is a glory of our Church. It remains one Church because of its traditional acceptance of certain pragmatic stances such as creative compromise, its one ministry, its single constitutional and canonical structure, its Book of Common Prayer. This pluralism reached down into the parishes even in a single diocese. And so, Mass was offered daily in one parish while in the next the Communion was observed on the First Sunday of the month. But even in the midst of differing eucharistic theologies everyone in both parishes [was] united in the conviction that by faith the body and the blood of the Lord were received.

The Anglican Church of Canada, after reasoned discussion and debate, has decided to resolve the issue of ordination of persons of female gender to the priesthood and episcopate by allowing [through] Synodical action the various dioceses in that Church to proceed toward implementation of the principle it has adopted or not to proceed. It has placed the matter where it belongs—in the Diocese, and near to the ordaining minister, the local bishop. For ultimately, after the canons and other prerequisites have been satisfied, it is the bishop who, by virtue of the apostolic ministry which is his, ordains. The final decision to ordain or not to ordain is his as in the tradition it always has been. And so the Ca-

nadian route toward such ordination is both theologically and pragmatically sound.

For a national church to endorse in principle the ordination of women to all Orders of the Sacred Ministry and then to allow each diocese the option of implementing such ordinations is, I think, an honest *via media* which the American Church would do well to emulate. In view of the confrontation tactics we have seen employed by some, the profound polarization in the Church (even in our House), this issue must begin to be moved from the national to the diocesan arena. The Church at large is looking to us, the bishops, to provide leadership in this most important area. It is my devout hope that the House will examine carefully the Canadian model and such others as may be discovered.

This House is in a position to do just that. The lawlessness, the breaking of covenanted relationships, undertaken by a few of its members, has not been copied by a single bishop with jurisdiction. The overwhelming majority of us have remained true to each other and loyal to the democratically constituted authorities of this Church. Our ranks have not been broken by the few. We, therefore, are in a position to move with honor, dignity, and in statesman-like fashion towards the discovery of means by which the present brokenness of our Church may be bound up.

Proposed resolution for discussion in small groups:

Whereas, The House of Bishops over the past several years has endorsed the principle of the Ordination of Women to the priesthood and episcopate with ever increasing majorities, and

Whereas, The principle and the implementation of it will come before the next General Convention, be it, therefore

Resolved, That this House investigate the various options before the Church for such implementation including the manner adopted by the Synod of the Anglican Church of Canada, and be it further

Resolved, That this House request its presiding officer to refer this matter to the appropriate committee of the House for it to investigate and study the possible options for the implementation of the Ordination of Women to the priesthood and episcopate and if possible to report back to this House the results of such study during its present session in order that its members may reflect theologically, pastorally and practically upon whatever model(s) or mode(s) of implementation may be possible for this Church to adopt in General Convention assembled should it choose to do so.

The Bishop of the Central Gulf Coast moved that the deadline for submitting resolutions on the Ordination of Women be extended until noon on Tuesday, September 23. Seconded by Bishop Gordon.

Motion Carried

COMMITTEE ON THEOLOGY

The Bishop of Ohio read the first part of a report from the Committee on Theology for information only. The report will be submitted later in its entirety to the House. (See Appendix I)

Appendix I

A NEW STATEMENT
by the
COMMITTEE ON THEOLOGY ON THE ORDINATION OF WOMEN

May 19, 1975

The House of Bishop's Committee on Theology has given further thought to the several theological issues which have emerged in the ongoing debate on the matter of the proposed ordination of women to priesthood in the Episcopal Church.

We offer the following reflections with respect to three matters in particular:

A. Reflections on the Majority Report of the Board of Inquiry

The Board of Inquiry, appointed to weigh charges of constitutional and canonical transgression leveled at the four bishops who conducted the July 29, 1974 ordination rite in Philadelphia, has raised the doctrinal question

"whether this Church's understanding of the nature of the Church and the authority of the episcopate permits individual bishops, appealing solely to their consciences, to usurp the proper functions of other duly constituted authorities in this Church . . ."

To this question from the Board of Inquiry we respond that in our

judgement there is an immediate
and formal correlation between the
powers of the ordained ministry
and the community within which
that power is exercised. To say a
correlation is found between community and the sacramental power
of the ministry is to say that each
refers to the other in order to be
itself; neither is itself in isolation
from the other.

The fundamental importance of
the correlation about which we
speak is a primary feature of the
Anglican Church's understanding
of itself as a Church. In the Episcopal Church all members, laity as
well as clergy, are essential participants in its sacramental acts and
its ecclesial decisions by virtue of
the gift of the Spirit each member
receives in baptism.

Within the Church no divinely
instituted order, clerical or lay,
acts in isolation from the other orders. The Church is a whole, each
member of it depending on the others. But each order has its unique
contribution to make.

The interdependence of which
we speak is especially evident in
ordination. For in ordination sacramental grace is given *for* the service of the Church as a whole
rather than being offered primarily
to an individual for his or her personal sanctification.

Ordination commissions servants of the Church for the
Church—servants whose primary
function is to enable the Church to
be itself and who must, therefore,
be recognized and accepted
throughout the Church. The commissioning achieved through ordination must, we believe, be
accomplished in such a way as to
be acknowledged publicly by the
Church.

While a bishop is called to exercise prophetic witness as his conscience, inspired by the Spirit, may
lead him (as indeed every Christian is so called), he is not free to
appropriate the sacramental structure of the Church to his own views
within the Church.

B. Comments on Theological Dialogue Since July 29

Since the July 29 service in Philadelphia, there have been a number
of statements out of a variety of
quarters dealing with the theological issues of that ordination rite.
None of them, which have come to
our attention, have asserted that
the eleven deacons presented for
ordination on July 29 are as yet authorized to serve as priests without
some further authorizing action by
the Church.

The most thorough and detailed
of these has been that produced by
the four theologians invited to
study the matter by the Bishop of
Rochester.

Several features of this Rochester Report seem most salient to
us:

First, we observe that quite different meanings are ascribed to the
word "validity" by the four professors when compared with the definition used by our Committee.
The Rochester Report contends
that the Philadelphia ordinations
were irregular but valid. In reaching this conclusion, however, the
Report seems to distinguish "validity" from "irregularity" in a more
absolute manner than our Statements do. In the Oaxtepec word-

ing, our Committee sees *"in-validity" as an extreme instance of irregularity.* And it is presumably with our definition in mind that the House of Bishops concluded that the Philadelphia ordinations do not meet the test of validity for ordination in the Episcopal Church. Therefore, the discussions of validity and irregularity in the two documents do not converge as might be hoped.

Second and as we have indicated under the first section of this Report, our Committee Statements emphasize an immediate and formal correlation between ministerial power and ministerial community (college). We do not find such a correlation in the Rochester Report, although an association between the two is admitted.

Third, in reaching their conclusions, the Rochester theologians assume the propriety of their own arguments for the theological possibility of ordaining women to the priesthood and episcopate. While a majority of the House of Bishops apparently agrees with the Report's contention here, it is also obvious that this issue has yet to be decided by the Episcopal Church in an authoritative way. The argument in the Rochester Report is clear and self-contained in a certain possible understanding of the term "validity" but does *not* thereby remove the ambiguities in the Philadelphia service.

Fourth, we are most encouraged to note that the conclusions of our Chicago and Oaxtepec Statements and those in the Rochester and in most other reports happily have some pragmatic coincidence in their conclusions. Both our Statements and Rochester, for example, understand that something more must be done before the "effect is enabled" (to quote Rochester) of the Philadelphia service. Our Oaxtepec Statement speaks of "completing"; Rochester speaks of "recognizing." Neither concedes that the eleven women who underwent an ordination rite on July 29 are now "priests *of* the Episcopal Church" (to quote Rochester again).

C. The July 29 Ordination After the Minnesota Convention

If the General Convention should state that the intention of the Episcopal Church as an ecclesial community is to allow the ordination of women to the priesthood and to episcopal orders, then the completion of the ritual act performed at Philadelphia on July 29, 1974 becomes possible.

Such a completion might be accomplished in several ways.

A prerequisite to any such endeavor would be the carrying out of those canonical procedures required for ordination to the priesthood within the respective dioceses.

Thereupon, two possibilities seem feasible to us:

1. A public act recognizing the sacramental elements found in the Philadelphia service and incorporating those elements in the now-stated intention of the Church to ordain women to the presbyterate. The proper context of the Philadelphia service now provided by the ecclesial intention, the previous rite would be sacramentally completed and the persons canon-

ically commissioned to function as priests in the Episcopal Church.

2. Another possibility, which commends itself to our Committee as decidedly preferable for pastoral reasons and for its reconciling power is Conditional Ordination.

Conditional ordination would recognize that indeed something of extra-ordinary significance did occur in Philadelphia.

A fundamental reason for our Church's concern about ordinations is the desire to assure both the ordinand and the people of the Church that the ordained person is indeed an *authorized channel for divine grace*. In this instance our concern is for those in the Church who have honest doubts about the validity or regularity of the Philadelphia "ordinations." Whether the doubts be justified or not, the matter of assurance is vital and is a proper pastoral concern of the whole Church. Holy Scripture bids the Christian to care about the qualms of the weaker brethren, and the example of St. Paul indicates that such care is a special responsibility for anyone in a pastoral office. Since the matter under consideration is the priestly office, such pastoral sensitivity is particularly appropriate.

Reconciliation is desperately needed in this troubled situation, a reconciliation effected both by the Church and by the individuals involved. The Church would be seeking reconciliation in this conditional ordination service by the decision to ordain women. In addition, the Church-at-large would be officially sharing as an ecclesial community an act from which she was excluded in Phila-

delphia. The participation of the individual ordinands concerned would be an impressive and healing contribution to the needed reconciliation.

The willingness of all parties to take this conditional ordination route might significantly assist in the ecumenical movement. It would prevent unnecessary complications in future ecumenical conversations, since it would leave no room for doubt that these persons were indeed ordained priests.

Conditional ordination would respect the integrity of Christians holding divergent views of the Philadelphia action; refrain from passing judgment on diverse convictions honestly and strongly held, and allow the Lord to determine matters beyond our capacity or desire to judge.

The Committee on Theology submits the reflections on the above three issues in the hope that it may in so doing assist the House of Bishops in the pastoral and theological leadership bishops are obliged to give in the controversy over the proposal to ordain women to the priesthood.

John H. Burt (Ohio) Chairman

George M. Alexander (Upper South Carolina)

William A. Franklin (Columbia)

Donald J. Parsons (Quincy)

Jonathan G. Sherman (Long Island)

Arthur A. Vogel (West Missouri)

William G. Weinhauer (Western North Carolina)

FIFTH DAY

Portland, Maine
Tuesday, September 23, 1975
The Presiding Bishop called the House of Bishops to order at 9:07 a.m.

The Lessons were read by the Bishop of Delaware. The Presiding Bishop led the House in prayers.

Philadelphia Ordinations

Bishop Welles presented a resolution on the Invalidity and Irregularity of the 1974 Philadelphia ordinations. The resolution was referred to the Committee on Theology.

Resolution on Censure

The Bishop of Maine, reporting for the Advisory Committee to the House of Bishops, moved the adoption of a resolution on censure. Seconded by Bishop Gesner, the resolution read as follows:

Whereas, the House of Bishops at previous meetings has affirmed its support of the principle of ordination of women to the priesthood and the episcopate, and

Whereas, the House of Bishops is committed to an orderly process under the Constitution and Canons of this Church, and

Whereas, certain bishops defied that orderly process, invaded the jurisdiction of diocesan bishops and deprived others in the Church of their proper and appointed functions, and

Whereas, we recognize that while a bishop is called to exercise prophetic witness as his conscience, inspired by the Holy Spirit, may lead him (as indeed every Christian is so called) he is not free to appropriate the sacramental structure of the Church to his own view within the Church, therefore be it

Resolved, That this House repudiates the actions of several of its members in conducting unauthorized ordination services, and deeply regrets the damaging and divisive and disrupting effect of their actions upon the life of the Church, and be it further

Resolved, That this House does hereby censure the Rt. Rev. George W. Barrett, the Rt. Rev. Robert L. DeWitt, the Rt. Rev. Daniel Corrigan, and the Rt. Rev. Edward R. Welles, and records this censure in the records of this House.

The Bishop of Southern Ohio moved that the words "may not" be substituted for the words "is not free to" in the 4th Whereas clause. Seconded by the Bishop of Ohio.

Motion carried

The Bishop of Massachusetts moved that the 2nd Resolve clause be deleted. Seconded by the Bishop of Rochester.

The Bishop of Central New York moved that the following two Resolve clauses be substituted for the final Resolve clause.

Resolved, That this House decry the action of the Rt. Rev. George W. Barrett on September 7, 1975 in the Diocese of Washington, and be it further

Resolved, That this House does hereby censure the Rt. Rev. Robert L. DeWitt, the Rt. Rev. Daniel Corrigan, and the Rt. Rev. Edward R. Welles, and records this censure in the records of this House.

Seconded by the Bishop of West Virginia.

Motion carried

The Bishop of Southern Ohio moved to reconsider the adopted substitute presented by the Bishop of Central New York so that the deletion proposed by the Bishop of Massachusetts could be considered. Seconded by the Bishop of the Central Gulf Coast.

Motion carried by 2/3 majority

The Bishop of Central New York now withdrew his substitute motion so that the motion of the Bishop of Massachusetts to delete the last paragraph of the original proposed resolution could be voted upon. The House considered the motion to amend the resolution by deleting the last Resolve.

Motion defeated

The Bishop of Central New York reintroduced his two substitute Resolve clauses. He moved the adoption and the Bishop of West Virginia seconded the motion.

Substitute motion carried

The amended Resolution as before the House read as follows:

Whereas, the House of Bishops at previous meetings has affirmed its support of the principle of ordination of women to the priesthood and the episcopate, and

Whereas, the House of Bishops is committed to an orderly process under the Constitution and Canons of this Church, and

Whereas, certain bishops defied that orderly process, invaded the jurisdiction of diocesan bishops and deprived others in the Church of their proper and appointed functions, and

Whereas, we recognize that while a bishop is called to exercise prophetic witness as his conscience, inspired by the Holy Spirit, may lead him (as indeed every Christian is so called) he may not appropriate the sacramental structure of the Church to his own view within the Church, therefore be it

Resolved, That this House repudiates the actions of several of its members in conducting unauthorized ordination services, and deeply regrets the damaging and divisive and disrupting effect of their actions upon the life of the Church, and be it further

Resolved, That this House decry the action of the Rt. Rev. George W. Barrett on September 7, 1975 in the Diocese of Washington, and be it further

Resolved, That this House does hereby censure the Rt. Rev. Robert L. DeWitt, the Rt. Rev. Daniel Corrigan, The Rt. Rev. Edward R. Welles, and records this censure in the records of this House.

The Bishop of Fond du Lac moved that the word "four" be substituted for the word "several" in the first Resolve clause of the proposed resolution. Seconded by the Bishop of Lexington.

Motion defeated

The Bishop of Newark called for Division. Seconded by the Bishop of Rochester.

Motion carried

The Bishop of the Rio Grande, joined by the Suffragan Bishop of Massachusetts and the Bishop of Newark, requested a vote by roll call.

The Presiding Bishop announced that members of the House could divide their vote on the three Resolve clauses.

The Secretary announced the vote placing the divided vote within the total as follows: Resolution I, 119-yes, 18-no, 7-abstain; Resolution II, 116-yes, 16-no, 12-abstain; Resolution III, 118-yes, 18-no, 8-abstain.

The Presiding Bishop declared that the resolution, B-21, as amended, on Censure, was adopted.

The Suffragan Bishop of New York requested and received permission for the following Preamble to the Resolution on Censure to be printed in the records of the House. (See Appendix I)

PREAMBLE:

Be it clearly known and understood that the House of Bishops of the Protestant Episcopal Church of the United States of America recognizes and states

(1) That it is not a part of the canonical judicial procedures of the Episcopal Church

(2) It affirms the canons of the Episcopal Church, in the whole and in every part, especially those Canons which provide for the establishment of trial courts for Bishops and Priests

(3) The House does, however, claim to itself the right to state its opinion as to the action of any of its members in non-judicial terms.

Ordination of Women

The Bishop of Maine, continuing the presentation of the Advisory Committee, moved the following Resolution:

Whereas, The House of Bishops at New Orleans in 1972 and at Oaxtepec in 1974 affirmed the principle of ordination of women to the priesthood and the episcopate; and

Whereas, the principle and the possible implementation of such ordinations will be on the agenda of the next General Convention; therefore, be it

Resolved, That the House of Bishops request the appointment by the Presidents of both Houses of an Ad Hoc Joint Committee to consider steps to be followed upon either approval or rejection of the ordination of women at the next General Convention.

Seconded by the Chairman of the Dispatch of Business.

The Bishop Coadjutor of Long Island moved the deletion of the first Whereas clause to this resolution, and the substitution of the words "ordination of women to the Priesthood and the Episcopate" for the words "such ordinations" in the second Whereas clause of the same resolution. Seconded by the Bishop of Northern California.

Motion defeated

The Suffragan Bishop of New York moved the addition of the words "meeting in interim meetings, the House of Lay and Clerical Deputies not being assembled" between the words "Bishops" and "at" in the first Whereas clause. Seconded by the Bishop of Guatemala.

Motion defeated

The Bishop of West Virginia moved that the resolution be tabled. Seconded by the Bishop of Fond du Lac.

Motion defeated

The Bishop of Washington moved to amend the resolve clause of the resolution, so that it would read as follows:

Whereas, the House of Bishops at New Orleans in 1972 and at Oaxtepec in 1974 affirmed the principle of ordination of women to the priesthood and the episcopate; and

Whereas, the principle and the possible implementation of such ordinations will be on the agenda of the next General Convention; therefore, be it

Resolved, That the House of Bishops request the appointment by the President of this House an Ad Hoc Committee to consider steps to be followed upon either approval or rejection of the ordination of women at the next General Convention, giving special attention to actions taken by other branches of the Anglican Communion.

Seconded by the Bishop of South Carolina.

The Bishop of Ohio moved to defer the vote on this resolution until after the House had received a report on plans being made for the Minneapolis General Convention. Seconded by the Bishops of Southwestern Virginia.

Motion defeated

The vote was taken on the motion to amend, moved by the Bishop of Washington.

Motion carried

The vote was then taken on the original resolution presented by the Advisory Committee, as amended.

Resolution adopted

The Bishop of Maine moved that the Advisory Committee be discharged from Resolutions B-9 and B-14. Seconded by the Suffragan Bishop of New York.

Motion carried

SIXTH DAY

Philadelphia Ordination

The Bishop of Ohio presented the Report of the Committee on Theology dealing with possible alternatives for the eleven women of the Philadelphia Ordination.

Appendix II

REPORT OF THE WELLES RESOLUTION
from the Committee on Theology, House of Bishops

September 24, 1975

The Committee on Theology has been requested to review and make recommendations with respect to a proposed Resolution offered yesterday by Bishop Edward Welles, retired of West Missouri. The resolution reads:

Whereas in classic Catholic theology for an ordination to be valid four requirements must be satisifed: there must be (1) the proper minister (a bishop who has himself been validly ordained priest and bishop); (2) the proper form (the correct words must be used); (3) the proper matter (the correct action must be performed); (4) the proper intention (the intention of the whole service must be to ordain a priest); and

Whereas in the Church of the Advocate, Philadelphia on June 29, 1974, those four requirements were satisfied, and

Whereas some of the normal requirements of the Canons of the Episcopal Church were not satisfied, and

Whereas in Chicago on August 15, 1974 this House did not make clear the distinction between invalidity and irregularity,

Now, therefore be it *Resolved* that it is the mind of this House that the ordinations in the Church of the Advocate, Philadelphia on July 29, 1974 were valid but irregular.

Members of this House will note that the theological issue underlying this proposed Resolution is one with which our Committee on Theology has dealt at some length in our Reports in Chicago, in Oaxtepec and on Monday last here in Portland. In each of these we have focused on the relation of ministerial power to the ministerial community.

Thus, for us, the proposed resolution involves more than the question of whether eleven or fifteen women are truly priests. The resolution challenges our understanding of what we are as a Church, how power is exercised in community, where decision-making authority is vested and who determines policy in this ecclesial community we call the Episcopal Church in the United States of America.

In our Oaxtepec statement our Committee said, "a bishop can legitimately function and be himself only within community for community, although his ministry derives from Christ in ordination, not from the community." In our Portland statement we have affirmed, "Ordination commissions servants of the Church for the Church—servants whose primary function is to enable the Church to be itself and who must, therefore, be recognized and accepted throughout the Church. The commissioning achieved through ordination must, we believe, be accomplished in such a way as to be acknowledged publicly by the Church."

These convictions suggest that there is an important dimension to every act of ordination which is not adequately touched upon by the four-fold scholastic criteria which the Welles resolution proposes. Thus, any attempt to define validity for Holy Orders purely in terms of this historic formulary (developed for a different age when theological issues facing the Church were of a different order) would be far too simplistic a route for this House of Bishops to follow now, in our opinion.

Current debate over the theological propriety of the July 29, 1974 service in Philadelphia has centered down on the word "validity" and the meaning we should give to it. Our Committee has sought, on two previous occasions, to throw some light on a proper understanding of that word and the varying meanings various people give to it. Indeed, our formal Report already given at this present meeting of the House has illustrated how four theologians (appointed by the Bishop and Standing Committee of Rochester) have used the word "validity" in a way sufficiently different from the definition used by us so as to suggest to many that their conclusions about the meaning of the July 29 rite are at odds with ours. In truth, however, we discover that their final conclusions and ours converge at approximately the same place though we use the same words differently.

If the proposed resolution, now offered by Bishop Welles, is to be seriously considered by this House, then let us first agree on what we mean by the word *validity*.

To our Committee the word means not so much "authentic in the eyes of God" (for indeed who among us can boast we can have such knowledge?) but rather an "understanding that the sacramental action is 'assured,' that its efficacy is certain" (to quote our Oaxtepec statement) by the Church for the Church—and even more precisely by and for the Episcopal Church in the U.S.A.

If we accept this latter definition, our Committee does not see how this House can affirm at this time the validity of the Orders offered in the Philadelphia service.

In saying this we do not dispute the felt presence of the Holy Spirit in that service nor the sincerity of the participants there. But we continue to believe, as this House affirmed in Chicago, "that the necessary conditions for valid ordination to priesthood in the Episcopal Church were not fulfilled" in that service.

As support for this view, we cite the reality of the present debate now under way throughout our Church over the propriety of ordaining women. Surely this is illustration enough that the certitude which the sacraments are meant to convey is still very much in dispute among us on this matter. This is a dispute which General Conventions in both 1970 and 1973 were unable to resolve but which must be resolved by some legislatively appropriate process if it is to be said that bishops seeking to ordain women can act in and for the Church.

Moreover, we ask: Is it possible for this House (even if we use the criteria urged by Bishop Welles) to affirm that *"proper intention"* was honored at Philadelphia when the three bishops *intended* on that occasion to do that which the Church they serve has in fact *not yet intended?*

Again, we ask: Is the only criterion for the *"proper minister"* of ordination the fact that he has been validly ordained a bishop?

Still again we ask: Can the mere use of the authorized ordinal be called *"proper form"* if the manner in which it is used contradicts its own provisions?

In summary, the criteria which the Welles resolution proposes as foundation for its enabling resolve are far too simplistically stated for the complex reality with which we are confronted.

In view of these deficiencies, we cannot recommend the Resolution and move to be discharged from further consideration of it, and this report be printed in today's minutes.

The Committee on Theology
The Bishop of Ohio, Chairman

Following the presentation of the report, the Bishop of Ohio moved that the Committee on Theology be discharged from Resolution B-23, on Invalidity and Irregularity of Orders. Seconded by the Bishop of Upper South Carolina. Bishop Welles moved that the last sentence of the Theology Committee's report on the Welles Resolution be amended so that the words, "and this report be printed in today's minutes" be added to the last sentence of that report. Seconded by Bishop Gresham Marmion.

Motion carried

The motion to discharge the Committee from B-23 was considered. (See Appendix II for the Report on the Welles Resolution)

Motion carried

The Bishop of the Rio Grande requested that his negative vote for the discharge of the Theology Committee from B-23 (The Welles Resolution) be recorded.

SEVENTH DAY

Report of Theology Committee on "July 29 Ordination"

The Bishop Coajutor of West Virginia moved that the House receive Section C of the Report of the Committee on Theology, entitled "The July 29 Ordination after the Minnesota Convention," with thanksgiving and that the report be given to the Church for continued study. Seconded by the Bishop of Arizona. (The report appears as Appendix I to the Minutes of the Fourth Day.)

The Bishop of the Rio Grande moved to amend the motion so that the report would be re-referred to the Committee on Theology to include another alternative incorporating the position of amnesty for the women ordained. Seconded by the Bishop of Michigan.

The Bishop of Central New York moved to amend the Bishop of the Rio Grande's amendment that there be a Special Order of Business set up later in the schedule for further discussion on the Theology Commitee's report, and also on collegiality of the House. Seconded by the Bishop of Southwestern Virginia.

The Bishop of Southern Virginia moved a substitute motion that debate at the present be extended for thirty minutes. Seconded by Bishop Gordon.

Motion for Substitute
for Amendment carried
Motion on Adoption of the
Substitute carried

Discussion continued on the floor for thirty minutes and then action on the motion before the House to receive the Report of the Committee on Theology, Section C, was taken.

Motion carried

CHAPTER ELEVEN

RENEWAL
(1980–   )

In the 1980s the American mood grew more conservative. The peaking and eventual decline of such social measures as the divorce rate, crime figures, and projected teenage drug use attested to a return to more traditional values. In the 1980 presidential election the Reverend Jerry Falwell, the founder of the "Moral Majority" political organization, led the way for a sizable group of evangelical Christians who abandoned the policy of noninvolvement in the political arena that had been standard for evangelicals since the failure of prohibition. While such politicized evangelicals did contribute to Ronald Reagan's victories in the 1980 and 1984 presidential elections, they were not immediately able to translate that election victory into remedies for what they perceived as the two major social ills—the availability of abortion on demand and the illegality of school prayer. Well after Reagan's second election victory, the 1960s and 1970s Supreme Court decisions affecting school prayer and abortion remained intact.

Mainline churches had lost membership in the 1970s. After 1980, however, there were signs that their downward trend was coming to an end. The 1985 Gallup report on religion in America showed the Lutheran and Episcopal churches leading the recovery.[1] The shared experience of the two churches contributed to their historic decision in 1982 to enter into an "interim eucharistic

---

[1]*Religion in America, 50 Years: 1935–1985* (Princeton, New Jersey: The Princeton Religion Research Center, 1985), p. 27.

sharing." Presiding Bishop John Allin (b. 1921) and three Lutheran bishops who resented the three Lutheran bodies involved in the sharing (The Lutheran church in America, the American Lutheran church, and the Association of Evangelical Lutheran churches) celebrated the new relationship at a joint Lutheran-Episcopal eucharist at the National Cathedral in Washington on January 16, 1983.

The Episcopal church benefited from the changed national mood in two ways. Evangelicals within the denomination enjoyed an increasing prosperity and influence, and some outside of it joined the church because of the corporate liturgical and theological setting it offered for personal faith. Southern Baptist pastor John Claypool, leaving the Second Baptist Church of Lubbock, Texas in 1985 to prepare for the ministry in the Episcopal church at ETS-SW, expressed the sentiments of many who had found a new home in the Episcopal church, when he noted that he had discovered "a greater emphasis on the sacrament, [a] sense of mystery, and a great sense of grace in the way the human condition [was] handled."[2]

By 1982 the Episcopal church had resolved, at least in principle, most of the major issues that had been before it in the 1960s and 1970s: women's ordination, prayer book and hymnal revision, integration, and the war in Vietnam. No longer arguing over how to define tradition, the church was once again able, as the 1979 prayer book catechism put it, to pursue "its mission as it prays and worships, proclaims the Gospel, and promotes justice, peace, and love."

One of the signs of this sense of mission in the Episcopal church was the increased health of the theological seminaries. They had fallen on hard times in the 1970s, when conservatives suspected them of being the source of unwelcome social activism and liturgical change, and activists condemned them for being unresponsive to the needs of the church and too bound by tradition. In contrast the early 1980s were a period of increasing stability for the theological seminaries. The three seminaries that had recently merged—Bexley, Philadelphia, and Berkeley—found viable ministries in their new settings. The Trinity School for the Ministry, whose opening in Ambridge, Pennsylvania in 1976 reversed the

---

[2]John Claypool quoted in *The Episcopalian* 150 (November 1985), p. 2.

trend of seminary mergers, secured accreditation in 1985. It was the first new accredited Episcopal seminary since the founding of ETS-SW in 1951. The 1982 General Convention's adoption of the "one percent resolution," which called for parishes to devote one percent of their budgets to theological education, created a more sound financial basis for the schools. The revitalized seminaries began to fill a slightly different function than they had in the decade before. No longer serving primarily as advocates for or opponents of basic changes in the church, they began to interpret the reorientation of the church to a generation of new clergy.

Seminaries joined other organizations within the church in fulfilling a similar function for the laity. At a time when 58 percent of the adult members of the church were not raised in the Episcopal church, this function was particularly critical.[3] Important efforts in this direction included Sewanee's Education for Ministry program (EFM), the newly formed American branch of the Society for the Promotion of Christian Knowledge (SPCK/US), the cursillo movement, the Colorado Lectionary Church School materials, Morehouse-Barlow's Anglican Study Series, and a new Church Teaching Series. Former Congregational clergyman John H. Westerhoff III (b. 1933), a professor of religious education at Duke Divinity School who was ordained an Episcopal priest in 1978, brought his considerable insights into faith development to the Episcopal church, contributing to one of the volumes of the revamped teaching series. At Virginia Seminary Locke E. Bowman, Jr. (b. 1927), ordained to the priesthood in 1984 after an ordained ministry in the Presbyterian church, organized the Center for the Ministry of Teaching in 1985, to equip those interested in Christian education, particularly of children.

At the same time Episcopalians took a new look at foreign missions. After a relative de-emphasis of missions during the 1960s and 1970s, organizations such as the South American Missionary Society (SAMS), the Episcopal Missionary Community, and Episcopal World Mission refocused the attention of the church on foreign missions. In December of 1984 representatives of these and other missionary organizations met with the Standing Committee

[3]"Report of the Committee on the State of the Church," *The Blue Book: Reports of the Committees, Commissions, Boards, and Agencies of the General Convention of the Episcopal Church* (produced for the General Convention by Seabury Professional Services, 1982), p. 320.

on World Mission to begin to map out a more coherent missionary strategy. Participants planned for regular annual meetings. Perhaps the clearest sign of the new priority of missions was the slate of candidates for presiding bishop presented to the 1985 General Convention by its Joint Committee for the Election of the Presiding Bishop. All four of those nominated had served in overseas missions. New Presiding Bishop Edmond Lee Browning (b. 1929) had served in Okinawa and Europe before election to the episcopate in Hawaii. Candidates William Carl Frey (b. 1930) of Colorado, Furman C. Stough (b. 1928) of Alabama, and John Thomas Walker (b. 1927) of Washington had served respectively in Central America, Okinawa, and Uganda before election to their present dioceses.

Domestically, Episcopalians regained a sense of confidence in their ability to establish new congregations. The Office of Mission and Ministry reported that over two hundred new congregations were founded between 1979 and 1984.[4] Province VII (dioceses in the states of Texas, New Mexico, Oklahoma, Arkansas, Missouri, and Kansas) led the way in numerical growth with a 7 percent increase in communicant strength between 1980 and 1982. Province VIII (dioceses in the states of Alaska, Arizona, California, Oregon, Hawaii, Idaho, Nevada, Utah, and Washington, and the Navaho Area Mission) recorded the second largest growth in the same period. The strength in numbers in the church shifted south and westward; the Gallup polls on religion in America showed that the percentage of Episcopalians in the South and West rose from 45 percent in 1971 to 51 percent in 1985.[5] Some members of the church began to call for a relocation of the national church office. The General Convention of 1985 did not move the office from New York City, but it did make it possible for the presiding bishop and executive council to take such an action, if they desired to do so.

At the same time that Episcopalians were giving new priority to both foreign missions and the planting of new domestic congregations, Hispanics led the way in a new emphasis on American language ministries. The 1985 Gallup poll showed a higher percentage Hispanic membership in the Episcopal church than in

---

[4]Margaret V. Uyeki, "Over Two Hundred New Churches in Five Years!" *Into the World* (New York: the Education for Mission and Ministry Unit of the Episcopal Church Center) July/September 1984, p. 1.
[5]*Religion in America 1935–85*, p. 35. *Religion in America 1976*, p. 47.

seven of eight other Protestant denominations profiled.[6] ETS-SW's Hispanic Studies program, established in 1974, helped provide clergy for the growing number of Spanish language congregations.

Foreign missions and domestic language ministries also contributed to a heightened awareness by Episcopalians of their sister churches within the Anglican communion. With the phenomenal growth of the Anglican church in Africa in the postindependence era, blacks became the largest ethnic group in the Anglican communion worldwide.[7] For American Episcopalians South African Bishop Desmund Tutu was a personification of this demographic change. Bishop Tutu, an ardent opponent of apartheid, was a highly visible figure on the American scene, speaking at the 1982 General Convention and receiving the Nobel Peace Prize in 1984, while he was spending a sabbatical in the United States.

Another sign of health within the church was an increased seriousness by Episcopalians about stewardship. In the period from 1975 to 1985 Episcopalians increased their giving by 294 percent, the largest increase of any denomination. By 1985 the Episcopal church ranked first among major denominations in giving by confirmed persons.[8]

Many Episcopalians in the 1980s used the word renewal as descriptive of the broad transformation that was taking place in their church. In the nineteenth century Episcopalians had favored the term renewal for what other Protestants referred to as regeneration—an adult affirmation of faith. The Roman Catholics, however, popularized the term in the 1960s as referring more to corporate than to individual transformation; the Second Vatican Council had renewed their church. In the 1960s and 70s reformers within the Episcopal church used the term for both the personal and institutional changes they advocated: the charismatic movement, ordination of women, liturgical revision, or social action.

Some of the reformers of the 1960s and 1970s had used the term with an exclusivistic connotation, but by the 1980s most recognize that only an inclusive general conception of renewal could revitalize the church. The Bishops who gathered in 1985 at

[6]*Religion in America 1945–85*, pp. 34–36.
[7]*The Episcopalian* 150 (October 1985), p. 15.
[8]"Good News in Stewardship Statistics," *Stewardship Report* (New York: The Office of Stewardship of the Episcopal Church Center) March 1985, p. 1.

the 200th anniversary of the first General Convention spoke not only to individual reformers within the church but to the whole membership when they called in their pastoral letter for "a renewed sense of our high calling."[9]

---

[9]*The Episcopalian* 150 (October, 1985), p. 15.

Index